It's Really Quite Safe

"It's Really Quite Safe!"

Capt G.A. (Hank) Rotherham
DSO, OBE, CM, RCN (R), RN (Ret.)

HANGAR BOOKS

Canadian Cataloguing in Publication Data

Rotherham, Geoffrey Alexander, 1906 -
It's Really Quite Safe

ISBN 0-920497-07-1

1. Rotherham, Hank, 1906-
2. Canada. Royal Canadian Navy - Officers - Biography.
3. Canada - History, Naval - 20th century. * I. Title.

V64.C32R67 1985   359' .0092'4   C85-099654-6

Published in Canada by
Hangar Books
Box 1513
Belleville, Ont.,
K8N 5J2 Canada

Book design by Harvie Brydon,
Cover design by Peter Mossman
Printed and bound in Canada by the John Deyell Company

Table of Contents

Foreword

Captain G.A. Rotherham (always 'Hank' to his many friends) joined the Royal Navy in 1920 -some three years after I took the same step. He quickly showed outstanding mental and physical qualities -the former by gaining first class certificates in all five examinations for Lieutenant's rank and the latter by playing for the Navy or for one of its fleets in many team games and for representing his service as a fencer. After the usual spell of sea service, mostly on foreign stations, Hank specialized as an Observer in the Fleet Air Arm, the branch of the service which the Admiralty had rebuilt almost from scratch after practically all the 55,000 officers and men of the original Royal Naval Air Service had been transferred to the newly-formed Royal Air Force in 1918.

Hank was never troubled by minor difficulties such as might be presented by his seniors or officials, and at once turned his active mind to solving some of the technical and operational problems of the period. Perhaps his most original and potentially valuable contribution to naval air warfare technique, which he worked on with a brother-officer (Flight Lieutenant A.P.Revington, later Air Commodore A.P.Revington, CB, CBE), was to develop the concept of High Level Bombing and put it on a proper scientific basis. Had these ideas been accepted and followed-up energetically, the striking power of the Fleet Air Arm could have been greatly augmented.

In 1939 Hank was selected to take the Staff Course, and to his intimates this seemed to be a favourable augury for early promotion to the rank of Commander. In the same year, at the very early age of 33, he got his third broad stripe. At the outbreak of war he was serving in *Courageous*, one of our few fleet carriers, and was aboard her when she was torpedoed and sunk off south-west Ireland by the submarine U-29. Fortunately, Hank survived that disaster, and next came to the Admiralty to serve as a staff officer. Hank then took part in the ill-planned and abortive expedition of September 1940 which aimed to set up General de Gaulle's Free French forces in Senegal, with control of the strategically-based naval installations at Dakar. As is well known, that operation ended in fiasco, although the establishment of Free French forces in the Cameroons had a far more happy outcome. The Douala episode described here earned Hank an OBE.

In May 1941 Hank was stationed in Hatston in the Orkneys when news came that the *Bismark* and *Prinz Eugen* had left the Baltic for the North Sea. On the 21st May the two ships had been sighted from the air in a fjord near Bergen, but the weather subsequently closed in. I see that in my book "The War at Sea 1939-1945" I described Hank as 'a very experienced naval observer', and it was precisely this experience that was needed when the Commanding Officer at Hatston decided to send a Maryland aircraft to search for the ships. Hank at once agreed to navigate the plane, and it set off on a most difficult and hazardous mission. Hank made a perfect landfall, and then searched the fjords near Bergen so thoroughly that he was able to signal with confidence that the enemy had sailed. This was exactly what the Commander-in-Chief wanted to know, and he had no hesitation in accepting Hank's report. He at once took the main fleet to sea, with results that have passed into history as one of the most thrillling sea chase sagas of all time. Throughout Hank's very varied service career I do not believe that he ever accomplished anything of greater value. It brought him a well-earned DSO.

In 1942 Hank went off to the Indian Ocean and he took part in the combined operation to seize Madagascar from the Vichy French. The chief purpose of the assault was to secure for our use the splendid harbour of Diego Suarez and so safeguard the convoy route to India and the Middle East. It was the first successful combined operation of the war, and it came at a time when our fortunes were at their nadir. Hank's next appointment was to command the naval air station at Katukurunda in south-west Ceylon, which was in the process of vast expansion as part of our effort to regain control of the Indian Ocean and the Bay of Bengal. Then he was called home to command HMS *Trouncer*, an escort carrier under construction at the Belfast yard of Harland and Wolff. On the way to join the Eastern Fleet, Hank directed a remarkable rescue operation in the Mediterranean when he saved the lives of most of the 450 persons aboard a ship striken by fire.

Trouncer was Hank's last war-time appointment, and his service had been of such distinction that contemporaries felt confident that his rank of Acting Captain, held for five years, would be confirmed by promotion to the substantive form and that, in due course, he would rise still higher in the service. In the event, Hank took the post of Director of Naval Aviation at Ottawa in 1946, when this part of his story comes to an end. In conclusion, I would say that I am very glad that Hank has written these memoirs of his naval service, and I feel honoured that he should have asked me to write a Foreword to them. Though I take leave to disagree with him on some of the points he has made, he is entitled to his view of people and events as I am, and I leave it to the reader to form a judgment between us.

Stephen W Roskill
Cambridge University,.April 1979.

Introduction

An introduction to an autobiography must be more explanatory than that of a novel. This story has been sixty years in the making and nearly five years in the telling. It is simply the story of a Naval Officer from the period of change in the post-World War I years to post-World War II years, when perhaps things did not change as steadily or as much for the better and they should have.

It is told from the point of view of a man who started in the old Navy of coal-fired battleships and graduated to the most modern aircraft carriers of his time. The Navy was his life and his joy, and he had small patience with those whose dedication and understanding fell beneath his standards.

It is a frank tale of both enjoyment and criticism, the former having a great deal to do with the association and happy community life most ships enjoyed, and the latter with the too frequent errors of judgment or lack of facilities that could have been avoided. It would probably have taken a General Staff of supermen with the knowledge and experience of many fields to have avoided all pitfalls, but it meant that many of those serving under them suffered from their mistakes. The two sides of the story come through, loud and clear, the two in balance, weighing more heavily on the side of happiness and the satisfaction of being able to accomplish what he did.

Deborah

Cadet G.A.Rotherham R.N., May 1924

Cadet
and Midshipman

In May 1924, at the age of seventeen, I was appointed as a naval cadet to *Iron Duke*. One of the last coal-burning battleships in service, she had been launched the day I turned five. Now she was the flagship of the Mediterranean Fleet, and along with four of my classmates from Dartmouth I went out to join her at Malta.

My first night on board *Iron Duke* I slept in a hammock on the upper deck under a full moon, with the gentle breeze wafting in the scents of an exciting new land. All around me the lights of cruisers and battleships were reflected in the calm waters of the harbour which was encompassed by the walls of the fortress, gleaming white in the moonlight. Rays of light shone out of the embrasures, giving the whole scene an almost theatrical quality. To a boy fresh from England it was all indescribably beautiful. Few young men can have had such an idyllic introduction to their new career.

Coal-burning ships such as *Iron Duke* had a peculiar cameraderie and discipline based on hard physical labour. When we took on coal every last man (including the so-called idlers such as the Chaplain, Paymaster and Major of Marines) was put to work shovelling coal, stropping up bags for the hoist, wheeling barrows, trimming coal in the bunkers, or any of the numerous tasks involved. Woe betide any man who shirked his fair share of the work!

HMS Iron Duke, one of the Royal Navy's last coal-burning battleships.

When not coaling-ship, a cadet's day was filled with instruction, duties, sports, and precious little social life. On our stipend of five shillings a day, out of which we had to pay for our messing and clothing, we could not have gone far in any event.

The twenty of us cadets and midshipmen on board (known collectively as "snotties", supposedly because they were too young to have learnt social graces such as not picking their noses) were placed in the charge of the President of the Mess, a young Sublieutenant. The Lieutenant Commander responsible for our instruction and general behaviour was dubbed the "Snotties Nurse". Although we had the official status of officers we were generally regarded as the lowest of the low. We were frequently reminded that we were of little value by everyone including the Commander, Herbert Fitz-Herbert, who began a detailed recital of what he thought of us by saying, "You so-called young gentlemen must realize that you are MUD."

We had a poor "Nurse" when I first joined, but Russell Grenfell later took on the job, and he was very tough. At first we hated him for he was as rude as a man can get, but by the time we parted company we had both respect and admiration for him. He and I later became friends and I have always felt that I learned a great deal from observing the way in which he handled a group of spirited young men. As one of us said following his departure, "He made us the best Gunroom in the Fleet, and we got him promoted to Commander."

As a Gunroom we won about every athletic contest that the Fleet had for Cadets and Midshipmen, and we had a great time doing it. At 5.40 am each morning we had to get off the quarterdeck with our hammocks while the hands scrubbed decks. Twenty minutes later we would play hockey --it was the only time of day we "Gunrooms" could get a ground to play on. We also played a great deal of water-polo and I was elated to make the team for the First Battle Squadron for there were some 4,000 men to choose amongst from the crews of the four battleships.

Of all our sports the one which I found the most fun was the "Crash Cutter Race". Each Gunroom entered a 12-oared boat with two masts supporting a standing lug mainsail and a dipping lug foresail. The race started with each boat at anchor, sails down and awnings spread. When the starting shot was fired it was down-awning, up-masts, up-sails, up-anchor and sail for half a mile. It took about a minute for us to get underway. At the end of the first leg the sails and masts came down, securing rigging as they all had to go up again, the oars went out, and we rowed for half a mile. The third ½ mile leg was under sail, followed by the fourth and final leg which we rowed. In this event you really had to look lively with oars and sails and masts crashing about your ears. Miraculously no one ever seemed to get seriously hurt, and everyone thoroughly enjoyed the mayhem, particularly the winners.

One of my first jobs on board *Iron Duke* was to be the Captain's "Doggie". That is, I was his messenger during any drills or when entering harbour. I had to carry any messages that he wished, rude or otherwise. Captain "Biff" Rose was an irascible man and not one to cross. I particularly recall one incident when he was conducting boat drills from the quarterdeck. All of the boats were sailing or rowing, as ordered, when the Captain instructed all boats to anchor. One of the boats dropped anchor, but unfortunately the water was too deep and she continued to drift slowly by us. Thinking that she had only lowered the anchor part way so that she might pull it up quickly when ordered and thus gain merit for smartness, the Captain called for his megaphone, which I carried for him, and hailed the boat,

"Mr. Tilley, veer more grapnel!"

"Aye, aye, Sir," came the reply, as the bowman let out the last few feet of anchor rope. It was not enough to catch the bottom.

"Mr.Tilley, do you hear me? Veer more grapnel!"

"All grapnel veered, Sir," came the reply.

"Don't argue with me: thirty days leave stopped!", roared the Captain, and so it was. As I have indicated, he was an irascible man, but not a bad one. We met again when I was serving in destroyers. He was relieved by Captain Forbes who subsequently became C-in-C of the Home Fleet in 1939-40.

Early in my time as a Midshipman I was lucky enough to get a picket boat to run --much to be preferred to spending hour after hour watchkeeping on the quarterdeck while we were in harbour. Manned by a crew of seven under the command of a Midshipman, these 52ft steamboats, capable of 16 knots, were the workhorses of the Fleet --we ran ours from 8 am. till late at night. Since we always had the same crew we became a close knit group. On one occasion the Officer of the Watch, having decided that I needed correction for slackness, sent me to the foretop for half-an-hour's meditation. The main attraction of this mode of punishment was the fact that the foretop was sooty from funnel smoke and so climbing it was a task well calculated to make a mess of a clean uniform. My crew, who considered this to be an unjust punishment, were furious, and I had a hard time trying to pacify them. In their own way they made amends for the injustice -they insisted on my coming to the Ship's Company dance at the Canteen, and there took turns to look after me at the bar whilst ensuring that I did not get drunk. I should add that I was much younger than they were.

Another incident occured shortly after I had transferred to *Resolution* and had a new picket boat and crew. One night when we were at a Greek Island we were sent inshore to wait for an escort to fetch some wayward sailor. The Coxswain asked if the crew could go ashore

A picket boat similar to that commanded by the author.

for a drink, but having some experience with the local rotgut I said, "Yes, Coxswain, they can go, but in pairs, and on condition that they only drink beer." The first two went off but were soon back. "That was quick," I said. "There was no beer, Sir," came the reply. I had discovered one of the greatest secrets of service life: that you can trust men who trust you. I continued to trust them throughout my time in the service, with great rewards: rarely was I ever let down. I continued to mix with, play sports with, and drink with my men whenever the opportunity arose, never finding that these moments of familiarity diminished my power of command. They were predictable, lovable, and always ready to follow and work as long and as hard as was necessary, but nevertheless impossible to drive, and they always liked to have a bit of a grumble.

Picket boat work provided a fascinating diversity of experiences. There was the routine work of going round the Fleet of eight battleships, cruisers and destroyers with correspondence, taking officers and liberty men ashore, towing sailing craft, or taking a tow of boats filled with men into an awkward berth and having to place each boat alongside. It was excellent training for ship-handling. Then there were the less routine events which were most memorable: going into Alexandria in 1925 after the Sirdar's murder and wondering whether we would be fired upon; finding the unlit channel through the reefs in our nighttime approach to Famagusta; entering Port Said at the start of the Suez Canal; going into Athens (or rather its port of Piraeus) with the Acropolis standing high over the city; the run into Pompeii, site of the ancient Roman city that was submerged in lava from Mount Vesuvius. There certainly was truth in the old slogan "Join the Navy and see the world."

The remainder of our circuit of the Mediterranean covered the more conventional tourist spots. I particularly remember Venice which we entered through a narrow pass into the main lagoon. From there the ship's boats went on to St.Mark's square with its cathedral crowned by gilded horses. We saw the Doge's palace and the Bridge of Sighs across which so many condemned men had passed. We even went to the Lido, haven of the rich, but here we did our share of sighing for everything was priced far beyond the shallow draught of a Midshipman's pockets.

The ship steamed on to Genoa, Villefranche, Valencia, Malaga and Barcelona. In Spain I watched my first bullfight, hoping that perhaps the bull might win, just this once. It didn't. One night while we were docked at Gibraltar we took our picket boat to Algecirras. There was a full moon and an unusually luminous sea, and porpoises played around us, each with its own luminous bow wave. My hard bitten crew wondered aloud at the marvels of nature and I asked myself what more a young man could have wished for on his first taste of life at sea. What indeed.

There were occasional reminders that there was a more serious side to life. One day as we were passing through a line of destroyers while returning to *Resolution* we saw all ships hoist the same signal —"Boat Capsized". We closed the nearest destroyer and asked where she was. The Officer of the Day indicated that it was off their

Top: HMS Resolution's 1926 water-polo team were cup winners. The author is at far right, front row.

Bottom: HMS Resolution.

starboard beam, and that one of the Flotilla's boats was enroute. Since our picket boat was both bigger and faster than any of the destroyer's boats we set off at full speed. We soon overtook the smaller boat and after a couple of miles we came upon the capsized 27ft whaler with its cold crew in the water. We pulled them out, bailed out the whaler, and towed it to its ship. We then returned to *Resolution* warmed by a signal of thanks from the destroyer which fortunately silenced the grumbles of those whose shore leave had been delayed by our unscheduled excursion. I got a "Well Done" from the Officer of the Watch, though I suspect that the thoughts of those who were kept waiting were somewhat less charitable.

The Boatswain's Call or Pipe was used when hoisting boats by hand. The Officer in charge would give the necessary orders, but in a strong wind his voice might not carry. It was then that the Boatswain's Call came into its own as its shrill notes pierced the fiercest wind. By listening to the note men knew when to hoist, when to walk, when to stop and when to walk back. When a 32 foot cutter with a full crew was being hoisted in a strong wind so many men were needed that it was not unusual to have two or three men with Calls spread along the line so that everyone would be able to hear clearly. In the days of fleets of sailing ships at sea, if the Admiral called all the Captains for a conference they would come alongside in their boats and be hoisted in by a Boatswain's Chair, the Boatswain's Call being used to issue the orders -a shrill rising note as they were hoisted up, followed by a low note as they were lowered on deck. This ceremony became the regular custom in harbour, and whenever boats came alongside. It did not matter whether the officer coming aboard was the Chief of Staff or a junior Lieutenant -only the Captain of a ship, no matter how humble, obtained the same historic greeting of the Boatswain's Call. Life on board a battleship at this time was such an ordered affair that men might, by choice, go ashore only once every three months even though leave might be taken every other day while in harbour. I can recall hearing one of my crew saying, "I think I'll go ashore here and that'll do me for the cruise." It was a very different service to that of later years when men rarely stayed on board if leave was available. In many ways it was still Nelson's navy.

During our first three years we were required to serve three months destroyer time, and so I was transferred to Wanderer of the Third Destroyer Flotilla. Most of our time was spent based at Gibraltar, working the Tangier Patrol with three other destroyers. Tangier, a place full of fun and sin, was under international control with Britain, France and Spain trying to shut off the flow of arms through the city to the "Riffs" -fierce Berbers fighting for independance against the French and Spanish. We took it in turns to spend a week in Tangier, during which time we would conduct a daily patrol between 9am and noon. Had I been a gun-runner I am sure I would have used the cover of darkness. From what our friends in Tangier told us, however, our patrols were little more than window dressing --the guns were apparantly passing through French and Spanish customs with ease provided that the traditional payments were proffered!

One other short diversion was an introduction to naval aviation for which I spent about a month aboard the carrier *Eagle*. Here I learned that pilots had only the wind to stop them when they landed --the aircraft did not have wheel brakes, and carriers were not yet fitted with arrester wires. At first it seemed to me that every landing must be a nerve-wracking event, but I was lucky enough to get a flight with a Royal Air Force pilot, "Farmer" Brill, and was relieved to discover that the aircraft soon rolled to a stop. The Blackburn Fleet Spotter was not a fast aircraft, its cruising speed was a mere 60 knots, one mile a minute, which if nothing else made the task of plotting distances flown simple. It was an ungainly aeroplane on the ground, standing so high off the deck that a knotted "manrope" was required to help the crew of four (pilot, observer, telegraphist and gunner) clamber aboard. I thoroughly enjoyed this first experience in the back seat, blissfully unaware that in a few years time I would be observer, telegraphist and gunner all rolled into one while travelling at twice that modest speed.

At the end of my three years of sea time I had to take an examination in seamanship. It was tough, but I managed to get through with a first class certificate -the reward

Above: A Blackburn Fleet Spotter.

Below: HMS Eagle, the carrier from which the author made his first flight.

was being able to go home on leave at last. The trip home was lengthy: by steamer to Syracuse, and then by train through Italy and France. As the swaying railway coach clacked its way through the countryside, however, it offered time for me to reflect on the lessons of those formative years. My first lesson, of course, was that cadets and Midshipmen were very low forms of life, but this was tempered by the second lesson that the relationship between officers and men was not all based on the blunt Prussian concept of giving and taking orders, and throughout there was that all pervading truth -'There are no bad sailors, only bad officers.' Finally I had learned how important it was that a junior officer use his initiative. In those days the chance of promotion to Commander was less than one in ten even if you didn't step out of line. The rule of thumb was that "If something happens and you don't know what to do, then for God's sake do something!"

Observing my seniors during those first three years brought me to recognize the truth of a saying attributed to Admiral Von Scheer of the German Navy in WW I, "Rules and Regulations are made for those that need them." Initiative was, perhaps, a dangerous commodity to those seeking promotion in a service where every last detail was covered by regulations and where conformity was the watchword. It was nevertheless essential for efficiency, and in time of war it was absolutely vital.

Sublieutenants' Course at Whale Island Gunnery School, February 1928.

Courses
and Cruisers

In 1927 young sub-lieutenants had to do an academic course at Greenwich before proceeding elsewhere to schools for gunnery, torpedo and navigation instruction. As with most of my contemporaries it was the Gunnery School at Whale Island that left the strongest impression. Whale Island, built on the dredgings of Portsmouth Harbour and with no proper drains --we used Thunder Boxes as toilets--, was headquarters of the Gunnery Branch of the navy. It was this branch that provided most of the openings to higher rank.

Gunnery and discipline have always gone hand in hand, and to succeed at Whale Island one had to demonstrate that you were smart yet submissive. All movement was done "at the double", everything had to be spotlessly clean and polished, and there seemed to be an obsessive interest in angles. The Parade Officer during my time was Brownfield, a man who was quite unable to cross the parade ground unless he was doing so either at right angles or at 45 degrees!

One instructor I remember well was our Gunner's Mate, a splendid character named Fulminger. To break the monotony of rote instruction he would frequently insert anecdotes of his own devising. If a superior hove into view he could return to the exact place in the text where he had left off. Less capable instructors, we noted, had to go back to the beginning of the paragraph.

Also on our curriculum was field gun drill, something familiar to anyone who may have watched a Royal Tournament on TV. There were all sorts of sporting opportunities. I managed to play field hockey and fence for the Navy during my year at Whale Island and was proud to end up with five first class certificates from the five courses, Seamanship, Greenwich, Gunnery, Torpedo and Signals.

I was now a Commissioned Officer, but I still had to do six months in a seagoing ship to qualify for a Watchkeeping Certificate which would allow me to keep watch on the bridge at sea alone. I had the good luck to be appointed to HMS *Durban* a light cruiser with six-inch guns that was attached to the America and West Indies Station. My voyage to join *Durban* was an adventure in itself for the ship was on the west coast of Canada at the time. I had to cross the Atlantic on board the Canadian Pacific liner *Montcalm* , traverse Canada from Montreal to Vancouver by train, take the ferry to Victoria, and then travel by bus to the naval base at Esquimalt. For me it was a superb trip -the Northern Lights were at their brilliant best as we sailed through the Gulf of St.Lawrence, and the Rockies presented an awe inspiring profile to the train and its passengers.

To be a real officer in a smaller ship was also a new adventure. The ship's complement was only about 400 men and so it was possible to know everything that was going on and to be close to both the officers and the men. Also on board *Durban* was Prince George (later the Duke of Kent.) I suspect that he was probably the reason for my presence, because the Admiralty seems to have believed that it was necessary to have an extra officer on board to cover absences whenever the Prince was fulfilling social engagements. Known as 'PG' in the wardroom, he was the Senior Watchkeeper but he never took advantage of his position to fiddle the watchkeeping roster —whenever he had to attend some social function he never demanded a relief; instead he would arrange a swap with a fellow watchkeeper. On the morning he left us he even kept the middle watch (from midnight to 4 am.) although the ship was scheduled to berth at 6 am. He was not a dedicated Naval Officer as his father had been, though he never shirked his job. Nor was he an athlete, though if he felt out of sorts he would put on a couple of sweaters and go for a five mile run; indeed he might have made a long distance runner. When the regatta came round he and two others demanded that they compete in the Wardroom Skiff Race for which honour there were few competitors as it was one of the least glamorous races. This tubby little boat was rowed by a crew of three, one as stroke, one with the skulls, and one as bow. He took the skulls and I have never seen such a raw pair of hands as his when he finished, in fact I don't know how he did it. He was well liked and we admired him.

The author with "PG" in HMS Durban at Bermuda in November 1928. The ship was in dry dock at the time.

It's Really Quite Safe

Santa Barbara, near Hollywood, was one of our ports of call and so a visit to the movie colony was inevitable. Our Captain, Guy Coleridge, did not want 'PG' to go, fearing adverse publicity. The attraction was too great for the Prince, however, and he went off quietly as soon as he was off duty. This indiscretion was discovered by journalists, and the next day when Coleridge and half a dozen of us officers drove to Hollywood there were headlines to the effect that "TWO CARLOADS OF SEA DOGS ARE ON THEIR WAY TO SAVE PRINCE". There was no need to save the Prince -he got back safely on his own. For me the high points of the day were a meeting with Billie Dove, (a gorgeous star of the time), seeing Douglas Fairbanks on the set of a swashbuckling drama, "The Three Musketeers" and having drinks with Charlie Chaplin.

While we were still off the coast of California the West Indies were battered by a hurricane, so we steamed at best possible speed to render what assistance we could. Enroute to Panama we encountered a tropical storm of our own and at times we were down to six knots with all hatches sealed and fans stopped. Between decks the heat was unbearable; the air so thick you could almost chew it. Through the Panama Canal we made 24 knots, increasing to 28 knots once we reached the open sea again and headed for Grand Turk and Nassau. It took us some ten days to get there, by which time the local inhabitants had repaired much of the damage. At Grand Turk Island the local dignitaries invited the Captain and Prince George to dinner, and at Nassau they came aboard to arrange games. Although we proved to be of no great assistance they were nevertheless reassured to know that we would come eventually if they were ever in real trouble.

Top: *Some of the officers of HMS Durban with actress Billie Dove. Seated (with legs crossed) is Capt. Guy Coleridge.*

Below: *Charlie Chaplin (right foreground) had no trouble making people laugh.*

HMS Durban passing through the Panama Canal.

After about six months we returned to England to recommission with a new crew. A few officers and men who had been onboard for a relatively short time stayed on to provide some continuity. I was one of these. Our new ship's company seemed to be a much more colourful and efficient lot this time. We were able to field far better teams at all games, and our officers were ready to take any entertainment in their stride, be it lively or dull. We were learning that on the America and West Indies Station, where showing the flag was the name of the game, the best resource a young officer could have was social and physical stamina. Our cruise took us around

South America, an area of the world where we were warned that VD was rife. Our ship's Doctor, Charles Savory, was a man with foresight —before we left England he obtained substantial stocks of condoms wholesale, which he subsequently sold for just three pence each. (This was long before the days when these items were free medical issue.) He gave a talk to the entire ship's company on the dangers and unpleasantness of VD. I recall vividly his admonition that although "its like washing your feet with your socks on" failure to use 'French Letters' would surely result in VD. "You won't like it," he said. "I know because I've had it!" I suspect that he was embellishing the truth for effect, but he certainly made his point. As a result our ship had fewer cases for the entire cruise around South America than another cruiser had at Valpariso alone. I learned from this that there is no point in pussy-footing around when you have a message to convey. It is better to be straightforward, perhaps even brutal.

Our time in Uruguay and Argentina was composed of a mixture of games, dances, shooting and sometimes marching through the streets on National Days. We often had trouble with the language as seemingly simple words seemed to have a variety of very different meanings. There were two highlights that stand out in my mind. Both took place at Rosario, (an Argentinian city approximately 100 miles up the Parana River from Buenos Aires), although both were very different. We had been told by several colleagues who had heard that we were going to Rosario that we must be sure to visit the "Round Table". This establishment was obviously unique to Rosario, and clearly nothing like King Arthur's Round Table. Some of us were taken to this place late one night —it was a visit which provided me with another first experience. The "table" was the pièce de résistance of this high class brothel: it was a large, slowly rotating dais with four divans set round its circumference. Each divan was adorned by a lovely naked damsel demonstrating her charms for the benefit of prospective clients and doing her best to encourage custom. I was still very young, but the experience was nevertheless invigorating.

South America showing some of the places visited by the author during his cruises with HMS Durban and HMS Apollo.

The other high point of this visit was a surprisingly clear lesson on the value of showing the flag. We had had a very good visit. I played three rugger matches and one hockey match, and danced every night until the small hours during the five days we were in Rosario. The day we left a small party of English businessmen came on board for a farewell drink, and then asked if they might say a few words. Feeling a little embarassed we agreed. Their spokesman said, "You will not mind my saying that you are not a very big ship, but you are a clean ship. Your men are well behaved, and you have beaten us at games. But that is not everything. You are the first British ship here since the *Glasgow* in 1918, and people here thought that England was finished, and trade was terrible. Though you have been here only five days business is booming again! Thank you!"

Durban's soccer team after their first match at Rosario. They defeated the Central Railway Company team 5-0.

It's Really Quite Safe

When I was in Ottawa after World War 2 I witnessed the same effect when an RCN cruiser was sent around South America. Response from all trade connections was very positive, but yet no more ships were ever sent. I have always found this very hard to understand --what better way is there for a navy to earn its keep than by developing overseas trade?

Our next stop was the Falkland Islands, a place we found inhabited mostly by Scots. Entertainment was simple and genuine: we chased penguins, played golf on the world's most southern golf-course, and attended a Pantomime conducted by the Governor. We were there in June, which at those southern latitudes (55°S) was mid-winter. We had pretty good weather although there was one day when we had a gale and had to keep anchor watch for 24 hours. Altogether we had a very happy visit with nice people who entertained us in their homes and whom we were pleased to entertain on board.

Left: The Governor of the Falkland Islands. Below: One of the many penguines that Durban's crew had fun chasing. Opposite: Durban's crew "invades" the Falklands.

The local Defence Force wanted to simulate the sighting of a ship so that they could exercise the call out of their men to oppose a landing. The drill was that we would fire a gun to mark the time of the sighting, after which we would leave the harbour and prepare for a landing two hours later, that being the time we estimated an approaching ship would take to reach shore from the time it was first sighted. Our Captain was staying ashore with the Governor and was being closely watched to see when he returned to the ship. To thwart this watch he used his bed sheets to climb from his bedroom window, and then made his way down to a boat waiting to take him to the ship. At dawn we fired our gun and left harbour. The islands are surrounded by a belt of thick kelp which would make it very difficult for any boat attempting to land if the locals were there with their guns. We had a great friendly battle in which both sides claimed victory, so everyone was happy.

It's Really Quite Safe

We went on to the Straits of Magellan. Enroute we met HMS *Caradoc* and enjoyed a mock battle, firing our guns at one another (angled off by a few degrees for safety.) We visited the town of Magellanes, and then went up the Patagonian Canals to Valpariso. These so-called canals are in fact fjords, so deep that there were only two places on the way where we could anchor. The scenery was magnificent. The only inhabitants were Patagonian Indians who visited the ship wearing very little clothing despite the cold. They would then beg clothes from us, hurry off to shore, doff them and return for more.

Of our stops along the west coast of South America I loved Valpariso and Lima, but was not too impressed with Antofagasta which was very arid. At the latter stop we were invited to dinner after we had gone ashore to ride horses provided by the Chilean Army. The dinner turned out to be a banquet to mark the end of the Army Rifle Competition, and we in our nondescript riding apparel turned out to be the guests of honour! Each of us was seated in the middle of a long table of Chilean officers who persisted in drinking toast after toast with us. They would call out "al seco", and immediately a dry glass would be refilled. We tried to reciprocate, but we were far outnumbered and definitely came off second best. They beat us to the punch when they toasted Cochrane, (their main liberator from the Spanish, who was actually a British Admiral), before we could claim him, but we then brought the house down by all rising in our somewhat tipsy dignity and toasting, "Chile - AL SECO."

Opposite, top: Monté Sarmiento, part of the beautiful scenery along the Patagonian canals.

Opposite, below: Patagonian Indians.

Right: The author sitting under the canvas awning on the quarter-deck.

It's Really Quite Safe

Going home to base in Bermuda via the Panama Canal we again came to Nassau. Here we were at anchor off the harbour with the Captain ashore for the night when, at dawn, we were hit by an unheralded wind of hurricane force. We had two power boats in the water but within minutes both had been torn away from us. The one sank alongside, while the other, a motor cutter, was tossed onto the coral reef astern of us where it quickly disintegrated. Our Commander did not at first appear to appreciate the danger we were in with the coral reef to leeward. Fortunately, however, the Captain came out in a tug which braved the raging sea on the bar off the harbour and called to us to raise steam and get out to sea at once. Inexplicably, the urgency of the Captain's order seemed to have evaporated as the message was passed down to the engine room.

On deck there was frantic activity as we secured for sea, turning in boats, reeling up hawsers, and closing watertight doors. Mike Evans, our Senior Engineer, just happened to come on deck for a breather and asked me what was up. I pointed to the reef and said, somewhat dramatically, "In not too long, Mike, we shall be on that reef unless you can claw us off!" Suddenly appreciating the situation he said, "My God!" and rushed off to the engine-room hatch where he shouted down an order to open all sprayers into the boilers. Soon reassuring clouds of black smoke were billowing from the funnels, but we were still not under way. Our anchor was dragging and we were being driven closer and closer to the reef. If we struck it I knew that it would mean the end of the ship, and in all liklihood the end of most of the crew as well. I was not feeling too optimistic -when I was asked by the forecastle officer what I thought of our chances I recall answering, "Frankly, practically nil." It was one of the few times I remember praying ferverently to God for help, for it seemed to me that divine intervention might be all that could save us. Perhaps our prayers were answered, for when we got up just enough steam to go slow ahead we were so close that the screws were churning up debris on the reef.

Top: Durban's motor cutter on the shoal at Nassau after the storm.

Bottom: The motor cutter as it was left after everything of value could be salvaged.

The remains of the motor boat which sank alongside during the storm being hauled aboard.

Although we had managed to save ourselves from the reef things were still in a state of crisis on the fore-castle. The ship was moving ahead, but the anchor had not been fully stowed when a green sea broke over the bow. All five men who had been ahead of the breakwater securing cables were seriously injured with broken bones. At the time I was at the break in the forecastle and rushed forward to help. I was right up in the eyes of the ship with Max Cunningham, our Gunnery Officer, and had just gathered up one of the injured lads when we felt the bow rear up before falling into a trough in the waves. We braced ourselves for the onslought of water, not that it would have done much good, but we were lucky. This time the wave splintered to heavy spray under the bow and we were able to scramble to safety before the next boarding sea could get us. I remember putting in a second prayer at that point. In retrospect that was probably the most dangerous experience I ever had in the service, more perilous than any of the wartime episodes in the years to come.

The most tiring time I had during my stay with *Durban* came during a visit to Vera Cruz in Mexico. The Captain had to make an official visit to Mexico City, so it was arranged that the rugby team would go as well. We made the two hundred mile trip on the night train and seemed to be pulling on blankets all night long as the train climbed from the steamy coastal plain into the mountains. After a gala lunch at an English club in the city we were taken out to the Country Club for the game. I found that at 6,500 feet above sea level rugby football ceases to be an enjoyable game -you can't get enough air to breathe and it is totally exhausting. After the game we recovered slightly with drinks in the Club locker room, before going upstairs for a thé dansant. There was just time enough to open some conversation with some pretty girls before we were whisked off to the city for another thé dansant. Once again we had just enough time to start to appreciate the female company before we had to change and go with the Captain to the British Embassy for dinner. During dinner I was almost roped into doing the rounds of the local night spots with the Japanese naval attaché, but I was rescued by the Third Secretary. We managed to get just two hours sleep before catching the train back to Vera Cruz. I would have gladly traded my position for that of one of the lower deck members of our team. While we ran from one engagement to another, they had more leisurely entertainment and had the time to enjoy the company of young men and women. What we did for our country!

Besides all the partying there was work and training to be done. The hero of one Admiral's inspectiom that we underwent was A.B.Pink. One of the inspecting officers, Commander Gilmore, was conducting a gun drill and called for a simulated gun misfire. Immediately everyone behind the gun had to jump clear while the charge was removed. On the order to do this from Pink, the breech worker, everyone moved except the Gunnery Officer, who evidently thought he was exempted. Pink, who had other ideas, ordered Gilmore to "GET OUT!" loud and clear. Afterwards Gilmore told me how pleased he was with Pink's reaction. "Of course I should have got out of the way," he said. Pink and I played rugger together and I often wonder what became of him. He should have gone far, but our paths never crossed again.

Right: HMS Durban at Houston, Texas.

Below: Durban's rugger team at Mexico City.

It's Really Quite Safe

The last International ceremony we took part in before
returning home in the summer of 1930 was the celebration
of the tercentenary of Boston's receiving its Royal
Charter from King Charles 1st in 1630. The Boston Tea
Party was forgotten and we were invited to take part in
the big parade. We fielded four platoons of seamen, the
Royal Marines and our ship's band, and we paraded
immediately ahead of the Black Watch Pipe Band from
Montreal. There were some 25,000 participants in the
parade that day, but the local papers gave us top honours
for drill, and the Black Watch got top marks for
appearance, so together we carried off the day.

In October 1933 I was appointed to *Hawkins*, a cruiser twice the size of *Durban* My stay on board was brief, which was probably just as well because I did not get on too well with Captain Holland. He did not like delegating authority, something I found out one thick night in the English Channel. I was on the bridge when the lights of a steamer appeared rather close on the starboard bow so that it was our responsibility to adjust course to avoid collision if necessary. Almost at once I altered course to a safe heading, and then called the Captain to advise him of the change. He was soon on the bridge and put me down severely for not calling him before taking action. That was not the *Durban* way of doing things, and considering that we were getting far too close for safety I judged it not to be in accordance with the Rules of the Road at Sea, but it certainly typified the attitude of many of the big-ship commanders of the period. I was not at all unhappy when, in May 1931, my appointment to a destroyer Flotilla Leader in the Mediterranean, HMS *Stuart*, came through.

Opposite, top: Officers who took part in the parade at Boston. Left to right: the author, Osborne, Max Cunningham, US Navy officer, Ben Bolt, Nugent.

Opposite, bottom: With bayonets fixed, Durban's ships company marches through the streets of Boston during the city's tercentenary celebrations in 1930.

Above: Durban's junior officers. Rear: Clouston, Hawkins, Maclean, Merriman. Front: Begg, Smith, Nugent, Rotherham, and Morgan.

It's Really Quite Safe

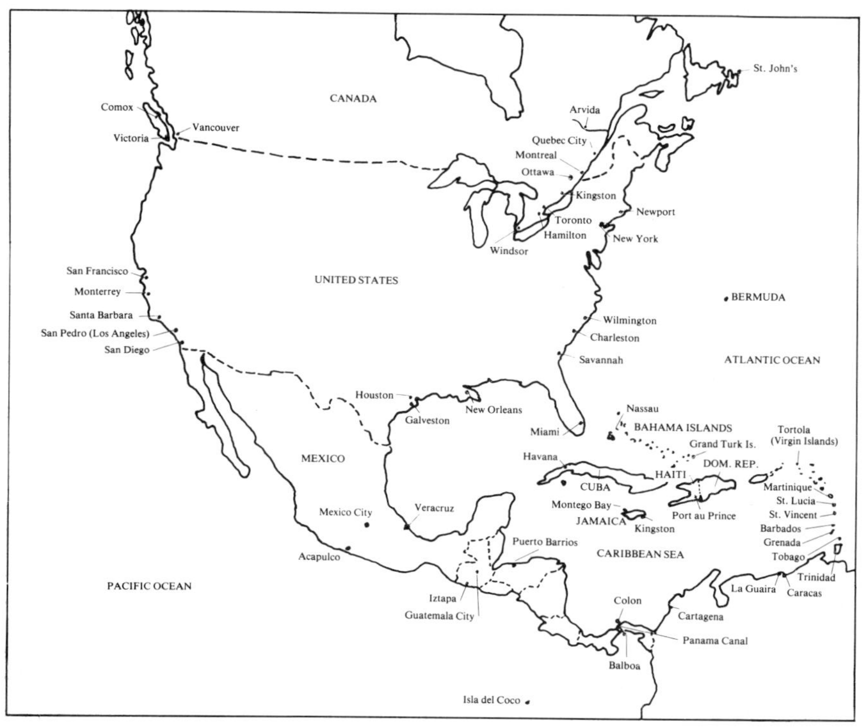

Destroyers

I joined my new ship in Malta. Since I was a little short of shore leave the Admiralty allowed me an extra week at home by arranging for me to travel by train across France and join the P & O steamer *Mantua* at Marseilles rather than board at Southampton. When I set off on my journey I discovered to my horror that I had packed my Passport in my trunk which was by then already at sea in *Mantua*. There was no problem at the Folkestone end of the cross-Channel ferry, and I decided that I would try to talk the French immigration people into letting me pass through their country. When we landed in France I explained in a mixture of several kinds of foreign phrases and a great deal of pantomime that the King wanted me urgently in Malta and would be furious if I was late, so would it be all right if I promised not to get off the train? The officials laughed at the performance and waved me through. Subsequent experience has confirmed for me that if you can make a joke with a civil servant of any nationality you can often get away with a great deal.

The promise not to leave the train probably saved me some trouble. A young Army lieutenant enroute to India had the splendid idea of getting off the train in Paris, having a night on the town, and then catching the express train to Marseilles in the morning. At the time I regretted that I could not go along, but when our liner left France without the young lieutenant I felt much better about it. I have often wondered what his Colonel said when he eventually showed up, and how much it cost him to book a new passage.

Stuart was somewhat larger than the other eight destroyers in the Flotilla, and because of its position as Leader it was commanded by a Captain. The other ships were organized into two divisions with each division leader being commanded by a Commander, the remaining ships being captained by Lieutenant- Commanders. I found Captain A.H.Taylor in Stuart to be both intelligent and kind. He was reputed to be an expert on the battle of Trafalgar and he had a thoroughly professorial air. He indicated that he was most distressed to find that I had a bad report from *Hawkins*, something which was news to me. It meant that Captain Taylor had to make quarterly reports on my conduct. After the first three month period, however, he sent for me and told me not to worry any further: his first report had settled the matter.

The other leading character on the ship was our Torpedo Gunner, a Warrant Officer named Jackie Jago. He was the life and soul of the Wardroom, always ready to lead a singsong or organize fun and games. The atmosphere was reminiscent of the family feeling I had experienced in the picket boat: it was a larger family, and just a little more formal, but there was that sentiment that blossoms in small ships --that we were all somehow on the same side.

A destroyer is a wonderful training ground for a young officer. The bridge was informal and because there were so few officers you were close to whatever was going on. You read all the signals and operation orders, and you were close to your Captain and to your men. The Coxswain, the Senior Lower Deck rating in the ship, was always available to discuss ship's matters and what the sailors would want. Having gone through the mill for some 20 years he certainly had more experience than the junior officers with just five or six years service.

HMS Glorious.

The destroyer's home in Malta was Sliema Creek, which was separated from the Grand Harbour, where the big ships lay, by the town of Valetta. This was very much to our liking as our way of living was different from that of the big ships, and we had some kindred spirits in the submarines which were berthed in the same creek. We of the Second Flotilla were especially favoured as we berthed in Lazaretto Creek, an offshoot of Sliema behind Manoel Island. This was delightfully private and sheltered from the gale force "Gregale" winds which occasionally ravaged the Grand Harbour and Sliema. On those days we were the only ones who could get ashore, and we were not loath to shout to our less fortunate friends that we were off to see their wives or engage in some other pleasurable activity.

One of the great sights of the time was that of the Fleet leaving port for a cruise. Out of the Grand Harbour under the ancient battlements of Valetta would come the Battle Squadron of six or eight ships, along with the aircraft carrier *Glorious* and the cruisers. Out to meet them from Sliema and Lazaretto creeks would come *Coventry* leading as many as 36 destoyers divided into four flotillas. The big ships moved majestically, each slipping its buoys in turn. The destroyers scuttled out from their congested creeks to join the battleships, probably needing no more signal than the time-honoured "Follow Father". They would gather speed as they moved out to sea and form up in perfect order in their stations ahead of the Battle Fleet. What a spectacle this massive exhibition of power was when seen from the battlements of Valetta. Magnificent and impressive as it was, however, there were many of us who had begun to realize that the days of the battleship were numbered. The aeroplane and the submarine would replace them in a short span of years. Now they were obsolescent —like actors past their prime, but still holding centre stage in a last gesture of defiance of time and technology.

The Rear Admiral Destroyers (R.A.D.) was Forbes, my Captain in *Iron Duke* and later to be C-in-C Home Fleet in the early days of the war. These were days of economy and so we never exceeded twelve knots, even during manoeuvers. It really was no way to train destroyers, but things changed when "Biff" Rose took over. He had been my first Captain, and he was an old destroyer man. When he gave an order we moved at full speed to carry it out. Overnight the spirit in the Destroyer Flotillas changed and we started to become efficient. We had pride. When Rose went round the Flotilla on Sunday mornings we vied with one another to be the best and cleanest ship.

In one Fleet Exercise our Flotilla was defending the battleships against torpedo attack from the other three flotillas which were making a massed attack. We steamed out bravely at 30 knots to counter the attack and quickly found ourselves too close to the attackers to turn away. We were obliged to steam right through another flotilla in line abreast with ships just 300 yards apart. Captain Taylor, who was not the greatest of ship handlers, was giving me helm orders when I heard the Navigator's quiet voice from behind me say, "Take her through yourself, Hank." This I did, and I don't suppose the Captain ever knew the difference. Passing other ships at a relative speed of 60 knots with just 100 yards between was exciting. You had to pick the hole to go through early in the game, and then hope that the ship next to you didn't go for the same hole!

Once we were sent to render assistance to a small Greek village that had been damaged by an earthquake. Shortly after we arrived the Greek Admiralty contractor came on board and asked if we wanted any beef. Since we had been sent to help supposedly starving people we were a little surprised. The contractor explained that although there was a shortage of meat in this village they could easily bring some in from Athens for us. Evidently the supply was limited only by the ability to pay, not by need.

During a winter cruise the Fleet lay in the sheltered harbour of Navarin. There was such a gale blowing that for the entire length of our stay we kept 'anchor watch' on the bridge day and night, and kept adequate steam in the boilers to give us low speed in case our anchor started dragging. I discovered that destroyers, with their rather light ground tackle and their habit of yawing in bad weather, were notorious for dragging their anchors. While we were there we watched the crew of *Glorious* play deck hockey each evening on their spacious flight deck. We were slated to play them in the final of the Caesar Cup* when we returned to Malta, and all the space we had for exercise was about ten paces on the quarterdeck. I am glad to say that despite our lack of training we still beat them.

During my time in *Stuart* I had to make a difficult career decision. The Admiralty was calling for volunteers for specialization as Observers, and I was intrigued because I believed passionately that aircraft were to be the prime weapon of the future. I also knew that I loved destroyers, so it was not an easy decision. I finally decided that I had a quick mathematical brain which should be made use of, so I submitted my application for Observer training. I knew that it would mean a complete change of life style from little ships to big ones, but I subsequently found that aircraft squadrons themselves had the atmosphere of small ships.

* *The Caesar Cup was awarded to the ship fielding the best hockey team and winning the knock out competition. Destroyer flotillas fielded a team as did each big ship. Cups were frowned upon by English Field Hockey authorities as leading to rough play in this robust game, and indeed I can vouch for this. The Caesar Cup was, however, a time honoured institution and the competition was the cradle of naval hockey. Any efforts to have it abolished were fiercely resisted and promises, if extracted, were tactfully 'forgotten'.*

It's Really Quite Safe

About three months before we were due to return to England our First Lieutenant went down with Malta fever, and he was very ill. There was no question of him coming back to the ship as he would have to be invalided home. I suggested to our surgeon that he should make this official in the hope that I would then be appointed First Lieutenant and inherit the two shilling and six pence a day allowance. The plan worked until the C-in-C stepped in to offer Captain Taylor a Lieutenant Commander as relief since I was so junior. Much to my relief Taylor declined the offer and I got my first real taste of the sweet and sour flavour of executive responsibility. For a twenty-five-year-old this was quite a coup. I found it rather strange to be President of the Wardroom by virtue of my position, although the Captain's staff were all far senior. They were all very helpful to the new boy, and I recall the Staff Gunnery Officer, Lieutenant Commander Michael Laing telling me an anecdote from his own experience to illustrate his point that some opportunities should be taken, and others declined. He had been offered a job in the Royal Yacht when he was a young Sub-Liutenant, but refused it, saying that he didn't want to be a damned flunky. He was appointed to a destroyer instead, which was subsequently sent to Cowes to act as a guardship during Cowes Week. King George V was sailing *Britannia* that year, and paid his customary visit to the guardship to inspect the ship's company. Near the end of the line of officers the King came across Laing, and eyeing him up and down he said, "Aren't you the young officer who refused to be a damned flunky?" Laing was speechless with fright and tried to sink through the deck. "Quite right, my boy. Quite right", murmured the King, moving on to the next in line.

I also received a good deal of help from all the First Lieutenants of the Flotilla, particularly Ruck Keene of *Viceroy.*, Tiny Stewart of *Winchelsea*, and Wingfield of *Venetia*. I certainly needed all the help I could get when the Admiral decided to inspect *Stuart*. It was the custom for a friendly ship to send over a party of experts to put the final touches to the clean up job while the ship's company were 'cleaning', ie. getting into their best

HMS Stuart off Southsea with paying-off pennant streamed.

clothes for the inspection. The party rendering this sort of last-minute cosmetic help would slip over the port side as the inspecting officer came up the starboard gangway.

At the end of her commission *Stuart* set off for home, and after a rough passage through the Bay of Biscay and the Channel anchored for the night off Spithead. At dawn, with no persuasion at all from their temporary First Lieutenant, the hands were over the side washing the ship down to make sure that it looked right to wives, girl-friends and the Home Fleet that might be encountered within the Narrows. The paying-off pendant streamed proudly in the wind as we entered port with the Southsea photographer bouncing along in his launch snapping photos that he would later sell to the crew. It had been a happy ship for me, and I left her with regret.

Before the Observers Course started, however, there was still some time to be killed, and so I was sent to *Sardonyx*, a handsome 'S' Class destroyer of about 900 tons. She had been in reserve since 1918, and had been recommissioned as a tender to the Signal School. Her task was to test equipment and to act as Duty Destroyer, although she was almost never called upon to perform the latter duty.

The ratings were classified as 'Harbour Service' and were therefore supposed to to have a long weekend off every month. As we spent days and nights at sea in the Solent these could hardly ever be arranged, even though we usually exceeded by far our economical and legal speed when on the move. To make up for the loss of weekends I allowed them to go ashore as soon as the ship was clean after we docked. It was small recompense, but they appreciated it. One morning we entered harbour after a couple of days at sea in dirty weather. The ship was simply filthy, so 'Clean Ship' was the order of the day. Early in the afternoon the Chief Boatswain's Mate (the Buffer) came to tell me that there was a soccer match arranged against another ship and to request that the crew be relieved of their cleaning duties. Since this was the first I had heard of the game I denied the request. Some time later he returned with the same request, which I again refused. On his third try, however, he won. "Look 'ere, Sir, about this soccer match, you know you're playing don't you?" I had been prepared to give in this time, but this was the clincher, and so we all went off and played soccer. We were winning the game, and just to make me happy our team put the ball at my feet with an entirely empty goal and yelled "Shoot!" I shot and scored one more goal. Everyone was content.

There were six destroyer tenders attached to various naval schools and we took it in turn to be Duty Destroyer, although as I have mentioned we were almost never called out. One day when it was our turn I had a hockey match scheduled in London, and managed to persuade my Captain to let me go since there was so little likelihood of our being called out. After the hockey game I was on my way to a party when I stopped to buy a copy of the Evening News and was astonished to read the headline "SARDONYX GOES TO SEA". Since there was nothing I could do about it at that point I hid the newspaper under my seat and went on to enjoy the evening. I discovered later that I had scarcely left the ship when it was ordered to raise steam and stand by to search for two sailing boats containing naval officers who were adrift somewhere in the Channel. An officer who had been in a third boat which managed to get back was sent over to the ship to tell the Captain where the others might be. As he was about to leave the Captain said, "What did you say your name was?" He gave his name, but the Captain replied, "No it isn't. Your name is Rotherham. You will find your clothes in your cabin!" When I returned to Portsmouth in the wee small hours *Sardonyx* was back. In the morning I went straight over to the Gunnery School from whence came my relief and swore him to secrecy, for both my Captain and I could have been raked over the coals if the hierarchy discovered that I had been granted leave when we were Duty Destroyer.

There was a nice old custom that merchant ships always dipped their ensigns to warships, then the warship dipped to the merchantman. The custom dates back to Stuart times I believe, when the British demanded this courtesy of the Dutch. It may go back even further than that. We were constantly operating in the Solent, the sea approach to Southampton where so many trans-Atlantic liners docked at the end of their voyage. We would frequently see one of these magnificent ships of up to 80,000 tons coming towards us. We would instruct a signalman to stand some ten feet or so from our ensign halyards, but not to touch them. Then we would wait, and without fail these great ships would dip their ensigns to us, a very little ship. Immediately our signalman would spring to the halyards and dip our ensign in return. I always felt great pride of service for this courtesy.

During my time in *Sardonyx* I learned much about ship handling because of the frequency with which I was able to watch my Captain bring the ship alongside. One day when we were coming alongside against a strong wind I learnt a particularly clear lesson. We had made several tries at slow speed, but each time the wind would catch us and blow us off. Then he realised what to do, and with full ahead, stop both, full astern starboard, we were there with no trouble at all. In such conditions the only thing to do is to use power, and with 27,000 horsepower in a 900 ton ship we did not lack it!

When the time came for my Observer's Course I had to

say goodbye to *Sardonyx* and to destroyers, my second love. Still, I was looking forward to working with aircraft. I had made the choice, and now it was up to me to acquire the skills needed to match my strong belief that naval aviation was the key weapon of the near future. I would be in on the ground floor and surely involved in all the development work that would be necessary.

Airborne

The Observer's Course started in October 1932. There were just seven students, all of us Lieutenants. I was pleased that all three parts of the course would be given in the Portsmouth area and that consequently I could continue to play hockey for the Portsmouth Services and for the Navy. The Signal School had the nearly impossible task of teaching us the complete theory of wireless transmission in the space of a few lessons. During this time we had to work up our command of the Morse Code to 22 words per minute in order to be able to read at a rate of 15 words a minute while flying. The Captain of the Signal School was Herbert Fitz-Herbert, previously my Commander in *Iron Duke*. His comments about our efforts (in a subject in which he of course excelled), were predictably terse. He told us that it was clear from our examination results that only two of us were doing any work, and that he had considered failing the rest of us. The truth was that the two "workers" had done very little -this sort of learning simply came easy to them. The rest of us had worked like dogs.

The second phase of the course was at the Gunnery School at Whale Island. Here we were delighted to be received as disciples of the art rather than as mere course-fodder. Spotting the fall of shot was, of course, an

Top: The 1932 United Services Hockey team at the Folkstone Hockey Festival. Rear: Collett, Morris, ?, Davies. Middle: Cronyn, Buck, Phillips, Rotherham, Dickens. Front: Rebbeck, ?.

Bottom: A Fairey 111F

essential part of enabling the gunners to hit their target, and observers were seen as valuable members of the team. We were pleased to see a spirit of ready co-operation developing.

Finally we went to Lee-on-Solent, which at that time was an RAF float-plane base. The place was a hybrid affair in every way with a mixture of Royal Air Force and Royal Navy personnel. The base was commanded by an RAF Group Captain and the pilots were RAF, but the small training staff were naval, as were the Telegraphist Air Gunners who had expertise in radio and Morse work. Generally the pilots seemed to think that Lee-on-Solent was some sort of punishment posting, although in my experience they were first rate people who did their best to help us. Half the day was spent on book work, and the other half flying in Fairey 111F float-planes over both land and sea.

One disappointment for me came late in the course. I had played hockey regularly for the Navy team, but had played in only one of the Combined Services Matches, so when it appeared that my season was ended I broke training. Then with no warning I saw my name listed in the Times as a player in the final trial for the English team. Although I did my best I failed to make the team. As fate would have it I was never again to be in England to get a second chance.

English winter weather was not very favourable for flying so I was glad to be appointed to HMS *Glorious* at the end of the course. *Glorious* was in the Mediterranean where I was sure to find weather that would permit plenty of flying to enable me to put into practice all that I had learned. When I joined the ship I was delighted to find that Flight Lieutenant A.P. Revington, formerly the Adjutant at Lee-on-Solent, was on board as a pilot, and that he had asked that I be assigned as his observer. I came to admire 'Rev' both as a man and as a pilot, and we became firm friends. This sort of cross-service association was typical of the period, for the Fleet Air Arm was made up of a mixture of Air Force and Navy personnel.

In those days the Captain RN commanding a carrier

usually had no previous knowledge of aviation, and the Wing Commander RAF had no experience of deck landings nor of Fleet Air Arm methods. It created a situation strangely reminiscent of the command structure of ships in Elizabethan times as described by E.Keble Chatterton in his book "English Seamen and the Colonization of America". He stated that "This division of authority between a Landsman in supreme command (being ignorant of nautical matters) and the Master (who had spent his time afloat) contained the very elements of trouble and disunity." His later words were equally apt: "But where the Captain was able to unite in his person the ability of Shipmaster and Pilot, then he was a genuine superman whose authority was unique." Four hundred years later a similar situation reigned and it was fortunate for us that some of our commanders were broadminded and adaptable men such as I found in Glorious.

About half the pilots, all of the maintenance crews and the senior pilot (a Wing Commander) were RAF. The Telegraphist Air Gunners and we Observers were all Navy (the RAF did not have such trades at the time.) At the lower levels we got on very well together, but in the higher echelons there was discord. Although the RAF was in charge of the Fleet Air Arm the top brass seemed to know that their sea-going days were numbered. There was little incentive to develop new concepts in naval aviation, the natural inclination was to channel new design work towards RAF needs rather than naval requirements. As one small example I recall that as late as 1938 we were still using the TF-T21C radios which had been in use twenty years earlier during the First World War! Also, it is my understanding that had not the head of the Naval Air Division been a close personal friend of Sir Richard Fairey and able to persuade him to go ahead with the Swordfish as a private venture we would not have had even that aircraft when war was declared.

Just how the FAA had fallen so low from the large and efficient Royal Naval Air Service of the First World War was explained to me in 1947 by Admiral Troubridge who had heard the story from Admiral Freemantle. After the First World War there had arisen a dispute between the

RAF and the Navy as to who should be in charge of naval air operations. The Admiralty was adamant that the RNAS should remain part of the Navy, but Lord Trenchard, head of the RAF, insisted that the Commander-in-Chief of the Home Fleet, Admiral Beatty, be consulted. The Admiralty did not take time to brief the Admiral since they assumed that a Navy controlled air arm was an obvious requirement. To their dismay Beatty is reported to have said that he thought aeroplanes were a nuisance and that he didn't care who controlled the air. In this almost casual manner the Navy lost control of the RNAS whose members were absorbed into the RAF. In the process they lost that vital ingredient of air-sea operations -that of aircrew understanding what ships were trying to do and having the best interests of the Navy at heart. From then on the Navy got second best aircraft and second best service. The Navy also lost experience in aircraft so that our developing officers grew up lacking knowledge of air operations. Naval personnel were not reintroduced until a few years later and were still under the direction of the RAF. Control of the Fleet Air Arm was not regained until April 1939, when it was very nearly too late to win the crucial Battle of the Atlantic. I later heard that Beatty very much regretted his hasty five minute decision and worked for five years as First Sea Lord to reverse his mistake.

In 1934, however, we were only vaguely aware of these matters of high policy, being much more concerned with the everyday business of our profession. During my time with *Glorious*, and later with *Furious* the most memorable characters were the Captain of *Glorious*, Ginger Royle, Commander Daniel of *Glorious* (later Admirals), and Camidge, our senior observer aboard *Furious*. Royle was much loved by his crew, and his wife was similarly popular with the officer's wives. Camidge weighed over 280 pounds and was famous for the great quantities of gin he could consume with no apparent effect.

In the aircraft carriers we were a team. The RAF pilots worked with us and helped to develop our techniques. Our Telegraphist Air Gunners were a magnificent breed of men. Cox was my first TAG, and since he had flown with many novice observers before I found him to be a great help. The RAF riggers and fitters were also wonderful. Not being seafaring men they were really out of their element, but nevertheless nothing was too much trouble for them if you needed some adjustment to make life easier. Often they would work all night to get our aircraft ready for the next day's flying.

There was a different way of life in the carriers where it was more precarious than most naval life, save perhaps the submarines. They always said that we were the most daring, but we pointed out that what goes up must come down, but what goes down did not have to come up. Everything was taken as a joke. If an aircraft went over the side, possibly in two or three pieces, it was a laugh -a drink on him. I don't think there was any other way to operate. In fact I never saw anyone killed landing on, and only one taking off, and I saw some pretty devastating crashes. So there is little doubt that the FAA and the submariners were the hardest living branches of the Navy, followed not too far behind by the destroyers.

Observers on board HMS Glorious.

If you did something silly you were usually said to have joined a Club. There was the Seven League Boot Club for those who plotted the speed wrong, the Where It Listeth Club for those who got the wind wrong and were blown off course, and many others. The Rat Club was reserved for those who, realising that their aircraft was going over the side, jumped out to avoid a swim. There was one remarkable member of this club, Edwards, nick-named the 'Chinese Ambassador' because of his countenance, who in Hermes decided that his aircraft would not make it and tumbled over the side. At the same instant the pilot, also having come to this same conclusion, opened up the throttle in the hope of getting airborne again, a possibility that Edwards had discarded as impossible. He staggered off, flew around and landed on to find his observer waiting for him. Since he had not been aware of Edwards impromtu departure he was somewhat shaken!

There was just one member of the Trapped Rat Club. An aircraft piloted by Dal Stead landed, and when he decided that it was not going to stop on the deck he jumped out leaving his observer in the aircraft -of this we obtained photographic evidence. Then the observer also jumped, in the nick of time, becoming the first and I believe the only member of the Trapped Rat Club. Remember that in those days the aircraft had no brakes and there were no arrester wires. If you joined more than one club you were termed a 'Man About Town'. It may have been childish but it kept one from dwelling on the dangers.

Glorious was a happy ship in which we were all delighted to serve. When she was sent home all of the aircraft and their crews were disembarked in Malta to await *Furious*. As *Glorious* left harbour the entire complement of the Squadrons, be they Navy or RAF, aircrew or maintenance men, were on the breakwater to say goodbye. Many were close to tears. In *Glorious* I had learned my trade -reconnaissance, navigation, spotting for guns and many other chores. I had also spent time photographing Flotilla torpedo attacks so that the exact behaviour of the 'fish' could be seen.

"Queen Elizabeth,"
at Thasc.

26th July, 1934.

Med. 33.

Sir,

I have the honour to inform you that I noted with satisfaction the good results obtained by "C" Flight of 803 Squadron in the High Bombing attacks on "Centurion." reported in HF/23/03/Air of 25th June, 1934.

2. The results obtained by the unit led by Lieutenant G.A.Rotherham, Royal Navy, were particularly good.

I have the honour to be,

Sir,

Your obedient Servant,

(Signed) W. W. FISHER.

ADMIRAL,
COMMANDER-IN-CHIEF.

Air Officer Commanding,
Mediterranean.
(Copy to Commanding Officer, H.M.S. "Furious.")

Above: *The C-in-C's letter —an interesting study in the prevailing chain of command.*

Opposite: *HMS Furious during WWII —note the camouflage and Albacore aircraft.*

After *Glorious* had left we were nominally attached to *Furious* pending her arrival in Malta. In the interval the old battleship *Centurion* was equipped with radio control and sent to the Mediterranean to be used for target practice. We were told to prepare for High Level bombing attacks against *Centurion* who would be allowed to take full avoiding action. We used flights of three aircraft and Rev and I led one flight. After a little practice we had great success in hitting *Centurion* hard, and the C-in-C, Admiral W.W.Fisher was kind enough to send us a congratulatory letter. The experience we gained was to be used later when more extensive pattern bombing was planned.

The letter from Admiral Fisher is, apart from its pat-on-the-back aspect, an interesting comment on the peculiar chain of command that applied to a Naval Air Squadron operating from a carrier in the thirties, (*Furious* had arrived by the time this letter was despatched.) It was sent to the Air Officer Commanding, Mediterranean, who was an RAF Air Marshal who probably had no idea what we were doing, with a copy to our Captain. It filtered down to us through the RAF General Office, Fleet Air Arm, HMS *Furious*. Only though goodwill in the working ranks could such an organization operate. Further examples of this chaotic system, which we were convinced could have been designed only by someone with a warped sense of humour, were abundant. For example, all Naval pilots carried both Naval and RAF ranks, which were not necessarily equivalent. All Naval pilots carried the suffix '(P)' after their Naval rank to show that they were qualified pilots and similarly Naval observers carried the suffix '(O)'. The RAF ranks took precedence when working within the squadron, or when detached to an RAF station ashore. When carrying out ships duties onboard Naval ranks applied. I recall one Commander RN who held only Flying Officer status in the RAF...he could command one of His Majesties ships, but in the air he was just tail-end-Charlie. We Observers, of course, carried Naval rank only since the RAF had no equivalent trade. In the RAF Pilots were God; Observers were nothing. This strange dual-rank system led to some amusing situations, such as the one that occured shortly after a Naval Air Squadron had been disembarked to an RAF station. In RAF Messes it was the custom for the senior officer present to go into dinner first when the meal was announced. In this case the Squadron commander was a senior Lieutenant Commander (P) who had only recently been promoted to the RAF rank of Squadron Leader. The squadron included a fairly senior Lieutenant Commander (O) carrying no RAF rank. The Mess Sergeant reported that dinner was served to a rather junior resident Squadron Leader who was nevertheless senior in RAF rank to the Squadron Commander. He took thought, then turned to the Lt.Cdr.(O) and said, "But you are senior to me." The latter agreed, but turned to the Lt.Cdr.(P) and said, "But you are senior to me." Again this was agreed, but the Squadron Commander, realising how junior he was as an RAF Squadron Leader turned back to the resident Sqn.Ldr. and said, "But YOU are senior to me!" The impasse was resolved by all three going into dinner arm in arm.

There was one occasion on which the system worked to our advantage. We were disembarked at RAF Station Manston at the time, and each day the senior officer present took command of the morning parade. One morning the senior officer happened to be a naval Observer, creating a situation that the RAF considered tantamount to sacrilege -ie. having a back-seat man in charge of their pilots. We were forthwith excused parades to prevent any recurrence. In the air the pilot was always in command

-even if he were a junior Pilot Officer with an experienced Lt.Cdr.(O) in the back seat. It was the pilot who would make decisions as to the policy to be adopted by the aircraft. As I have said, it was only through the goodwill of the lower ranks (and thank God there was plenty of that), that the system worked at all.

Eventually I could claim to be in the first flight of back-seat men, one of those the Admiral's Staff would wait to hear from to resolve any conflict in the reports of enemy position and movement given by other aircraft. Each observer was assigned his own letter as part of his aircraft's call sign to enable the fleet to know who was doing the reporting. The call signs were made up of three letters -the first identified the Carrier, the second the observer, and the third the duty being carried out.

A Blackburn Baffin, one of the many types of aircraft in which the author flew.

I flew in all types of aircraft besides my own with Rev, and one of my responsibilities was the training of new pilots in sea work. One new Flight Lieutenant was not very good at steering an accurate course. This made getting lost a very real danger, so he was not very popular among observers. I suspect that he felt that it was rather infra-dig to be asked by a back-seat man to be accurate. On my first flight with him he only managed to keep within some five degrees of the proper course. We managed to find the ship again, but it was clear to me that some drastic emphasis on the importance of accurate steering was required. But for that flaw he was completely competent. That evening when we were all having a drink in the ward room I wandered over to him and said casually, "Spoode, if you don't keep a better course tomorrow when we are going out over 100 miles we shall probably get lost. I hope you don't mind." The result was immediate. From that day forth he steered a commendably accurate course.

Sometime later Lt.Cdr. Tony Colthurst joined the squadron as its Commander, and shortly afterwards we were teamed up as a flight crew. I was really too young to be the Senior Observer of a squadron, but Tony and I got along very well. We became evening drinking companions which led to our collaborating on ways to develop the efficiency of the squadron, particularly in high level bombing.

High level bombing was an art that had been neglected by the RAF, probably because it was easier to bomb accurately from lower altitudes. For a bomb to have the speed on impact necessary to penetrate heavily armoured decks, however, it had to be dropped from at least 10,000 feet. Even dive bombing from lower altitudes could not achieve the required speed. Thus high level bombing was an essential part of Naval air operations.

Our two main concerns were finding an accurate wind so that we could adjust our aim accordingly, and dropping our bombs in a pattern that would give us the best chance of making a hit. I found the wind-finding methods taught by the RAF at Lee to be somewhat naive. We were supposed to make three runs over the target from different directions dropping practice bombs, and to deduce the wind direction from where they fell. How one could hope to do this with a formation of aircraft and still maintain any element of surprise was beyond me. If there was any enemy air cover or anti-aircraft fire it would be tantamount to suicide. The method we adopted was to wait until we were about 10-15 miles from the target and then send an aircraft ahead to drop a sea marker and fire a smoke puff for us to fly through and make our calculations for an accurate wind.

Whatever method of wind-finding was used there were bound to be errors, and our primitive bombsight with its temperamental magnetic compass was difficult for even an expert to use. It appeared to me that a squadron intending to bomb a ship or other target where penetration was needed would have to make the utmost use of its very best bomb aimer and have all bombs dropped simultaneously from aircraft arranged in a formation that would produce a pattern calculated to result in several hits. The formation we eventually devised produced a pattern of bombs 450 feet square, with bombs spaced 90 feet apart. We figured that a battleship with a length of 700 feet and a beam of 100 feet would sustain 5 or 6 hits from such a pattern -virtually any large target could not avoid being hit.

Eventually we were ready to try out our refined procedures on *Centurion*. On the first try she was told to steer a steady course and we got six hits. Then she was allowed to take whatever avoiding action she liked and still we got our six hits. We carried vertical cameras so that there could be no arguments over the hits scored. There is no doubt in my mind that we proved the method as effective, but unfortunately the knowledge went no further than those who were immediately involved. The RAF, under whose command we nominally operated, apparently did not consider it worth following up, and the Navy, despite the commendations of the C-in-C Mediterranean Fleet, did not see fit to record the methods and procedures we had developed. Early in the war, when I was with *Courageous* , we had intended to use the method on *Scharnhorst* and *Gneisenau* because our crews had not yet had any torpedo training. That opportunity fell through and never presented itself again.*

* *I was told recently by a colleague that in the Pacific Fleet they would have preferred to use their Avengers for high level bombing because they made poor dive-bombers. There was no information available to them about pattern bombing, and there was no time for experimenting in the midst of all the action.*

It's Really Quite Safe

I would not like to leave the reader with the impression that with one well trained crew per squadron it was possible to go out and sink any ship in sight. Our formation consisted of two flights of six aircraft in a flat V. Good formation keeping was essential; pilots had to follow every little variation in course and still maintain their station. The dropping of the bombs had to be co-ordinated down to small fractions of a second. Even at our very modest speed of 90 knots (a snails pace by todays standards) we were covering 150 feet per second so timing was critical: 0.6 seconds between each bomb's release. We spent a great deal of intensive practice in the hangar trying to hone the mixture of hand and radio signals to be used and determining the reaction time between brain and hand. It was very much a team event. In hindsight I would have liked to have spent the years leading up to 1939 designing a bomber and bomb sight for maritime use. It would have entailed a gyro rather than magnetic compass, a system to release bombs at predetermined intervals and radio voice communications between aircraft. As it was, the routine for dropping bombs was, for lack of proper equipment, very clumsy: lying on my stomach I would signal by hand to my Telegraphist Air Gunner who would then release the key on his morse transmitter, and other aircrew in each accompanying aircraft would release their bombs, hopefully all at the same time as mine. (We carried only two Observers, in the Leader and half-Leader; TAG's made up the rest.) It took a lot of practice to get it to work, and the whole exercise lacked a good scientific approach. Nevertheless the exercise created intense enthusiasm in the squadron. We knew that the new Swordfish aircraft, capable of carrying three 500 lb bombs, was in production and we felt that we were testing new procedures for it. For the first time our Air Gunners had a real job to do and our practice sessions onboard ship were fun. Everyone would be there trying out the procedure with radio keys, earphones and dummy bomb release quadrants while their mates would shout advice --too slow--too fast-- encouraging the others to get all the intervals just right. Taking into account the needed accurate formation flying, (Rev, the half-Leader had to be exactly 360 ft behind the Leader), and the accuracy required of the Telegraphists, not to mention the two with cameras as well, everyone had to be on his toes.

While we were disembarked to Manston for a training period we had a pilot with us (who shall remain anonymous) who was well known for his prowess with women. It was said that in Malta he had danced one night with an officer's wife at the Sliema Club, and that later that night he had made his way to their house, climbed onto the bedroom balcony and had his evil way with her right there while her husband lay unwittingly nearby in a deep, alcohol induced, sleep. At Manston a young Flying Officer who had served with us previously arrived on some RAF job, bringing with him his lovely young wife. He then had to go off on some other assignment and both Tony and I were incredulous when we overheard him in the Mess asking our notorious Don Juan if he would look after his wife for the few days that he would be away. For a moment we were struck dumb, then Tony turned to me and said, "Hank, if I had a bag of buns I wouldn't give it to an elephant to look after!" From then on the wife became known as the 'Bag of Buns'. I later asked our lothario how he had behaved, to which he replied, "Well Hank, you can't refuse, can you?"

During the latter half of my time with *Furious* I was in charge of the Midshipman's Short Air Course which was designed to give junior officers some knowledge of what we airborne types did for a living. We explained to them the many jobs we had, as well as the difficulties and problems which we encountered. Of course they had all heard about the accidents that happened from time to time, so we always tried to reassure them that the dangers were not too serious. One of the young men who took the course, Midshipman Stukely, was evidently not 100% convinced -he put a cartoon in his log book of a very dilapidated string-bag aircraft which had a cow's udder as a bomb and a red nosed observer with a shotgun in the back (presumably me). The caption he wrote was "It's really quite safe you know." He may not have believed it, but the fact of the matter was that these relatively light and slow aircraft were not killers. As I

Midshipman Stukely's cartoon.

said earlier I never saw anyone killed landing on a carrier, and only one fatality on take-off. It really was quite safe. As always the sea itself was still our greatest enemy.

While I was with *Glorious* we had gone with the fleet to Gibraltar. Enroute we had steamed into a nasty sea which had almost stopped the destroyers because of the short length between waves. As we had been able to straddle at least two crests at a time the sea had meant very little to us. After we left the Rock and moved into the Atlantic, however, it was an entirely different story. There was a strong gale with very long seas. The destroyers could ride the longer swells quite comfortably, while *Glorious* had to heave to. We took one big green sea over the bows which dished in our lower flight deck and smashed open the hangar door. Six aircraft in the hangar were concertinaed into the space of two, and a wire

Top: The upper flight deck and bridge of HMS Glorious.
Bottom: The waves continuing to pound at the bow of Glorious after a big sea had buckled the lower flight deck.

Top: When a heavy sea smashed in the hangar doors a number of aircraft were destroyed. A badly damaged Osprey and Nimrod are visible here.

Bottom: The waves continuing to pound at Glorious.

hawser reel was tossed onto a seaman. I arrived in the hangar just after the wave had struck and immediately gathered a small working party with a chain hoist to try and rescue the seaman. Miraculously he was unhurt -two projections on the bulkhead had taken the weight of the reel and kept him from being crushed to death.

During this storm Spoode (the RAF pilot) wanted to go on deck for fresh air, and so he opened a watertight door to the batteries, not too far above the waterline on the lee side, and took his deck chair with him. Fortunately for him some sailors aboard our attendant destroyer *Searcher* saw him come on deck and then watched in horror as he was sucked overboard by a wave. It was much too rough to lower a boat but they went alongside him and he was washed onboard. They grabbed him to safety and then let us know what they had fished out of the sea.

Once again I played in the Caesar Cup hockey competition, this time for **Glorious**. We won the Cup and I found it gratifying to reflect that on the only two occasions in which I played in this competition I was on the winning team, for the standard of play was very high. I also had the honour of being the Captain of the Mediterranean Fleet team when we played the Home Fleet.

We cruised around the Mediterranean, visiting many of the spots I had first seen when with *Stuart*. One of the highlights of this tour was playing cricket on the island of Corfu. This had become a long standing tradition in which the game was played in the middle of the town square with cheering spectators sitting at café tables through which one occasionally had to chase a ball. We usually lost these games, or did badly, for the pitch always seemed to behave oddly when it was our turn to bat -one could never tell which way the ball would bounce. Eventually one of our observers, "Baron" Bingley, caught on and insisted that he umpire the next game. He also insisted that if we won the toss we should have the locals bat first -they always liked us to be the first to bat. When we did win the toss there was a great deal of consternation amongst the Corfiotes -they had to roll up the mat on the pitch and sweep away all the small stones that they had placed strategically so that the ball might bounce erratically. Baron also made sure that he kept an eye on the pitch during half-time so that the stones could not be replaced. In fact he stood on it! That day, we won.

Another favourite place of mine was Athens. One weekend that we were there the British Embassy threw a party, following which the Captain, Ginger Royle, led his officers around the town. At the best nightclub, the 'Tabaris', we numbered 43. I came back to the ship with Commander Daniel just before the hands fell in at 6.00 a.m. I managed to get an hour or two of sleep before having to be on the Flight Deck for Sunday morning Divisions. As we waited for the Commander to arrive to inspect the Divisions we heard the bells of the aircraft lift coming up with his entourage. It reached deck level, and after a very brief pause went down again. The Commander had said, "Too much light, send them away. Down lift." Indeed it was a very bright sunny day, and with none of us feeling too well after a night on the town it was a welcome decision.

Furious, when we joined her, was quite a contrast to *Glorious*. She was not one of the best carriers and her Captain didn't much care for aircraft. Apparently he was in constant fear of accidents and rumour had it that he had not wanted the appointment in the first place, but was told that it was either this or nothing. Strange, I would have thought that command of a carrier would have been a plum appointment for which there would have been no difficulty in finding many eager applicants. Luckily a new Wing Commander, Digby Johnston, was appointed who was able to supply the moral support that the Captain needed. Without confident and experienced command no ship can be efficient and happy.

After we had joined her, *Furious* was transferred to the Home Fleet. Enroute to her new base she took part in a week long exercise in the Atlantic. Every day we flew our recconnaisance aircraft twice, launching the first sorties at dawn, and recovering the second wave at dusk. As the days passed I noticed that the pace of drinking in the Wardroom was noticably higher -crews were winding down after the strain of long flights out of sight of the ship. The Captain was asked how the aircrew were standing up

to the strain, which was one of the purposes of the
exercise. He replied that they were tiring, and that the
observers would be the first to crack. He was not
intending to be derogatory towards observers, he was
simply aware of the stresses they had to cope with. If you
can imagine trying to navigate accurately for some three
hours at a stretch over open water while sitting in an
open cockpit with the wind roaring by at 100 knots
perhaps you will understand. Apart from the fatigue
caused by the physical discomfort there was also a good
deal of psychological stress from the gloomy prospects of
survival if you did get lost.

When an "enemy" ship was sighted the co-operation
between pilot and observer really came into play.
Accurate navigation could be temporarily dispensed with
because you knew your position when you found the
"enemy", and you would report her estimated course and
speed. By keeping her plotted we would be able to take
our departure relative to her position when we left. This
coincided with our primary task of keeping our fleet
informed accurately of her movements. We also had to
locate any consorts. As the pilot worked around her as
unobtrusively as possible, using whatever cloud cover was
available, the observer would be kept busy plotting and
reporting her position and movements to the carrier. The
approximate location of any consorts could usually be
estimated from knowing the type of ship spotted. The fact
that we observers were ships officers gave us an
understanding of the ways of ships so that we knew where
to expect consorts, and we could anticipate their
reactions to whatever circumstances prevailed. We also
had a better understanding of what information was vital
to our ships to enable them to make contact. We often
contemplated when it would be worth taking extreme
risks, even to the extent of shadowing a target to the last
drop of fuel and hoping to be rescued after the battle.
After all, if *Jervis Bay* could steam out to almost certain
destruction to save her convoy, why should not the
captain of an aircraft make a similar decision.*

* *See footnote on following page.*

It's Really Quite Safe

Once we were back in England we spent a few months operating around the coast. Part of the time we were again at Manston, in Kent, which had a grass field large enough for us to take off and land in formation. There was a squadron of Vickers Virginia bombers there, and these splendid veterans would occasionally lumber into the air on a fine morning. Rearmament did not seem to be progressing very quickly, despite the fact that tht the newspapers were full of warnings about the Fascist menace in Europe. A visit to the bombing range at Catfoss in Yorkshire lent reinforcement to this thought, for it was here that I discovered that the RAF were not using any method to find the actual wind -they simply relied upon the Met Man's word as gospel. During the same visit we complained to a visiting Air Marshal about our bomb sight which, in our view, was a lamentable device whose compass might start revolving if vibrated. With a little juggling I was able to make it do just that for his benefit. (It scarcely needs to be mentioned that vibration was an unavoidable condition of flight in those days.) The Air Marshal told us that this was the first complaint he had ever heard on the subject. Perhaps this was because in the RAF the device was operated by 'Other Ranks' whose opinions were not given much consideration. At a later date I was in touch with Professor Pollock-Brown, who was the inventor of a simple automatic-pilot. I asked whether he thought he could develop a bomb sight with a gyro stabilized compass which might be accurate for some five minutes after it was triggered. He replied that it

* *HMS Jervis Bay, an Armed Merchant Cruiser, was the surface escort for a trans-Atlantic convoy that came under attack from the German heavy cruiser Admiral Scheer. Disregarding the mortal danger to herself, she steamed out to give battle, inviting certain destruction, while hopefully saving the convoy she was there to protect. The convoy turned away under cover of smoke floats and did indeed escape. The action of Jervis Bay was considered to be in conformance with the highest traditions of the Navy. By another brave act many of her ship's company were saved. S.S.Stureholm, a Swedish Merchantman with the convoy, turned back to look for survivors despite the risk of encountering the Admiral Scheer, and rescued 68 men. Captain Olander of Stureholm said of Jervis Bay, "There she rode like a hero." A similar remark might have been made of Stureholm. Heroism is not confined to warships.*

would be quite easy. It is unfortunate that this had not been done in the long days of peace. If it had, bombing would have become a science. Instead we were stuck with an object that made high level bombing a dubious art.

I was also surprised at the attitude of some of the pilots on the light bomber squadron that was there with us. I overheard one pilot, who was complaining about his bomb-aimer, suggest that the good bomb-aimers should be shared around so that the pilots would have an equal chance to get good marks. There seemed to be no recognition that bombing was a crew event that required careful coordination between pilot and aimer. To bomb accurately the aircraft has to be aimed to allow for the wind direction and speed, and since at that time the bomb-aimer could not steer the aircraft himself during the final moments of the approach, the deftness of last minute course corrections depended entirely upon the quality of voice communications between the crew. The fact that our aircrew were often constant companions, which enabled them to come to complete understanding of each other's ways, and to develop trust in each other, helped most effectively in the development of a bombing crew; and indeed of a crew that could give efficient service in any set of circumstances.

Its Really Quite Safe

HMS Apollo at full power.

H.M.S. Apollo

I joined *Apollo* the day she was commissioned for the first time. She was one of a class of two, (her sister ship being HMS *Amphion* , and her first appointment was to be with the America and West Indies Squadron. Her Captain was Martin de Meric, a destroyer man with a few eccentricities: he hated noise, did not drink, called all his officers by their first name, and liked to wear as few clothes as possible in the tropics. Under his command Apollo was probably the first ship to encourage its sailors to wear only shorts and caps so that they kept healthy and did not suffer from prickly heat caused by sweaty clothes. He was a marvellous ship-handler, a friend to us all and greatly beloved.

The Commander was Alf Russell, who had been the Gunnery Officer when I was in *Hawkins* . Our Gunnery Officer was Bertie Hinds, one of the finest officers I ever had the pleasure to serve with. Alas, for some reason the Admiralty did not see him in the same light, and he was passed over for promotion to Commander. He was high spirited, and it may well be that he had offended someone in authority at one time or another. The Royal Marine detachment was commanded by Micky Rogers, (who later stood as best man at my wedding), and the pilots were Ted Stokes, (later relieved by Jimmy Garnett), and Wally

Blackwell. Wally was without question the best pilot I ever had the good fortune to fly with. These men were, I think, the core of the ship and in very large measure responsible for the fact that *Apollo* was a hard working, efficient and happy ship. I spotted for the guns and never saw a salvo fall further than 400 yards from the target even though the range would often be in the order of eight miles. *Apollo* never failed to straddle the target with her third salvo. Her torpedoes ran straight, her aircraft flew constantly and our Admiral told us that if he had to choose a cruiser to fight a battleship he would choose *Apollo* every time.

One of the criticisms we aviators faced from the 'salt horses', (those officers with no trade specialization), was that we seemed to consider ourselves a breed apart and not really part of a ship's company. As the senior flyer I had a talk with Alf Russell and obtained his agreement that we should all take a real part in the work of the ship, including Action Stations. Of course my action station was the aircraft, and until take-off I would have to be on the bridge to be up to date with what was going on so that we could be of the greatest use when we were airborne. Only one of the two pilots could be with me, however, so the other would, and should, be able to take some part in the battle. Both my pilots were given gun turrets to train. For normal routine they each had a part of the upper deck to look after, while I was both the 'Mate of the Upper Deck', (with overall responsibility for cleanliness), and Sports Officer, the co-ordinator of games. I am glad to say that the crew was, in general, addicted to sports. We never failed to field a team for any sport demanded by the squadron or any of the ports we visited, and we were always a force to be reckoned with.

We were sent to Portland for the ship's work up. The direction-finding equipment had to be calibrated, and there were the usual chores of testing guns and torpedoes to be taken care of. For my part there were tests to be done on getting airborne from the catapult before we could go on to develop floatplane techniques. The catapult was fixed, and because it could not be pointed into wind trials were needed to see if it was safe to get airborne with a 30 knot cross-wind, (a very possible condition with the ship at full speed.) The Admiralty sent out a special pilot for the trials, but since a second crew member was neccesary to be able to hook the aircraft on to the retrieval crane when returning to the ship, I got to go along for the ride. The day of the trial the cross-wind was the required 30 knots with the ship stopped. We left the catapult at about 55 knots, just a shade less than flying speed. With a little height to trade for airspeed we would have flown away successfully had it not been for the fact that the wind shifted so that it was slightly up our tail. As a result we did several beautiful salmon leaps from wave to wave before the Kestrel engine managed to drag us into the air. Nevertheless, the conclusion was that the Osprey could be catapulted no matter what the ship was doing and no matter which way the wind was blowing.

During our time at Portland we normally kept our aircraft in a small seaplane hangar ashore so that we could fly whatever the weather or state of the sea. One day we were to take the aircraft over to Lee in order to have the compasses swung to eliminate errors due to aircraft magnetism. The weather was not the best, but we decided that we would go anyway and so went ashore as the ship was leaving harbour. Once ashore we discovered that one of us had forgotten to bring the compasses for the back seat which were set in their stands on the side of the cockpit for use in the air. They were removed when not needed to avoid the danger of their being damaged. At first it appeared that there was no alternative for us but to wait till the ship returned and then go on board, confess our goof and eat crow. It occurred to me, however, that I might put the poor weather to good use, so when the Captain enquired why we had not gone to Lee I replied, "Well Sir, you had told us not to take any risks and as the weather was so bad I thought that you would prefer us to go another day." Fortunately for us the Captain fell for this line, even commending me for our admirable caution. Thereafter we could do almost as we pleased as long as I told him that it was safe.

Working-up at Portland was a fairly dull business with

only the occasional amusing incident for relief. One day while we were going round and round in circles calibrating the direction finding equipment and getting very bored, the Shambles light-ship which was nearby fired a gun. We consulted the "Admiralty Pilot", a book that described the coast and its dangers, looking for some explanation. It confirmed that, on occasions, the Shambles light-ship would fire a warning gun. There seemed to be no apparent danger, but we cautiously stopped what we were doing and steamed gently over to the light-ship. The Captain raised his megaphone and called out to the light-ship crew who were leaning over the side of the vessel but without interest in anything in particular, "Shambles ahoy! Did you fire a gun?" A broad Dorset accent replied across the water, "Yeeees, that's right." "Why did you fire a gun?" "Why, we allus fires a gun on the first o' the month." There seemed to be no adequate reply, but de Meric, determined as ever to have the last word, called out a crisp "Merry Christmas" as we went back to our task.

Once our work-up was completed we were sent to Gibraltar to temporarily replace a cruiser which had been ordered to return to England to recommission. The Spanish Civil War was underway at the time and the Admiralty wanted to maintain the strength of the Mediterranean Fleet. We enquired which battleship had the best hockey team, challenged them and duly defeated them handily. Bertie was also a Final Trials player for England and Wally too was up to this standard.

Furious was operating off Gib. at the time and there was a rather spectacular crash. An aircraft flown by Tony Colthurst was landing on at night and struck the round-down. I had flown with Tony a good deal and found that his night eyesight was not too good. When landing at night I used to watch the approach sector lights (white for too high, green for correct glide path, and red for too low), and talk him down. Occasionally when I saw a red light I would call out loudly, "Get up you bugger, get up!" On this particular occasion it seems that his observer did not have a good grip on this procedure and Tony flew right into the deck. The engine broke off and the prop flew down the deck, the starboard main planes fell off onto the quarter deck, and the rest of the aircraft with its crew of three went over the side and into the drink. Their destroyer, ever vigilant bless them, had them out of the water within minutes, with no serious injuries. I saw Tony a couple of days later at the Rock Hotel -we had a few drinks and spent a happy evening together. He complained that his legs were rather sore because the fuel tank had folded back on them in the crash and he had had a hard time getting out. Tony was a wonderful fellow to work with and his death later in the war was a sad blow to me.

On arrival in the West Indies we took on board Admiral Matthew Best, as his flagship, HMS *York*, was returning to England to recommission. He brought with him his staff, one of whom was Charles Thompson who doubled as observer and operations officer. It was suggested that I should go home with *York* while he took over my job. This did not suit me, and I appealed to de Meric who agreed that I should stay.

Matthew Best was a very broad thinking Gunnery Specialist. It was he who developed the cruiser vs. battleship tactics which were used during the Battle of the River Plate, tactics which might have been put to good use by Admiral Holland when he engaged *Bismark*. Best was a small man and rather a tyrant when on duty. He drove us hard but he was always entirely fair and prepared to listen to the objections or proposals of junior officers; he and de Meric made a wonderful team. When off duty his mischievous side would show and he would happily lead us off for a good time.

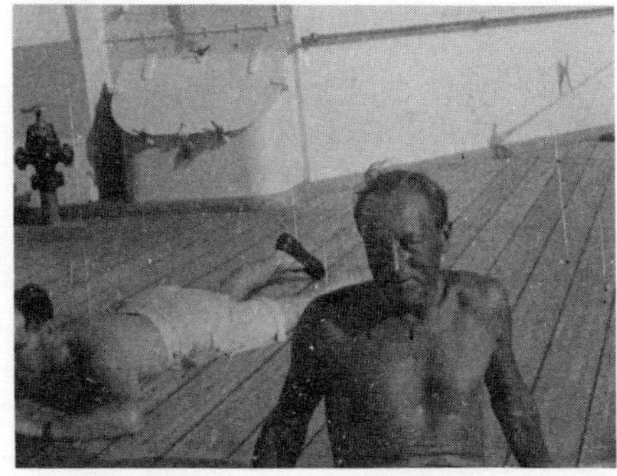

Captain Martin de Meric taking some sun. His dark tan is evidence of the fact that in the tropics he seldom wore more than shorts and shoes.

HMS Apollo enroute from Victoria to Vancouver with Governor General Lord Tweedsmuir on board. The Vice Regal flag is flying from the masthead.

We cruised up the west coast of the USA and Canada, stopping at San Diego, San Fransico, Vancouver and Victoria and numerous smaller ports in between. Our visit to Victoria happened to coincide with that of the Governor General, Lord Tweedsmuir (John Buchan). When we sailed for Vancouver it was arranged that we should give him passage and so we had the honour of flying the Vice-Regal flag from our masthead during the short trip. While in Vancouver the Governor General's Aides de Camp used the Vice-Regal train for accomodation and I was one of three invited there for drinks one evening. When it was time for us to leave for another official function in town we were offered the "other half", and being our usual weak selves in these circumstances we succumbed to assurances that there really was time. When we eventually did insist that it was time to go we were sent off in an RCMP car whose driver had been instructed that we really were in a hurry. With a gleam in his eye he set off through the streets at a terrific speed, rivalling Jehu, that hot rod charioteer of biblical days, in his performance. Fortunately for us he was a skillful driver and we arrived safely but very much in need of another "second half".

The camp at Comox.

From Vancouver we cruised north to Comox. Here we spent a month under canvas at the army camp while we used the rifle range for target practice. We then returned to Victoria for a second visit. Victoria was one of our favourite places and the night before we left everyone was ashore till late saying fond farewells to their friends. The next morning we left harbour at about 8.30 a.m., just in time for morning divisions after leaving. It was my turn to read prayers. As I was not feeling too well and sensed that many others were in a similar condition I read the prayers for the sick. I got a rather sideways look from Commander Russell, but he said nothing.

In the Georgia Strait we had our first aircraft accident. Wally got the toes of his floats into a wave on landing and the aircraft flipped onto its back. No one was hurt, but the Osprey was a write off. This meant that until we could get a replacement at Bermuda we were down to one aircraft.

Further south at Monterey I came down with undulant fever which lasted for a couple of weeks. As a result I

While in Georgia Strait one of Apollo's Ospreys came to grief on landing. No one was hurt, but after the aircraft had been recovered it was judged a complete write-off.

missed out on the cricket match against Sir Aubrey Smith's team at Hollywood. This was a disappointment for in my capacity as sports officer I had made arrangements with him on our trip north. Sir Aubrey was a delightful host and I heard many a glamorous tale after the event. I was about to be landed to the care of a U.S.Navy hospital in San Pedro when my fever broke and so I was allowed to stay with the ship as a convalescent as we returned to Bermuda.

By this time I had had plenty of opportunity to put my new found skills as a photographer to the test, and to discover some of the problems of working in the tropics with the ship's distilled water. There were no professional photographers onboard *Apollo* as there were on the carriers. Here I had to do all my own developing and printing in a little cubby hole under the catapult where the bulkhead often got to more than 100°F. To compensate for the softness of the distilled water we were provided with liquid 'hardeners' but I found that these had very little effect. The soft water would strip the emulsion off the plates which was most demoralizing after one had spent hours in the air to obtain the photos in the first place. Eventually someone suggested a solution to me, and armed with a block of ice and the salt shaker from the Wardroom I was able to process my photographs without further trouble. It was the salt that was the key -even cold distilled water stripped the emulsion. I wondered what practical experiments the experts had conducted to prove their products. Our reports on the subject seem to have been ignored, for no Admiralty instructions were ever published so that others might benefit from our experience. Perhaps our solution was not scientific enough for them.

During our stop in Norfolk we were challenged to a Tug-of-War by the U.S. Services, who had a cup for International Competition. My Physical Training Petty Officer and I went into a huddle to try and figure out a way we might win. We knew that we would be up against their largest and heaviest men and we did not think that our scratch team could compete. Our only hope was to use the 'lock' -something which can only be used efficiently by experienced men. In the 'lock', instead of leaning back pulling the rope with both hands and with arms straight, each man changes his stance so that the rope passes across his thigh with one hand pressing down on each side to 'lock' the rope there while he leans back digging his heels into the ground. This takes the strain of the arms and back and makes it very tiring for the opposition to pull you out, while in turn you are having it relatively easy. You are not allowed to go into the 'lock' until the pull has started, and then it must be done very quickly, man by man, so that at any one time only one man is not pulling. It is this transition period that takes skill and requires experience. We had no trouble getting volunteers for the team, but we had to train them hard for the few days that we had available. The 'lock' was allowed by Royal Tournament Rules but not by Amateur Rules. Fortunately the different rules were not quoted on the same page in our Royal Navy Sports Handbook. Being very careful not to show our opposition the alternative rules we got them to agree that our handbook was the Bible of sports and that Royal Tournament Rules should prevail. As an apparent expert I was even elected Umpire.

The first pull went to the Americans, although not too easily. Our team of willing volunteers went into a lock beautifully and it took the Americans some time to pull them out which I was encouraged to think would help tire them out. They almost won the event with the second pull, but just six inches short of victory they gave out and were pulled back over the line. The third pull was a foregone conclusion -they were beaten almost before they started and the cup became one more addition to our overcrowded trophy case.

We always offered the cup for a challenge when we met U.S. troops but we were never taken up. Just in case, however, our team kept in shape. A little international competition was a wonderful thing for morale. Although we may have been just a teensy bit underhanded to take advantage of the rule differences, I felt that it was part of our duty to look good. Looking at the obvious differences in weight I'm sure that our team must have looked very good to the uninitiated.

The author, ready for pick up by the ship, sits on the mainplane with his safety hook over the leading edge.

One of the main assignments of the air department was to establish the maximum safe speed at which aircraft could be retrieved from the sea. In the past the procedure had been for the ship to slow down to recover its aircraft, but with the threat of hostilities looming closer the Admiralty was concerned with the risk that slowing down posed to the parent ship. In calm waters at low speed there was little difficulty: the ship steams along, the aircraft taxies alongside, the observer hooks on to the crane and the aircraft is hoisted in. In mid-ocean with the ship at, say, 15 knots or over, things are a trifle more complicated. The aircraft has to land between the ship's bow and stern waves as taxiing over the stern wave at high speed could be disastrous. If the wind was in the right direction landing between the waves was relatively easy. Alternatively the ship could execute a sharp turn which produced some relatively smooth water and flattened the stern wave to some extent. Whatever method we tried taxiing up to the ship at 25-30 knots was a bumpy process.

While taxiing up to overtake the ship the observer had to climb up onto the mainplane in order to pick up the hook from the crane and connect it to the aircraft slings. Sitting on the wing just a few feet from the whirling propellor while the aircraft bucked around in the waves was an exciting proposition and we had to devise a means of making it safe for the observer -after all if he was lost there would be no way to recover the aircraft. Matthew Best suggested a padded hook which the observer could hook over the leading edge of the mainplane. This hook had a strop at the end through which the observer could put his arm. He could then sit facing aft with his legs hooked under the trailing edge and have both hands free for the critical job of hooking on. I tried this out with the aircraft taxiing at 30 knots and found that it allowed me to sit securely with both hands free -one to hold the slings and the other to grab onto the hook. Our problems weren't over, however. At speeds over 15 knots the bow wave was so close to the ship that no matter how far aft the crane was trained we were put in a position where the toes of the floats were actually riding the bow wave and the wing tip was just a few feet from the side of the ship. Any surge ahead or turn towards the ship could cause disaster so our time in this hazardous position could only be brief. The Admiralty-approved pick-up mechanism on the crane was the next stumbling block. It was complex, requiring three hands to operate. It was also slow and subject to jamming. As an alternative we obtained a long chain which replaced the Admiralty device. The bight of this was held by a seaman who dropped it to me as soon as we were under the crane. Once I had it hooked on, the winch driver hoisted us up at full speed. It worked like a charm and we were out of the water in seconds. We went on to try the procedure at higher speeds but unfortunately the chain we were using was not strong enough and one day we dropped an aircraft. The Dockyard made up another chain which they guaranteed to stand up to anything we could do, but before we could proceed with our trials the Admiralty directed us to cease using the chain and use only their patented crane gear. They claimed that the jerk on a chain would be too much. If they had ever seen how the crane jib bent as it took up the strain they would have realized that there was no jerk, chain or no chain, but you cannot tell their Lordships these things. The experiment stopped at 16 knots and that was that, although I feel that with a little further research we could have made pickups safely at up to 25 knots.

We also found the Admiralty unsympathetic to the use of our claw hook. We had reported our findings but the official reply was that the idea had been tested and found to be unnecessary. It was not till some time later, when I was back in the U.K., that I discovered the reason for this strange decision: the hook had been sent to HMS *Albatross*, a seaplane carrier used for experimental work. They had tried it out with an RAF aircraftsman doing the hooking on, and in the calm waters of the Solent at 6 or 8 knots he had seen no need for it! Of course we went on using it, life was too precarious without it.

For me this particular cruise was notable for three events: I met my future wife and got married; I had some close shaves when flying; and I took part in what I believe to have been the first use of aircraft in riot control. The first of these events ocurred when we arrived in Bermuda. My cabin-mate, Dicky Dakeyne decided to have a party. His girl was down from Montreal and he arranged for her to bring along a date for me. I was waiting for them at the bar of the Bermudiana Hotel, and as soon as I saw them arrive and realised which of the two young ladies was Dicky's girl I knew that he had made a mistake in asking me along. His girlfriend was Debbie Stairs, whom I later married. I'm glad to say that nevertheless Dicky and I remained fast friends, and he found himself another sweetheart.

Dicky Dakeyne, who made the mistake of introducing his girlfriend to the author.

It's Really Quite Safe

One of the difficulties with which we had to contend
was a lack of spending money. Most of our meagre pay
had to be spent on dress uniforms and civilian clothes
which all had to be of a sufficiently high standard to
satisfy our seniors and to enable us to meet with people
at the top of the social ladder. Besides this we had to
have working uniforms which were adequate for both
tropical and cold weather conditions and for work in
heavy seas. Fortunately for us we were very well
entertained by generous people in most of the places we
visited. We often met English businessmen who were only
too glad to be able to meet with someone who could speak
their language. The spread of English traders throughout
the world ("that nation of shopkeepers") has most certainly
been a major factor in making English the present day
language of commerce.

The only way we could afford to repay this hospitality
and to entertain the many attractive young women we met
was to invite them onboard, give them a personally guided
tour of the ship, and arrange for supper in our cabins. I
wound up with a double cabin to myself which gave me
more room than most, so I often arranged supper parties
with Micky Rogers or some of the others. These parties
were a lot of fun and very popular.

One of the perks of being an officer aboard ship at
this time was to have a Royal Marine servant. They were
of course paid extra. During this commission my man was
Jackson, a very pleasant and dedicated individual who
always looked after my wife like a father. One day he let
me know that he was going ashore for the evening. I told
him I was pleased because he didn't go ashore much, and
asked if he could find another of the Officer's Servants to
fill in for him that evening since we had some friends
coming onboard. "Oh no, Sir," he said, "No one is going to
clean up your cabin after one of your parties but me. I
will not go ashore tonight." Nothing I could do or say
would make him change his mind. When I think back on all
the dirty dishes, cigarette ashes, etc. that we left behind
I realise just how much I owed to men like Jackson
throughout my career in the Navy. Those that still survive
are scattered throughout England and are very hard to

Apollo's Ospreys, tied together with a White Ensign during their fly past at the Coronation Parade in Jamaica.

find. I think that that is one of the saddest things about service life -it is so difficult to keep track of ones' friends.

During the Spring Cruise we stopped at Jamaica to celebrate the coronation of King George VI. We took part in parades and conducted a flypast with the aircraft tied together with a White Engign between us. Most effective. During this time I had two close calls. The first one occurred when Wally and I were returning to the ship which we had arranged to be in the lee of one of the islands to avoid the short and nasty sea which is kicked up by the Tradè Winds. Such a sea can be fatal to a float plane unless the ship can give a lee, so we were very fortunate that we were in the lee of the island when the engine suddenly quit. Wally did a marvellous forced landing on smooth water. In the second episode we were about to be catapulted off the ship into (or hopefully over), a similar short sea. The procedure was for the pilot to test his engine, and when satisfied that everything was

HMS Apollo anchored at St.Lucia.

OK, signal the catapult officer, George Best, who would then order the gunner to place a cordite charge in the catapult breech. When this was done George would wave a flag around his head to tell the pilot to run up his engine. As soon as the engine was run up the pilot would give a "thumbs up" with his left hand and then immediately bring that hand down to the throttle. George would then bring his flag down sharply, the gunner would fire the charge, and we would be off on another flight. On this occasion George was just about to bring his flag down when the engine cut dead. I looked around apprehensively from my back seat and was relieved to see that George had raised his other hand to hold the flag so that the gunner could make no mistake as to his intentions. Then I heard him shout, "Take that ---- charge out!" It had been a close thing -being catapulted at over 50 knots into a trade wind sea would not have been much fun. Both of these incidents were attributed to dirty gasoline.

Passing up the west coast of Martinique we were able to help perpetuate one of the Navy's traditions that dated back to the Napoleonic Wars. At that time the French fleet was based at Fort de France in Martinique. To lessen the chance of their being intercepted by the British

Apollo's Ospreys on the waterfront at RCAF Station Trenton.

fleet commanded by Admiral Rodney, which was anchored in Rodney Bay at the north end of St.Lucia, the French would haul up close to the shore after rounding the south point of the island, and pass inside Diamond Rock. The Rock was a very small island a few hundred feet high with a precipitously steep shore line. To force the French to pass to the seaward side of the Rock where they would be easier to attack Rodney decided to occupy it. Cannon were hauled up to the top with the aid of block and tackle, and it was commissioned as HMS *Diamond Rock* and manned by seamen of the Fleet. It was held for several years against all attempts to recapture it.

To commemorate this gallant occupation, after the garrison had been withdrawn it became the custom of passing RN ships to salute the Rock as they would any other HM ship. The hands on deck would be piped to attention and would salute this emblem of history so that its remarkable defence might not be forgotten.

That summer we went to Montreal, in company with HMS *York*, for a two week stay. I arranged for our aircraft to visit Ottawa, the RCAF base at Trenton, Toronto, Hamilton and Windsor. York's aircraft joined us and we had a great time being fêted everywhere we

Above: The author (right) and his fiancé (seated) take a break between tennis matches with friends (Pricey and Mike Phipps) at Knowlton.
Opposite, top: The Niagara Gorge.
Opposite, bottom: An Osprey over Niagara Falls.

went. We flew over Niagara Falls and obtained some marvellous photos. When I got back to Montreal Debbie and I were formally engaged, something which I have never regretted. The ship was scheduled to be at the America's Cup races in Newport, and Debbie and a friend had arranged to meet me there. Unfortunately rioting broke out in the West Indies and we were dispatched to see what help we could give, and never got to Newport. This was Debbie's first taste of the uncertainty of service life.

It's Really Quite Safe

Our first stop was Trinidad where we were to relieve Ajax so that she could continue her South American cruise. By this time the trouble was in hand and our services were no longer required. During our short stay we were asked by an oil company if it would be possible for us to produce a photo-mosaic of an area for them. We did not carry the fixed vertical cameras normally used for this sort of work, but we decided to see what could be accomplished with our hand held camera. We flew to the area and I selected half a dozen or so spots to photograph, reckoning that, centered on these, my photographs would cover the whole area. Then I directed Wally to each in turn, giving him the word as we arrived in position. On my signal Wally would roll the aircraft onto its back and I pointed my camera at my chosen spot, hanging by the tail pendant to my parachute harness the while. It was probably a foolish risk but it worked. The mosaic was not at all bad and I had found that vertical photography can be done without sophisticated apparatus.

I should probably explain about our parachute harnesses. The pilots had seat packs, -they sat on their chutes and so were attached at all times, but not so the observers. Seat packs were just not practical in the back seat where we had to move around. We flew wearing just the parachute harness because the chest-pack was simply too cumbersome to work with, (it was there in a rack to be hooked on in an emergency). The harness had a tail pendant which could be attached to the floor of the aircraft to keep one from being bucked out of the plane in bumpy weather. There was a quick release in case you ever had to jump. I never felt the need to hook on my parachute, and had the quick release let go during our photo session I would have been on my own with no parachute.

The oil company asked if they could pay for the job but I told them it was not necessary, although they could send me a wedding present if they liked. Alas their generosity did not extend that far.

We were then called to Barbados where the unrest was continuing. We landed our Marines who then looked after security in Bridgetown while the local police went out into the countryside. Our job with the aircraft was to quarter the island twice a day, flying at about 2,000 feet and looking for signs of trouble. There was sporadic trouble all over the island, which we would report by radio. We would then come down low to show a presence, moving on whenever the police arrived. One day we found a very nasty looking gang at the north end of the island moving across the countryside armed with a motley collection of weapons. I called in a report and then turned things over to Wally. He dove at them, pulling out just a few feet above where they lay flat on their faces in terror. It was later rumoured that we had killed a few. We had touched no-one, but I suppose its always possible we may have scared some to death.

The next day we sighted a very large crowd moving along a road. This group seemed to be well behaved, but since we were under orders to report any concentrations I radioed in our sighting. Jimmy Garnett, who had replaced Ted Stokes a month or two earlier, asked if he could do a beat-up. I told him to wait until we saw which way they would turn when they came to the crossroads ahead. They turned neither left nor right, but went straight on into a church! I had to correct my signal to read "Church party only". That took a lot of living down with the police, who pulled my leg unmercifully. It was an object lesson about how difficult it is to tell from the air exactly what it is that is going on on the ground.

The police told us that we should do our best to avoid a forced landing as the blacks hated us. We never passed a group of men, no matter how small, without circling them to make sure that they had seen that we had seen them, and they knew that we would be out checking on them twice a day. There were a number of isolated houses where we had intervened to help, and these we used to circle until someone came out to wave and show that all was well. Once things had quietened down and we were told that we could cease our patrols, we made one more flight to drop messages of farewell to these houses. We received several invitations to tea or drinks (depending on their way of life) and we accepted those that we could. We also received a number of letters of thanks which I found so rewarding that I have kept some to this day.

After Barbados we continued with our normal cruise program which this time included showing the flag up the Amazon. We went 1,000 miles up this mighty river to Manaos, the centre of what was the world's first rubber-producing area. Here they tapped wild rubber trees, and Manaos became a boom town in the late 1800's and remained so until rubber tree seeds were smuggled out to start plantations in Malaya and Ceylon.

The city was most imposing, including its magnificent 19th century opera house, which was by this time deserted. As I recall it was hot as Hell, with a temperature that remained steady at 100°F both day and night, along with a humidity of 100%. It was the humidity that got you down, there was just no way to cool off. Manaos is actually on a tributary of the Amazon, the Rio Negro. It was so wide that when we slipped we went ahead at 25 knots, put the wheel over and did a 180° turn well within the confines of the river. Had we wanted to do so we could have gone a further 1,000 miles up the river to Iquitos.

Apart from a handfull of towns there is little to be seen along the river but jungle. At the time there was only about 10 miles of road in the entire Province of Amazon which was about 1,500 miles wide. Strangely enough, on these roads you drove on the left, whereas in the rest of Brazil one drove on the right. Each night we dropped anchor, on a couple of occasions by towns, but in most cases just in some broad reach of the river. At Belem, at the mouth of the river, we had to be careful to wear proper clothes. The locals considered open neck shirts and shorts to be immoral, so our sun bathing had to be confined to the side of the ship out of sight of the townsfolk. One other item I recall was the problem caused by the heavy make up worn by the local girls. They liked to press their cheeks against our chests while dancing and no amount of washing seemed to be able to get rid of the rouge marks from our white mess Jackets.

One character whom we met while playing tennis at Belem was a very anglicized Brazilian. He told us that he had taken part in several revolutions, (a pastime which

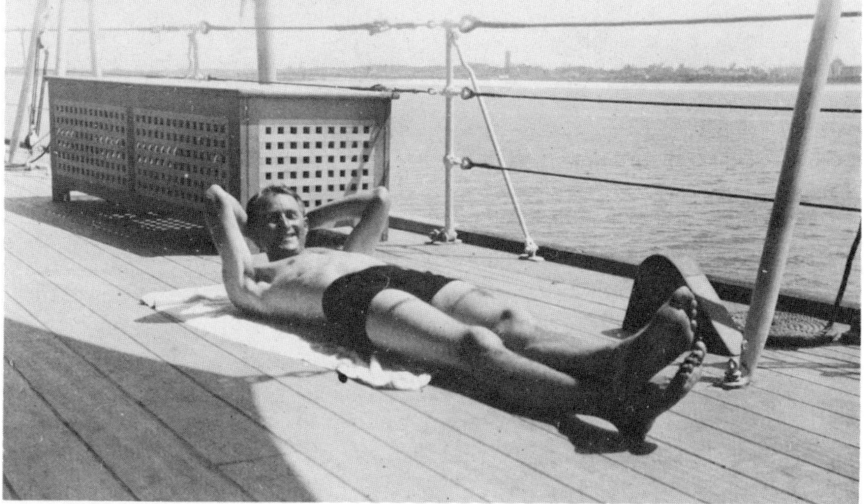

*Top: An aerial view of the Amazon river...miles and miles
of miles and miles.*
*Bottom: The author sunbathing during Apollo's cruise up
the Amazon River on the 'out-of-sight' side of the ship.*

seemed to be regarded as some sort of a game to
Brazilians, much like rugger to ourselves), but he had
decided to leave that work to younger men. King Edward
VIII had recently abdicated and he raised the subject in
the Mess one evening, saying, "You have no idea how
lucky you are. You had a man who was no good to you,
and you now have a very fine man in his place." He
proceeded to tell us several stories of the Prince in
Brazil, stories which never made the newspapers. Having
crossed the Prince's trail on several occasions I heartily
agreed with his verdict. Certainly one heard nothing but
praise for Edward's brother, King George VI.

After our trip up the Amazon we returned to the West Indies, and it was here that we had our worst aircraft crash. We were at Tortola in the Virgin Islands, and had decided to do some night flying practice. Both aircraft had gone up and were to land alongside the ship using the ships lights as a flare path. I was onboard controlling when the first aircraft, flown by Jimmy Garnett returned. Jimmy decided to use his emergency wing-tip flares to see how useful they would be for landing and wound up flying straight into the sea. The investigation revealed that with the oily calm and very transparent sea Jimmy could not see the surface and had actually been trying to land on what was the bottom, some 45 feet below. It was a foolish mistake which he would not have made by day. In glassy calm conditions the prescibed technique was to reel out the trailing antenna, set up a steady slow descent until the aerial hit the water, and then throttle back and flare for a landing. As it happened neither Jimmy nor his telegraphist were strapped in as they should have been, and they were catapulted out of the aircraft on impact, just before the mainplane folded back over the cockpits. They came back to the ship waving happily. Total damage was one broken collar bone, one stiff knee and one aircraft totally destroyed. I flew over the site with Wally the next day and was able to see the aircraft, looking as though she was lying on some moorland, obviously broken. Although she was 45 feet under water I was able to take some excellent photographs of her. The sea was practically invisible -it was no wonder that Jimmy did not see the surface with his flares.

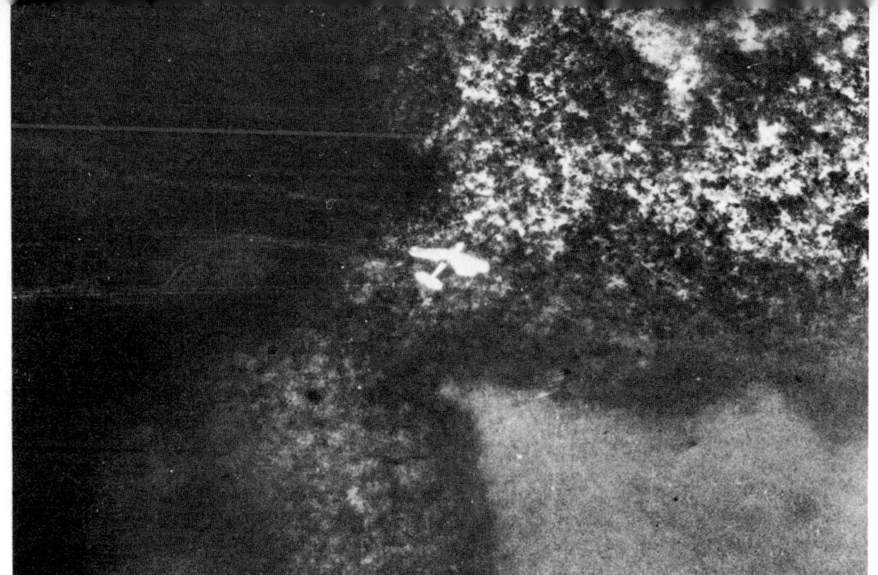

Opposite: Wally Blackwell at the controls of Osprey K5760. The aircraft is flying over the almost transparent sea of the Carribean.

Top: The wreckage of the crashed Osprey lying on the sea bottom some 45 feet under water.

Bottom: The wreckage is hauled aboard.

When we were at our next stop, Bermuda, the Admiralty, who had become impressed with our ocean landings, wondered just how rough a sea we could land on successfully. They selected an old Fairey 111F float plane that had been used for target towing at Bermuda, and told us to test it to destruction in rough water. I'm not quite sure whether it just never occurred to them that the crew might come to grief when the aircraft was destroyed, or whether they felt we were expendable. The choice of aircraft was equally uninspiring. We could understand that they did not want to spare one of our Ospreys, but choosing a Fairey 111F which had a notoriously weak undercarriage on floats didn't seem to make much sense. A volunteer pilot was called for, and naturally Wally volunteered. I became an involuntary hero as someone had to go along to hook the aircraft on to the recovery winch after each trial landing. We started inside the reefs where the seas were not at all bad, and were then to go to rougher waters outside. Our first landing was in a sea which would not have given the Osprey any trouble at all, but when I checked the floats I found a buckled strut. That put a satisfactory end to the test, and there were no more such stupidities.

Opposite and above: Apollo in drydock at Bermuda.

During our stay in Bermuda the ships frequently practiced their surface-to-surface and anti-aircraft gunnery. Whenever the battle practice target was out all ships would take it in turn to shoot. We always spotted for *Apollo's* surface shoots, and as they were very good my task was made easy. One day *Exeter* (later of Battle of the River Plate fame) followed Apollo in practice so I tuned in to her frequency and we moved over to watch her shoot. Since I could not hear her aircraft on the radio I called her up and asked if she would like me to spot for her. "Yes please," was the reply. *Exeter's* shooting was always bad, but this day was worse than usual. To my horror her first salvo fell so far short that I had to give her a correction of 1,500 yards, a distance far too great to estimate accurately. Purely by good chance, however, I was plum right and her second salvo hit the target.

The sea erupts around a towed target during gunnery practice.

Opposite: On the author's wedding day in October 1937 the ship hoisted the traditional wedding wreath.

Later, at the Battle of the River Plate the *Graf Spee* chose to fire at her instead of the two 6" gun ships. Thank heaven they did not know her reputation as surely she was no great danger to them. Commodore Harwood was still in command so I wrote to him with congratulations on his victory and he wrote back with thanks, saying, "I wish I could have called you over to spot as I did in 1937." A kind thought.

The gunnery people asked me if I could devise a method of spotting for anti-aircraft fire against a sleeve target towed by an aircraft. From the ship it was easy to see the line of fire, but it was near to impossible to determine whether the range was accurate, ie. whether the shells were bursting short of or beyond the target. I decided that if we flew under the towing aircraft so as to be clear of the towing wire we could observe the bursts and record their position relative to the target using 'clock code'. The first time we tried this I discovered that the rate of fire was too rapid for me to both spot and record, so Wally had to fly with one hand and write on a knee pad with the other...I was talking as fast as he could write. I was keeping pretty busy, but the ships, *Exeter* in

particular, kept addressing signals to me. I could read the damn things while doing something else, but to reply I had to drop everything and concentrate on the morse key. (We were not using voice transmissions at this time.) In exasperation I signalled *Exeter* and asked her not to send me any more signals. This seemed a bit too impertinent to my urbane Harwood and he was about to make a very rude signal to me when his Chief Yeoman of Signals stepped in to my defence. "You know, sir," he said, "he's pretty busy -he's doing your job, my job, the telegraphist's job, and the Gunnery Officer's job". The situation was saved.

In October I went to Montreal to be married, and I had ten days leave for our honeymoon. We then returned to Bermuda which was a pretty good place to start married life. However we had only two weeks there when Ramsay MacDonald died. He had been on a cruise ship with his daughter Shelagh and they brought his body to Bermuda. It was decided in England that since he was a former Prime Minister his body should be brought home aboard *Apollo*, accompanied by his daughter, who in turn would be chaperoned by the wife of our Paymaster-Commander, Mrs. Pearce. On passage we took it in turns to ask them for a drink in our cabins and to provide some relaxation for Shelagh who was a very nice girl. I felt very sorry for her -first she had to follow her father to the cathedral in Bermuda where he lay in state, then to *Apollo* where his coffin was placed on the quarterdeck with an honour guard of sailors with arms reversed, there was a similar ceremony when we entered Devonport followed by going ashore to be greeted by civic authorities, thence by train to London to be received with ceremony followed by a lying in state at St.Paul's, and a final train journey to Lossiemouth in Scotland where he was at last laid to rest. It was a long grieving, and she underwent it all with dignity and patience.

In the spring of 1938 we were lucky to have a cruise down the east coast of the United States. Debbie and Mrs. Russell followed us by various means. Our first port of call was Norfolk, Virginia, followed by Wilmington, North Carolina. We loved Wilmington, and they loved us, to the extent that the local paper published an article headlined, "One hundred years ago it took 100 British ships to capture Wilmington, but this year HMS *Apollo* has done it by herself". It was here that we discovered that enchanting southern custom that required that for the first year of marriage a new bride would sit in the place of honour to the right of the host. Mrs. Russell took relegation to second position very well. Debbie, however, was not too happy about being referred to as "The lovely little English bride". After all, Canadians have their pride.

When we arrived off the entrance to Cape Fear River, on which Wilmington is situated, we had just completed a full power trial and all boilers were still connected. A pilot came aboard and when he arrived on the bridge the conversation went like this,

"Good morning Captain."

"Good morning pilot. What would you like?"

"Full speed ahead Captain." (He obviously was not used to warships.)

"Do you know what that means pilot?"

"Why no Captain."

"Thirty-two knots. Is that what you really want?"

"No, Captain, please no!"

HMS Apollo doing 25 knots off St.Thomas.

Realising that the power we had was far more than he was accustomed to he allowed de Meric to handle the ship, telling him what dangers to avoid and what currents to expect. This was very much to de Meric's wishes, for he hated the ship to be in someone else's hands. Even more so he hated ever seeing a tug, as he always wanted to do things on his own. If a tug became too demanding that we take her line he would become quite speechless with anger.

Between Charleston and Savannah, which was a day trip, Margaret Russell and Debbie came with us. Since this was strictly taboo they were kept out of sight when we entered harbour, and their "arrival" was announced an hour or two after we got alongside. The Governor of Georgia came onboard, and while he visited with the Captain we entertained his naval ADC in the Wardroom. Alf and I discussed with him the best hotel for us to go to, telling him which one had been recommended. "That one is no good," he said, "You should go to the Savannah Hotel", and he told us that he would reserve rooms for us when he went ashore. When we later went to the hotel we were shown into a vast suite with two bedrooms, two bathrooms and an adjoining drawing room. It was lovely, but at what cost we wondered. Did he mistakenly think British naval officers were rich? Alf went down to the desk to check and returned with a broad grin -the ADC owned the hotel and there was no charge at all! That's what I call true southern hospitality.

The local Chamber of Commerce put on a magnificent oyster roast on the banks of the river for the entire ship's company. The roasting fires were burning in pits beneath moss covered oak trees, and there were many willing hands to serve the oysters which opened as they steamed. There were large pots of melted butter in which to dip the oysters before popping them into ones mouth. These were a special breed of oyster that grew on the roots of mangrove trees along the river banks, and although small they were most delicious. It was a wonderful party, paid for entirely by the city, and I hope that we showed our appreciation. Looking back on the fine hospitality that we received along that coast I often think that we were too inclined to take it for granted. Now I have a much better appreciation of all the work and goodwill that went into it.

While we were with *Apollo* we did a great deal of sailing, and Alf and George Best kept our boat's sails in excellent condition so that we did very well in the squadron races which were held in Bermuda when all the ships were together. On two occasions I organised our boats to race across to the Yacht Club in Hamilton with crews of two officers in whalers and three in cutters. Here we stayed for a somewhat liquid lunch, and then let Yacht Club members take the tillers while we crewed for them on the race back to the Dockyard. This was followed by a party at our club which made for a cheerful day.

On the first of these occasions a very well known American yachtsman by the name of Sherman Hoyt sailed one of our slowest whalers to victory. Although he was extremely wealthy he usually dressed in old sailing togs

and managed to look rather scruffy. On one occasion he
was turned away from the Bermudiana Hotel because of
his dress, much to their mortification when they found out
who they had rejected. I later met him at a wedding and
mentioned that if he was still in Bermuda the next week
we would be bringing the cutters over to the Yacht Club.
Although he had been planning to return to New York he
immediately said that he would stay for the event. I was
rather astonished that a well known yachtsman who sailed
in the top racing circles would bother to stay to sail in a
service cutter, and I had to ask why. He replied that he
much preferred drop-keeled boats to anything else.

In this last race he drew the cutter that I had brought
over. In one way this was a pity because it was the
fastest boat and he was by far the best helmsman so it
was almost no contest. On the other hand it was an
education for me to be able to see how beautifully he got
the boat balanced and how steady he was with the tiller.
There was a good strong wind, and where I would have
been constantly moving the tiller to counter the boat's
movements under the gusting winds his hand was steady
and sure.

*Above: The Regatta winner was "Cock of the Fleet"
-this was Apollo's day.*

Previous page: Apollo on Regatta Day.

He told us stories from the days when he was defending the America's Cup against Sopwith, the British skipper. Sopwith was ahead rounding the last buoy in the deciding race, and when the American yacht rounded the buoy the crew decided that their only chance of winning would be to try to split tacks with the *Endeavour*. They agreed that if Sopwith turned to cover them they would all go below for lunch as they would have no chance of beating him. Luckily for them Sopwith did not cover, and they won the race and with it the cup.

Another very amusing story he related was of a day when he sailed in King George V's racing yacht *Britannia*. He had gone below for a snack and was sitting at the table in the cabin when *Britannia* went about and heeled over sharply on the new tack. The door of the toilet sprang open and Queen Mary shot out, landing on his lap. She looked at him and said, "Mr.Hoyt, you must be even more embarrassed than I am!" At the time he told us this story he said he was writing a book, but that since Queen Mary was still alive he could not include this incident.

The last time Debbie and I saw him was in 1958; he was walking along the streets of Charleston in his old yachting clothes with his gunny bag over his shoulder, a very lovable character.

It's Really Quite Safe

114

Waiting for War

When I was in *Apollo* I had applied for a Staff Course and consequently I was sent to Courageous to await the appointment. She was the Home Fleet carrier, based at Portsmouth, and very little that was remarkable happened during my time with her, apart from playing rugger for the Home Fleet team. During the period of the Munich negotiations we were sent to Invergordon where a considerable force had been assembled in case the talks should fail. While there I was told to take a flight of aircraft from the ship back to land, and thence, via any route of my choosing, to lead them back to make a dummy bombing attack on the cruiser *Sheffield* which was approximately 15 miles off shore. After we had completed the exercise and returned to the carrier I went to file my report. To my amazement I was not asked where I had taken the flight, I was told in exact detail the course we had taken and our times at each turning point. I had no idea how they had obtained the information. It was not till sometime later that I realised that we had been tracked by the first seaborne radar which was under trial in *Sheffield*. This was in the fall of 1938.

The development of this invaluable invention appeared to be very slow. I can not recall that *Courageous* had radar in 1939, and certainly it was not until the end of that year that we received the first experimental set (RDF) in an aircraft at the Service Trials Unit. I have read that while *Sheffield* had just received a very good set in 1941, *Norfolk* had a very poor one.

While *Courageous* was in Portsmouth I witnessed an event which I felt illustrated the innate common sense of the average British citizen. At the time Debbie and I were living with my brother, a solicitor in Winchester, at his home in the village of Littleton. One evening we were in the village Pub with a cross-section of the local inhabitants ranging from the manager of the racing stables to labourers, and the topic of discussion turned to the need for conscription as people were getting worried about the possibility of war. Conscription was passed by acclamation by these men, which was at least six months before the Government started to move on it.

My Staff Course, which would last a year, started at Greenwich in January 1939. The Royal Naval College is in a beautiful parkland setting along the River Thames, and several of the buildings were designed by the renowned architect Christopher Wren. The Staff Course was housed in one wing of the old Greenwich Palace, with the remainder of the building being occupied by the War Course for Captains and more senior officers, and by courses for Engineers and Sub-Lieutenants. Debbie and I lived in a flat in Dartmouth House on the hill above the College which gave me a lovely country walk through Greenwich Park to and from classes each day.

Officers from all branches of the Navy attended the course, as well as a few from the Army and Air Force. We also had a number of Canadian, Australian and Indian naval officers with us. I found the work extremely interesting. The discussions were generally lively and we were encouraged to disagree with our instructors if we held opposing opinions. We had experts from all fields and it was amusing to see officers asking for help from an expert in one field one day, and then have the roles reversed when another problem arose. We visited the RAF Staff College for a few days and found their students to be horrified with the freedom of speech we were allowed. For them the instructors' word was law and not to be

The last pre-war staff course in 1939.

queried. To me this seemed a very strange concept considering the fact that the more senior students were often of equal rank with their instructors and that frequently students would have specialized knowledge and experience that the instructors did not. Our work load was heavy and we often worked late into the night on projects. These tasks were invariably interesting, and we learned a great deal about solving problems by taking all known facts into account. The more we learned, however, the more certain we became that war was coming. The general consensus was that it would probably happen before our course ended.

It's Really Quite Safe

The Admiralty had the Painted Hall renovated as the new Wardroom Mess while I was there. Greenwich was the repository of all the "retired" silverware from the fleet and there was a great deal of wonderful antique silver including busts of such naval heroes as Nelson, Drake and Hawkins, all of which was well displayed on magnificent new tables. The King came down by Royal Barge for the official inauguration dinner and it was a marvellous sight with the painted ceiling and all the sparkling silverware. We carried on with our usual events (although with the King there they became slightly exaggerated) including billiards, bowls, cards, and a sing-song. The King throughly enjoyed being back with his old service -so much so that he was almost two hours late leaving to return to Buckingham Palace by car. It was a great evening.

A few days after the opening dinner the Wardroom put on a second dinner, this one for all the workmen. It was at our expense and we served beer in copious quantities. The chap who sat next to me opened up after a couple of beers and said, "Sir, I worked on that there ceiling and when we started there was two naked women there, but the Office of Works can't 'ave that, Sir, so we 'ad to paint a 'diaphamous' (sic) veil across their most important parts." He pointed them out, and sure enough, bureaucracy had struck again. It was rather late before the evening wound up and we ferried the men home. One fellow asked me to drop him off a few doors from his house so that he could creep in without waking his wife. It didn't work though, she heard him and the bedroom window shot up and he, (and anyone else who was within earshot), got an earful.

One of the more interesting aspects of the Staff Course was the Dining Club. Eminent men were entertained to dinner in the Painted Hall, following which they would address us in one of our lecture rooms. This was capped off by a question period and drinks. We had some most interesting lecturers, one of the best being Mr.Kirkpatrick, the Third Secretary of the British Legation in Berlin. He had attended Chamberlain at Munich, but after the first day had asked to be excused as he said he found it very hard to stay in the same room as

Hitler, whom he described as 'an evil man'. He told us quite bluntly that war was coming, and left us with the words, "Well, gentlemen, goodnight, and keep your powder dry!" As far as we could see very few preparations for war were being made, the Government's head seemed to be firmly set in the sand.

Another noteworthy speaker was the United States Ambassador, Joseph Kennedy. We were concerned about the entry of the U.S.A. into the war which we believed to be coming, as did the Ambassador. He assured us that America would come in, and in response to an enquiry as to whether there would be much difference if Roosevelt were not re-elected, he said that he thought they would be in well before the election came about. I later found this hard to reconcile with his attitude once war had been declared. One of the last questions put to him came from one of our backbenchers who asked, "Mr.Kennedy, do you not think that the United States is rather like Ferdinand the Bull?" When the Ambassador replied that he did not understand, our questioner explained, "Well, Sir, the U.S. is a very strong bull, but it does rather like to sit around and smell the flowers." Mr.Kennedy was not amused.

Our first three month term was soon over and we all went on leave pretty sure that we would not be back. We were right, it wasn't long before I was appointed to *Courageous* to prepare for war.

It's Really Quite Safe

Three Months of War

Histories of the Second World War tend to show that not much happened before mid-1940, but that was certainly not my experience. I was involved in a frantic struggle to get *Courageous* battle-worthy. She was an old ship, and since she was just coming out of refit she was manned largely by reservists. Our Swordfish aircraft had to be brought out of storage; compasses swung; radios tuned in the air and we even had to buy batteries from shops in Portsmouth because Naval Stores hadn't enough. While we were busy with all of this, new aircrew joined us one by one. Although individually each was trained, it would be some time before they worked together as a team, as a squadron. Only a few training flights has been conducted before war was officially declared. We were based on Devonport for anti-submarine work in the Western Approaches. It was in this area that our merchant ships were being homed individually, and German submarines were known to be operating here.

The German battle cruisers *Scharnhorst* and *Gneisenau* were reported at sea and we were ordered to deal with them. How, we wondered? Although on paper we were a torpedo squadron entirely capable of handling the situation, the fact of the matter was that we had had no torpedo training. I felt rather like a nineteenth century 'forlorn hope' sent off to batter at the gates of an enemy stronghold with my bare hands. It was decided to use pattern bombing -this would only require a single trained crew, while the rest simply followed suit. True enough, our squadron commander Simon Borrett had not been with us during our bombing experiments, but at least we had half an expert crew. We hurriedly set about excercising the procedure in the hangar. However, before we got the only chance to use in war what we had developed in peace, word came that the initial reports were false -the German ships had not sailed. A little disappointed we went on to our next job, cruising around in the Atlantic with an anti-submarine screen of four destroyers trying to keep the submarine pack submerged while the many merchant ships not yet in convoy raced for safety.

It was at about this time that I made one of my more classic 'faux pas'. The Admiralty had decreed that we should use the 'SYKO' re-coding machine to re-code all radio transmissions from aircraft. Normal practice had been to use the 'Self Evident' code, a simple code that enabled us to make very short signals describing what we had seen. It was, however, very much like it's name -self evident to one and all. The SYKO was intended to render the signal difficult to read unless you had a similar machine to receive and decode the transmission. Considering the fact that we only broke radio silence when we saw an enemy, and when he almost certainly had seen us and therefore knew that we must be reporting him, I could never see much value in the attempt at secrecy. Even in the best of conditions an Observer in the open cockpit of a reconnaissance aircraft had a difficult time coping with the effects of vibration and rushing winds. I could see that under operational conditions when trying to report on the presence and movements of the enemy our Observers would be under a great deal of pressure and that the re-coding would cause many errors. My fears were borne out by the number of confused signals that were sent during training flights, so when for some reason he had called me to his cabin, the Captain asked me, as Senior Observer of our squadron, just what I thought about it I did not mince my words. Sadly he replied, "I'm sorry you think that, Rotherham. I invented it." He was obviously a signalman used to the relative serenity of a ships bridge or a coding office and I can not believe that any observer had been consulted. Nevertheless he was very understanding and gave me a drink.

One day a submarine was sighted by one of our aircraft on the surface some 70 miles from our ship. It was apparently agreed that two destroyers were adequate escort for us (having served in destroyers I would have strongly disagreed with this decision), so the Captain (D)* took off with the other two destroyers to hunt. I am afraid that the call of fame had made him overlook his main objective which was the safety of *Courageous*. Since he later rescued me I suppose I should not be too critical.

We afterwards heard from German radio reports that when we turned into wind to land our aircraft on we ran past a submerged submarine just out of range of his torpedoes. The U-boat captain must have been very frustrated at the time, however as soon as we had recovered the last aircraft we turned back and ran close past him.

Two destroyers were not adequate to the task of protecting us, particularly not during turns at high speed when their Sonar was blocked out by water noises. I was on the bridge planning a search for the next day and watching the landing on of the aircraft that had been out on patrol. We had no sooner turned back to our original course after the last aircraft had safely landed than there was an explosion and clouds of fumes drifted up from below. It was just one torpedo, but I could hear the roar of water flooding in and breaking down bulkheads. The ship listed to port and before long the order to abandon ship was given. I went down to the radio room, for I doubled as Signals Officer, made sure that everyone there was clear, then went on down the starboard ladders. I met a Warrant Officer, rather elderly and a bit frightened. "I

---

* *The '(D)' in Captain (D) indicated that he commanded a Destroyer Flotilla —normally comprised of a Leader and eight Destroyers.*

Top: A Swordfish circles to land on Courageous. Judging from the smoke the ship had been hit.
Centre: Still under way, but with a pronounced list, Courageous is taking on water and is doomed.
Bottom: Men scramble to get off the ship before she goes down as her escorts close in to rescue survivors.

can't swim, Sir", he confessed. The destroyers were close now, and I thought to myself that the years of playing water-polo were finally going to pay off. I gave him my life-jacket. I never did see him again and often wonder what became of him.

The ship kept on going over to port, and I made my way down to the starboard bulges where a few others had gathered. A young Sub-Lieutenant suddenly said, "I'm going down to my cabin to get my flask..." He was in our squadron, and I had heard him joke about keeping something ready for just this sort of emergency. He began to clamber awkwardly back up the side of the ship. This was so stupid with help close at hand that I was suddenly angry and shouted, "Come back you bloody young fool! It'll be hell down there with everything falling about." Nothing I said had the slightest effect, however, and he disappeared from view. I never saw him again. Apart from this one piece of foolishness though there was no panic. Some brave men on the other side of the ship slipped into the water and unhooked a cutter as the ship heeled further. Their work saved many lives later.

The ship lurched forward and seemed to shudder beneath us. She was obviously going under, so I dove in and did a fast fifty yards to get clear. I stopped, and looked back while treading water. The stern reared vertically in the air, with all four propellors stopped. I thought it strange that they were not turning. I could see two men clinging to the the ensign staff at the very extremity of the stern ...they were waving. Courageous went with a rush, and rafts and baulks of wood came up to the surface with sudden violence. I could see the two destroyers quite close, and a merchantman lying stopped a little further off. There was a raft not far away.

I was swimming towards the raft when I saw two men in the water and turned aside to help them. As I took hold of the first the other floundered around and got hold of me by the shoulders. I shook him off roughly. "Can't take you both...", I told him. He agreed breathlessly and let go. I towed the first man over to the raft, but when I turned back for his companion he had gone. Once aboard the raft I realised just how cold it was, my teeth were chattering and I could not stop them...another lesson learned: if you are going to be shipwrecked keep your coat on. The raft began to get overcrowded, and as the merchantman was by now much closer and had its accomodations ladder down I plunged into the sea once more and swam to her. She was the Ellerman liner *Dido*. Our two ships doctors had reached her before me and the first task was to take a young seaman who had a mangled foot down to a cabin for emergency treatment. I was asked to bring two others to act as anesthetic. The seaman was given a bandage to bite on, and while I lay across his chest to restrain him the others pinned his legs as the doctor stitched his foot back into place. He was extremely brave and only murmured at the worst of the pain.

Dido had been homeward-bound and was short of food, so we were soon transferred to the destroyer *Inglefield*. I wore the Master's spare working trousers and the Mate's oldest coat, and was grateful for both in the four days that it took Inglefield to get us home, hunting submarines enroute. (The Irish ports which were close at hand were not available to us.) There was an understandable tendency to see submarines behind the crest of every wave and the frequent manoeuvering and changes in speed did nothing to help our dreams.

We exchanged a lot of stories in those four days, the best I heard coming from our Commander Flying, Commander Conolly Abel-Smith. He said, "Well, Hank, I got trapped in the batteries when she went down, but eventually got hold of something and pulled myself clear. About half an hour later I saw a brown light which eventually turned out to be the top of the sea." Exaggeration or not, he must have gone a very long way down.

As soon as we arrived in Portsmouth I called my parent's home where Debbie was staying with our three month old son. It had been four days since they had received news of the sinking of *Courageous* and hope for my survival was begining to fade. Debbie took my call and was so overcome with joy that she ran out onto the golf course next to the house shouting the news and gave our neighbor, Dr.Cameron, a very sound kiss. I gather he waited the rest of the war for a similar event. I went straight on leave, still wearing the old clothes borrowed from Dido's crew. When my mother later took them in to be dry cleaned the cleaner remarked about the dirt and oil engrained in them. She explained that they belonged to a survivor from the Courageous, at which point the little man drew himself up to his full height and said, "Madam, they will be cleaned at no charge. I owe it to my country." We received letters of thanks from the owners when we had returned them -they had not expected ever to see them again.

The two weeks leave I was granted went by in a flash, but we did manage to hastily arrange for our son Tony's baptism. I was then instructed to report to the Service Trials Unit at Lee-on-Solent. They had a motley collection of aircraft for use as test-beds for new equipment. The Fairey Albacore was to be evaluated, and there was a Swordfish fitted with an airborne radar set to undergo trials. I also became involved with an automatic pilot and a dive-bombing sight. My boss was Robin Kilroy, a brilliant pilot. Among the other officers on the station were theatrical luminaries Ralph Richardson and Laurence Olivier. Richardson had to make a forced landing one day and was met by a mob of pitchfork-armed locals who suspected he was an enemy agent. As he said later, "They paid no attention to my claim to be an actor in uniform, and in fact that just increased their suspicions. What tipped the scale in my favour was the old flying helmet I was wearing -it resembled the type shown in the Biggles stories written by W.E.Johns: fiction was stronger than fact." We had three other pilots, one of whom had been sent to us by the Admiralty because he had a great deal of civilian flying experience, though he was now in uniform. He had other talents!

Initially I was kept flying all day long on the dive bomb sight tests, and I found the experience very hard on the back. Normally an observer could position himself however he pleased to best counter the G-forces experienced when pulling out of a dive (which could be as much as five times the normal pull of gravity). During these tests, however, I had no alternative but to sit facing forward so that I could read off all the specially fitted dials. The strain was terrific and years later when I was in *Trouncer* I still needed a chair on the bridge because I found standing for any length of time most uncomfortable. As a result of the tests we condemned the sight and it was not adopted. The only moment of light relief came when our civilian expert put a bomb through the roof of the canteen at RAF Calshot whose bombing range we were using. It was only a seven-and-a-half pound practice bomb, and no-one was hurt, but he was still not very popular. I suppose that he helped add to the RAF's fund of jokes about the bombing accuracy of those flying sailors.

It was inevitable that the Albacore we were testing should be compared with the Swordfish it was designed to replace. The 'Stringbag', although obsolete, had shown signs of becoming one of the great maritime aircraft of the war. Some of our first impressions of the Albacore were not good, its sliding rear seat canopy had its disadvantages as it interfered with the splendid all round view you get from a Swordfish, and we found that the aircraft's intercom system consisting of fixed metal voicepipes did not conduct speech very well —communications were unacceptably garbled. Our protests to Admiralty were greeted with an instruction to "make them work" which we did not find particularly helpful. Eventually I found a solution -a length of garden hose which I purchased in Portsmouth worked admirably.

We flew the Swordfish that was fitted with airborne radar out over the Channel looking for targets to test it with, but found that we wasted a great deal of time because targets were so scarce. Eventually I persuaded the Operations Room at Portsmouth to phone us whenever a large ship was coming up-Channel. To preserve security they would just mention that it would be "worth flying" that day and we would set off to look for it. Truth to tell, the set did not work very well in those early days and it soon had to go back to the research people for modification.

We had quite an experience with the Pollock-Brown automatic pilot we were given to test. It had been designed by a scientist at Farnborough, but for some reason he had been unable to get it developed beyond the experimental stage. It was a simple hydraulic device, its pump being driven by a propellor fixed to the side of the fuselage. At first we had a great deal of trouble with it, so we had our Artificers (instrument technicians) strip it down. They found that it had been sabotaged with a handful of steel filings -evidently someone did not want it to work well. From that point on we had no trouble with it. I flew with Lt.Cdr. Esmonde* while we were testing the device. He was an ex-Imperial Airways pilot and expressed the opinion that it was a better auto-pilot than the Sperry equipment of the day.

Despite the fact that it worked well for us, our ex-civilian expert claimed that it just wouldn't function properly for him. One day he landed and complained that each time he engaged the autopilot the aircraft would bunt even though the controls were trimmed all the way over to maximum climb. I asked him to take me up so that I could have a look to see if I could find out what was wrong. Once we had levelled off at a safe altitude I opened up the device so that I could watch what was happening inside and then asked him to give it a try. Sure enough the aircraft went into a steep dive. We levelled off and tried again, with the same result. Once again I asked him to check his controls, and then try again. This time, as he read off his control settings to me, I unfastened my harness and carefully climbed forward so that without him knowing I was able to look over his shoulder as he engaged the autopilot. As I suspected his controls were set hard to the 'DOWN' position. He was deliberately trying to sabotage the test. "You bastard!", I exclaimed, "Get back to the airfield!"

We later had a very forceful talk in the office when I questioned him about his actions. As far as I was concerned he was much too experienced a pilot to have done what he did purely by accident, and coming right after the iron-filings incident -well, it stank to high heaven. He left the squadron shortly thereafter, and I

* Esmonde was awarded a posthumous VC later in the war for his courageous attack on Scharnhorst and Gneisenau when they broke through the Channel.

believe he did not remain long in the Service. Years afterwards, when I was stationed at Katukurunda in Ceylon a Sergeant Pledger joined the Air Station. I thought he looked familiar, and he confirmed this when he said, "Don't you remember me, Sir? I was in the next office when you were talking to Lt. ————." We remained friends thereafter.

The Wilhelmshaven Raid

Although our test work was full of interest and often needed both our skills and ingenuity to make some new development practicable, it did not satisfy our desire to use our expertise to strike a blow directly at the enemy. I for one had a score to settle. In our spare time Robin Kilroy and I mulled over some ideas and came up with a scheme to destroy the dock gates at the German naval dockyards at Wilhelmshaven. Six Swordfish would be used, armed with torpedoes and flown by crews who had been trained to fly in the dirtiest of weather and achieve the highest standards of accuracy with the placing of their torpedoes and in navigation. Although the dock gates were the initial objective we felt that the attack could be diverted against any major warships that might be lying in Schillig Roads. The limited range of the Swordfish was a problem, but we thought that this could be overcome by having the aircraft catapulted from cruisers which would then retire at speed. The aircraft would fly in under the cover of cloud and rain, and following the attack would fly back to a predetermined spot near a navigational buoy where they would ditch. The crews would then be recovered by a waiting destroyer. The later development of the overload tank would have enabled us to get home safely.

It's Really Quite Safe

The plan was put up to Admiralty, but it was not approved. There was a spin-off, however, for the Air Ministry decided to adapt our plan. As far as I can tell they must have heard of our scheme through the RAF Liason Officer whom the Admiralty had consulted with regard to its feasibility. Out of the blue I received a signal telling me to drop everything and proceed immediately to RAF Mildenhall where I would be temporarily attached to a Wellington bomber squadron (No. 149 Sqn.). As there seemed to be some urgency Robin tried to fly me there, but the weather clamped down and we had to land near London. I finished the journey by train and taxi, and was met at the squadron door by a young pilot who exclaimed excitedly, "Thank God you have come! Now we shall know what to bomb!" Upon further enquiry I found that they intended to bomb German warships in the Schillig Roads. The only fly in the ointment was that none of the pilots could distinguish a warship from a merchant ship from the air, and at this time there were no other back-seat officer aircrew who could take that decision. I was to provide them with the neccesary capability until a permanent replacement could be found. The RAF had come up against the problem created by always having the pilot as the aircraft commander, a problem that the Navy had solved years before. In December 1939, however, the RAF was still not ready to accept that the pilot and the aircraft commander need not be one and the same.

The day after I arrived at Mildenhall I went flying with the Squadron Commander, Wing Commander Kellett, to get aquainted with the Wellington and to find out from what position in the aircraft I would be able to get the best view. The cockpit view was not bad, but when I lay down in the bomb aimer's position in the nose of the aircraft I found the view superb. It was so much better than I had found in the Fairey 111F in which I had done all my high bombing that my fingers itched to be on the trigger. After the flight I mentioned to the CO that if by any chance his regular bomb aimer should go sick I would be delighted to drop the bombs for him. To my surprise he replied, "You can anyhow, if you like." I refused at first, thinking that he and his bomb-aimer were a team that should not be disrupted. I was somewhat taken aback at his explanation that as CO he rarely flew with the same crew twice. I was still concerned that the Wellington flew considerably faster than I was used to, and that I just didn't have the same amount of experience as the squadron's bomb aimers. In response to my question on this latter point the CO indicated that some had probably dropped up to 30 bombs in practice, but that most would have dropped less than that. I therefore told him that since I had lost track of how many hundred bombs I had dropped I would accept the position gladly. And so it was that I became a bomb aimer in a Wellington with only a few days to practice the art before going into action.

On my second day with the squadron I asked if we could do a few runs over their bombing range and was surprised to find that we seemed to be the only aircraft requiring any practice. I was also a little disturbed to find that no one seemed to think it necessary, or even desirable, to send a reconnaissance aircraft to find out whether there were, in fact, any warships in the Schillig Roads. It seemed to be taken for granted that since the German fleet had lain there in the First World War it would certainly continue to do so in the Second. The last shock of the day was to find that Britain's first line heavy bomber would be carrying just three 500 lb bombs* on the planned raid -the same load a single engined Swordfish could carry. Just why the maximum load of 4,000 lbs of bombs was not carried I never knew.

After a few days wait for the right weather the raid was launched. Our squadron joined the aircraft of two other squadrons (Nos. 9 and 37) over the Wash, and we set course with a force of 22 aircraft. Two of the original 24 aircraft had had to turn back with engine trouble.† We flew at 14,000 feet, and if any of the crew wanted oxygen there were tubes to suck through, something like

* *500lb. Semi Armour-Piercing bombs were carried.*

† *The leader of 149 Sqn.'s second vic turned back with engine trouble, and his number 3, apparently not seeing the Aldis signal to formate of the first vic, followed him faithfully back to Mildenhall.*

milk-shake straws. Wellingtons had yet to be fitted with oxygen masks. Our intended track was to take us to a point some ten miles to the north of a small low-lying island off the coast due north of Wilhelmshaven and well south of Heligoland Island. From time to time as we flew along the Squadron Commander asked me how well the other aircraft were keeping formation as he could only see those that were close to his side of the aircraft.

Eventually we reached the ETA for our turning point and headed south towards our target. Looking ahead with my binoculars (I had the only pair in the aircraft) I made out a coast ahead and asked what this would be. Our navigator, a young pilot with about 60 hours flying time and no specialist navigation training replied confidently, "The coast of Germany". Looking again I could not see any low-lying land, just cliffs which made me think we were approaching Heligoland, which indeed we were. Instead of turning to the south of this island we were well to the north of it and as a result we sailed overhead at 14,000 feet in full view for all the world to see. So much for the element of surprise!

We flew on across Schillig Roads, where there was nothing but a couple of merchant ships, towards the Wilhelmshaven dockyards where the heavy battle cruisers *Scharnhorst* and *Gneisenau* were secured alongside. The prearranged signal that we were going to bomb was for the lead aircraft to dive 1,000 feet, and then level out and drop its bombs. This was a manoeuver not calculated to improve the bomb aimer's accuracy. One of the aircraft had mistaken the merchantmen for naval vessels however, and dropped their bombs prematurely. Our aircraft had a good run in and when I had the battlecruisers nicely lined up in my sights I pulled the trigger. Nothing happened. As we turned away from the target I checked with the pilot, and I can still remember his exasperated gesture when he realised that he had not armed the master release switch in the cockpit. This was, to put it mildly, extremely frustrating. It meant that I lost my only chance of dropping a bomb in anger and thus I failed to settle my score directly. Ironically this blunder may have saved the CO from a court martial because the RAF was at that

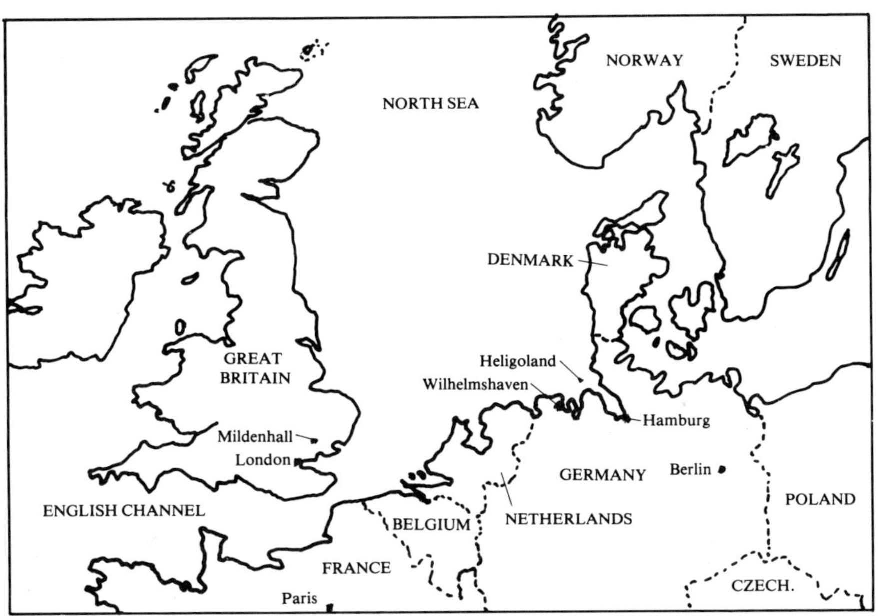

time still prohibited from bombing any target which might endanger civilians and the naval dockyard was embedded in a sizeable town. Furthermore he had been briefed to attack only warships in Schillig Roads and so the bombs dropped on the merchant ships were also "out of court". Although these rules sound totally ridiculous in light of all that followed, they were taken seriously at the time.

The Germans, playing by a much more realistic set of rules, were pounding at us with anti-aircraft fire and their fighters were buzzing about. The Wellington next to us went down in flames, and in all we lost twelve of our twenty-two aircraft. Our squadron suffered the least because we were in the lead and our defensive fire was controlled by radio, but the rear aircraft took heavy casualties.

I was very glad to see that my replacement, Lt.Cdr. Phillimore, was waiting when we returned to Mildenhall. At the debriefing I did my best to stop the man who had bombed the merchant ships from claiming credit for his attack since the photos taken at the time would show clearly that they were not warships. He persisted in his claim and in the end I had no choice but to leave him to his disciplinary fate which I presumed would follow. As far as I was concerned the entire raid was a black comedy of errors and I was so furious at this senseless waste of life and of opportunity that I decided to put my thoughts down on paper.

They had failed in three functions: command, navigation and bombing technique. I had been horrified at their apparent lack of appreciation of the necessity for practice and for the development of high precision bombing methods. As the Royal Air Force as a whole had not appreciated their inadequacy, however, it is perhaps hard to put the blame on an individual squadron. They lacked any method of accurate wind-finding, something which was critical to navigation over the sea where there are no visual clues to one's position, and essential for high altitude bombing. Indeed bombing without accurate wind information is mostly a waste of time. Individual bombing is similarly ineffective unless the crews are highly trained. Pattern bombing, on the other hand, provides a large spread of bombs and compensates for a multitude of errors. It is hard to think of circumstances where it is not the most effective form of attack on a ship or concentrated target. A close formation also improves the concentration of fire when defending against fighters. We did not consider that enemy anti-aircraft fire was sufficiently accurate to be given serious consideration when tactics were being decided.

In light of the obvious ineffectiveness of RAF navigation over the sea it is interesting to recall one RAF document which stated, "It is understood that the Navy has devised a method of windfinding over the sea, but this is not considered to be of use to the RAF." Even over land our windfinding method could have been of great value to them.

I began my report by pointing out that the pilot of a Wellington was unable to see all of the aircraft in his formation and ensure that they were keeping station properly. Nor was he able to oversee the navigation, for the navigator worked in a little cubbyhole down a short passageway where he had no outside vision. It was my opinion that a neophyte pilot with only 60 hours of flying time needed supervision. I suggested that a senior pilot should fly the aircraft while the squadron commander should be able to see his squadron, move about the aircraft and maintain general control of the mission. In the Navy whoever was the most senior officer on board the aircraft was in command and responsible for policy and the efficiency with which a task might be conducted.

I went on to set out methods for pattern bombing, complete with radio procedures and details of how to find the wind velocity either by an individual aircraft or by a squadron without disrupting formation. I also pointed out the foolishness of setting out on a raid without first finding out if there was a target to be bombed. In our case the results had been reminiscent of the Charge of the Light Brigade.

In my opinion a bomber squadron of this type needed to be commanded by a man who combined the talents of a good pilot, navigator and bomb aimer. If any of these qualities had to be discarded I recommended that the need for pilot efficiency be discarded first. One man could certainly be navigator and bomb aimer, and since the raison d'etre for a bomber squadron is to find and destroy targets I would have put full emphasis on these talents.

Having completed my report I handed it to Wing Commander Kellett and after a short discussion I left for London where my presence had been requested by the Admiralty. In London I was interviewed by a group of the top brass, including the RAF's Liaison Officer, and then I was able to go home.

When I had left for Mildenhall I had told Debbie that I was off on some experimental work, which turned out to be closer to the truth than I had imagined. My friends had played along with my story, and she had been quite surprised by the amount of attention she received from other wives on the station who had come in to help her bath the baby and do other household chores. When my friends knew that I had survived the raid and was coming home, in spite of the rather grim newspaper headlines, Robin Kilroy and Butch Judd came over for the evening in the hopes of getting a first hand report. They were very disappointed to find that I would not tell them a thing until the next day after I had been able to give Debbie a full account. She took it all very well, after all there was nothing now to worry about.

On New Years's Eve, just a couple of weeks later, we were having a small celebration because it was also my birthday. Tommy Stevens showed up at the door, uninvited and I told him, "Tommy, go away. You weren't asked. However, as you are here perhaps you had better come in." "I am indeed coming in," he retorted, "You have just been promoted to Commander." I was surprised and delighted -it was a very young promotion. I wondered whether my Wilhelmshaven report had helped -sometimes it is worth taking risks.

A few days later I was summoned to talk to the Air Officer Commanding Bomber Command, Air Marshal Ludlow-Hewitt. I went with some trepidation considering that my report had been very critical of the RAF. I went to see the AOC accompanied by the naval Liaison Officer, a Captain R.N. The Air Marshal told me that he had heard that I was critical of the operation and asked me to tell him about it. I started in, and each time that I hesitated the Captain would say, "You also had something to say about ------." Obviously they were familiar with my full report. The AOC heard me out most cordially, thanked me for my suggestions, complimented me on my recent promotion and I went on my way feeling lucky not to have been given a hard time. Air Marshal Ludlow-Hewitt was obviously a very broad minded man.

I have often wondered whether my representations to Wing Commander Kellett, and later to the Air Marshal, had any effect in changing the manning and techniques of the bombing force. They must have realised that the raid had been a disaster in both concept and execution, and that their methods needed examination. I hope that they took into account that the criticism levelled came from someone with a good deal of experience, and rank almost equal to their Squadron Commander, and that they did not dismiss it out of hand because I was Navy. I do know that the RAF eventually employed officers as navigators, but what other changes were made I can not say.

Cravenly I had failed to tell the squadron that I may have been initially responsible for the idea of this lamentable raid, and I had hardly done sufficient pennance. Nevertheless I would rather have led the attack in a Swordfish, choosing my weather.

The impact of the Wilhelmshaven raid faded slowly, and with the passage of time I grew to suspect that I had been somewhat unfair to the RAF who were, after all, having to pick up operational techniques as they went along. Years later I met Lt.Cdr. Phillimore (my replacement at Mildenhall) at a reunion in London and he suggested that I should write of my experiences with Bomber Command for the Naval Review. I agreed that I would if he would do the same. This he did, and it was a devastating report -his experiences were even worse than my own.

This was the end of a very happy, hardworking and interesting time at Lee. A great deal had been packed into three months. My next appointment was to the Admiralty which promised to offer plenty of interest at this unpredictable period of the war.

It's Really Quite Safe

At The Admiralty

When I was given my new job at the Admiralty in January 1940 I sent Debbie and the baby to stay with my parents at Godalming, in Surrey just south of London. I used the Public Schools Club in Picadilly for my evenings, had breakfast at my digs on St.James St., and usually lunched with a friend somehere in Whitehall near the Admiralty. Save for the blackout London appeared to be operating in almost peacetime fashion. One's pay did not run to much amusement, but fortunately I found that although my club's bridge stakes were higher than I liked, the standard of play was such that I could take part without fear of unbearable losses. This way of life continued until the start of the Norwegian campaign and the fall of France. At that point work became much more intense and there were days on end that I did not leave the Admiralty except for meals. The era of the Phoney War and leaflet raids was over.

At the time of my appointment Winston Churchill was First Lord of the Admiralty, Admiral Sir Dudley Pound was First Sea Lord, and Vice-Admiral Tommy Phillips was the Vice-Chief of Naval Staff. The Fifth Sea Lord, whose responsibilities included all air affairs, was Rear-Admiral 'Ginger' Royle, my former Captain from *Glorious*, a man for whom I had the greatest respect and admiration.

It's Really Quite Safe

Another former Captain of mine, Admiral Sir Charles Morton Forbes, was in command of the Home Fleet. His sailors had dubbed him 'Wrong Way Charlie' because he always seemed to turn the wrong way when he left harbour. He had little use for aircraft, and when he led the fleet on a foray into the Heligoland Bight (just as in the First World War days) he took the aircraft carrier *Ark Royal* with him primarily because it had such an excellent anti-aircraft battery. The first day that they came under heavy air attack the carrier was not allowed to fly off fighters. Despite the Fleet's heavy anti-aircraft fire the attacks continued with no enemy losses. On the second day he allowed *Ark Royal* to launch its fighters and bombing of the fleet came to a halt. Old sea dogs took a long time to learn new tricks, and unfortunately he was by no means the last of the type.

Winston Churchill's presence at the Admiralty was responsible for that peculiar institution known as the "Midnight Follies". Churchill kept unusual hours, and was fond of calling meetings very late at night or early in the morning. One of these meetings was described to me by a friend who had attended. Churchill, who had had the benefit of an afternoon nap, was wide awake and dominated the assembly. Pound was half asleep, and Tommy Phillips sat on the edge of his chair like a naughty schoolboy called into the study to explain his conduct. Signals sent following these meetings were often countermanded next morning after they had been seen by the Staff. I once asked a friend in the Home Fleet how they had coped with this frequent countermanding of orders. He laughed and explained, "After a while we always put any signal that originated after midnight to one side: it was sure to be cancelled just after nine in the morning when the old hands came to work and had time to think things through."

My job in the Naval Air Division was nominally to prepare an analysis of the results of training exercises, but as there were very few such exercises in wartime I turned my hand to looking at the searches made to detect blockade runners. I analysed one such search and found that there had been much duplication of effort when searching for an enemy moving in a known direction. It is perhaps too easy to criticize the work of others done at sea from the quiet of a comfortable office. An old friend, Terrence Shaw, told me later of one such a search in which he had been involved. They had come across a ship which could have been an enemy, but which was wearing British colours. They descended for a closer look. "Then," he said, "I had no hesitation in calling my carrier and reporting a blockade runner or raider; never before had I seen so many high powered binoculars on the bridge of a merchant ship!" How careful you must be when dealing with a flying seaman.

I was not very happy with the job I had been given, and after I had complained about it I was told to work half time with the Operations Division. This brought me into close contact with the Director, Captain Harcourt, and his Deputy, Ralph Edwards. I was quickly brought into the midst of what was going on, including the War Room where the position of every ship was plotted. Being the only aviator attached to the Division I found that I was called upon frequently. Ralph Edwards became a close personal friend and his early death not too long after War's end was a sad loss to me.

Then we heard that Norway had been invaded. The Norwegian campaign broke with actions at Bergen, Trondheim and Narvik. We had some cruisers not too far from Bergen and they were ordered to flush the Germans out. Then someone wondered whether the Germans had sown any mines, and despite the depth of water which made that a very doubtful prospect, our ships were recalled. I had a vain hope that they had passed the point of recall, but regrettably they had not. Of course there might have been some risk from the shore batteries, but these were very antiquated and the Germans had hardly had time to man them and get them into action. Many of us in the Operations Division were very disappointed that we had missed the chance of a quick success which would have been a great boost to the Norwegian's morale. We felt that the risks had been worth taking.

At the time of the Norwegian campaign I was able to participate in some small way with the decision-making process. It is always difficult to determine, even well after the fact, whether or not one's actions have had any impact on the course of the conflict. The following stories may serve to illustrate.

The first serves to underline the point that staff officers cannot make correct decisions if they are not familiar with the capabilities and limitations of the weapons they have at their disposal. In this instance the weapon was the Blackburn Skua. Designed for both the fighter and dive bomber roles it suffered from the inevitable restriction of being really good at neither. It was not fast enough to be an interceptor fighter, but it could be used successfully as a "goal keeper" over the fleet and indeed a Skua had claimed the first enemy aircraft to be shot down by the Fleet Air Arm in World War Two -a Do 18 on September 25th, 1939. Skuas of Nos. 800 and 803 Squadrons at Hatston had sunk the German cruiser Konigsberg in Bergen Fjord, and had shepherded our cruiser *Suffolk* home after she had been damaged by bombers off Stavanger. RAF Fighter Command had been asked to provide fighter cover, but single-seat fighters do not find navigation over the sea easy, and they had not managed to find her. A telephone call to Hatston, however, got the Skuas off the ground immediately, and being two seat aircraft with navigators they soon reached her and kept her from further danger. There now came a request from the RAF to employ one of these squadrons for a raid on the airfield at Stavanger from which enemy fighter aircraft were operating.

Without consultation with the Naval Air Division the Admiralty agreed to this request -I only heard about it because by chance it was my turn to sleep in the office. I thought about the chances of the raid being a success, and then began to think about the range of a Skua carrying a 500 lb bomb. I pulled out a chart of the North Sea and measured the distance from Hatston, in the Orkney islands, to Stavanger. My heart contracted: it was at the very limit of their effective range, rather further than Bergen, and they had sometimes returned from there virtually out of fuel; and as they were to be performing as dive bombers, their target being the runway, they would have

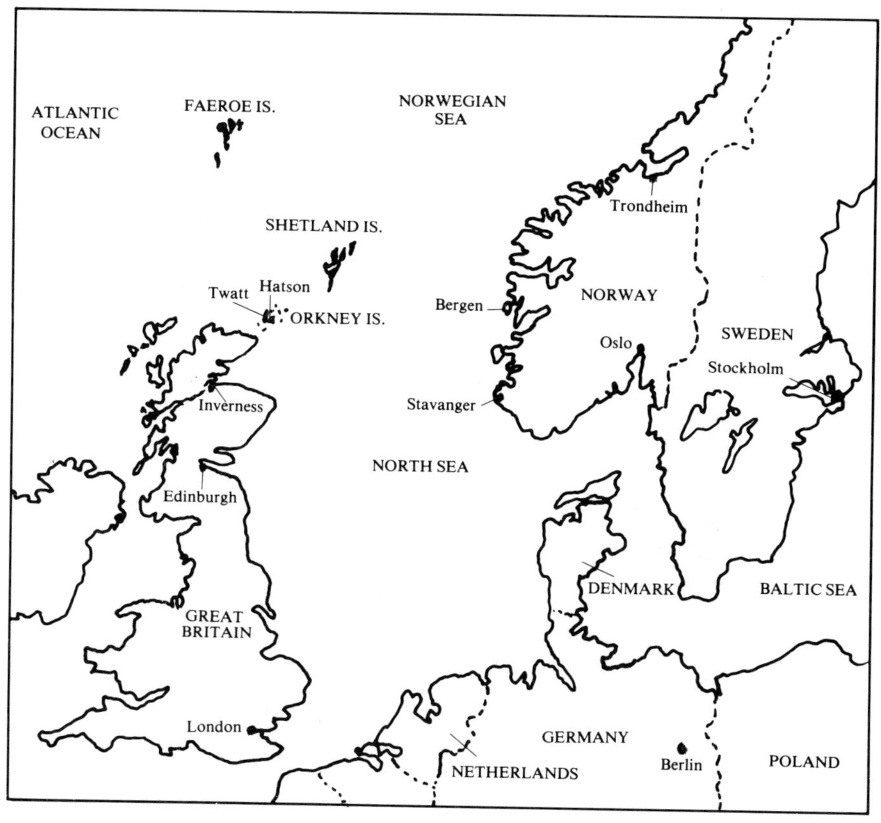

to go in high, where they would be vulnerable to radar detection, and be prepared to dodge fighters which outclassed them. (Stavanger had a fighter airfield, unlike Bergen at that time.) In my estimation, if they had to fight using full power they would not have enough fuel to get back to Hatston: we would lose the lot. The raid was due to take place the next day so I had no time to lose.

It's Really Quite Safe

I managed to find Tommy Phillips, the Vice-Chief of Naval Staff and spoke to him. He asked whether I did not like the concept of the raid and I gave him a firm "No Sir." Rather than ask for the reasons for my objections he enquired whether there were any Captains in the building. I went off to try to contact one of our three Captains by phone, but as luck would have it none could be reached. In desperation I called Rear-Admiral Royle and outlined the position. "All right, Hank", he said at length, "I'll take care of this one." Shortly afterwards I got a message from Tommy Phillips to cancel the raid, so I rang Hatston and gave them the good news. Phillips called for me once more. "Is the raid cancelled, Rotherham?" "Yes, Sir." He turned over on his folding cot and said, "Good, now I can sleep soundly." He never did ask for my objections to the raid, but I felt that saving a squadron of aircraft and their crews was well worth a snub from a Vice-Admiral.

Then disaster struck with the loss of *Glorious* on June 8th. The Captain, d'Oyly Hughes, who had made his name in submarines in the First World War and had been

HMS Glorious.

146

awarded the VC, was not a flying man. He had violent disagreements with his Commander (Air), J.B.Heath, with whom he was incompatible, about the use of his aircraft. *Glorious* was a most unhappy ship which can probably be put down to these internal differences. As a result of their disagreements Heath had been landed in the UK to await Court Martial and the ship sailed north to evacuate Hurricane fighters from Narvik without him. Despite their having no deck landing gear all of these aircraft made it on board safely, a very good job.

Then I understand that d'Oyly Hughes requested to be detached south without waiting for adequate escort. The reason for his haste is obscure. In his book "Operation Skua" Major (P) Partridge, RM, claims that *Glorious* was short of aviation fuel, and that they were anxious to return the Hurricane squadron to the UK since they could not be expected to operate from the carrier. There were other rumours, however, that the Captain's main interest lay in pursuing the Court Martial of Commander Heath. Regardless of these possible reasons, for her own protection this ship should have waited for an evacuation convoy returning to the UK. Incredibly the High Command agreed to d'Oyly Hughes' request and she was sent south with only six Swordfish onboard and with an escort of only two destroyers. As *Courageous* had discovered, two destroyers can not even provide security from submarines. Who was finally responsible for allowing this virtually defenceless ship to sail south through waters which were open to the enemy we do not know. Perhaps they assumed that d'Oyly Hughes would use his few Swordfish to fly defensive patrols, but he did not. No aircraft were flown off, indeed thy were not even ranged as a striking force in case the enemy should appear. So there was no warning when inevitably *Scharnhorst* and *Gneisenau* appeared over the horizon, nor was any defence possible. As a result we lost a fine old ship, two destroyers and about 1,500 men. Poor Heath, whom I knew quite well, spent the next few years demanding a court martial to clear his name, but there was no Prosecutor and no doubt the Admiralty did not wish to bring too much of this affair to light. Eventually, I am glad to say, he was promoted to Captain.

It's Really Quite Safe

One sad foot note to this tragedy came about because the German broadcast announcing the sinking also said that they had rescued survivors. This was not true, but the news stopped ships being sent immediately to help, and so many died who might have been saved. The Germans had rescued no one. It was a despicable dirty trick. Eventually some 30 survivors were picked up on Carley rafts. One of these, I am glad to say, was the CO of the Hurricane squadron.

I had often heard critical remarks in the Operations Division, including some by our Directors, but that night the conversation could only be called Red Mutiny. The Division had a small bar for the comfort of the Duty Officer in peace time as this office was always manned. It had not been closed for the war, but was naturally little used. That night, however, it was in full use. We mourned our friends and we damned the stupidity which had caused the loss of this fine old ship.*

Meanwhile *Ark Royal* had been working off Norway, attacking shore concentrations and troops moving by coastal craft. Then *Scharnhorst* and *Gneisenau* were reported in Trondheim harbour. This was a large, almost landlocked body of water and ideal for torpedo work. To the Naval Air Division's amazement, without any consultation with us, the Admiralty suggested to the Fleet that they should try to destroy these ships using aircraft but that the Swordfish were not to be used. The only other carrier-borne aircraft available were two squadrons of Skuas. Being dive bombers, their bombs could not penetrate these ships' deck armour. They could pierce the decks of *Konigsberg*, a 6,000 ton light cruiser, but not those of *Scharnhorst* and *Gneisenau* which were classed as battleships of 26,000 tons. We forecast the probable hits and losses, and implored the Admiralty to cancel the signal concerning the Swordfish. If these aircraft got in they should sink both ships with their torpedoes without trouble -being at anchor the German ships would be unable to take any avoiding action. If the Skuas flew high as cover, and the Swordfish flew as low as posible, hopping

* *The whole story has been detailed in a book by the well known Naval historian, Captain Stephen Roskill.*

over the land promontory and immediately going down to their torpedo dropping height of 30 feet, their chances of being detected would be minimal. The Skuas, flying high, could act as dive bombers, or in the case that opposition was met, they could release their bombs and act as fighter protection for the Swordfish which were to be the real killers. Further, their presence would divert attention from the low level attack, leaving the ships as sitting ducks. The Skuas might have taken a beating, but it could have been no worse than what actually transpired.

We managed to persuade the Admiralty to make a signal, but all they would do was ask the C-in-C of the Home Fleet if he would use the Swordfish if he was allowed to. His only air advisor in the Flagship was his Wing Commander RAF, Liaison Officer, and whether he asked *Ark Royal* we do not know, however his reply to Admiralty was, "NO." In his book "Operation Skua", Major Partridge RM states that he and his fellow Skua squadron Commanding Officer, Lt.Cdr.(P) Casson, disliked the prospects of the operation for the Skuas alone as much as we did. He thought that the only possible approach that would give a chance of surprise was one at low level, unfortunately impossible for dive bombing Skuas (but ideal for torpedo dropping Swordfish). In his account Partridge makes no mention of possible use of the Swordfish being considered, so it appears likely that the Admiralty's second signal was not passed to *Ark Royal*.

The doubt was compounded, however, by the unusual procedure followed. Partridge, as CO of 800 Squadron, got his orders for the attack directly from the Admiral Commanding the Carriers -Partridge being called to see him by the Commander Flying. The Admiral told him that he was sending both Skua squadrons in to attack the German ships and that he should discuss the attack with Casson, CO of 803 Squadron. This departure from usual procedure is strange. Normally the Captain might be expected to call a conference with his Commander Flying and Commander Operations, together with both squadron CO's and their Observers, where the attack would be planned with the benefit of all possible naval flying experience present. The Admiral would attend if he wished. Perhaps, though conjecture is dangerous, everyone knew the impracticability of this raid and wished to avoid discussion which could further depress the Skua crews -their CO's had already forecast 50% losses as a minimum, as had we at the Naval Air Division in the Admiralty.

A simultaneous attack on the nearby Vearnes fighter airfield by RAF Beauforts from the Shetlands was arranged but the impracticability of this must have been evident. The Skuas had nearly 300 miles to go (their extreme range) and the Beauforts 450 --co-ordination would have been next to impossible. In the event only a small force arrived, a little early, and merely sufficed to alert German fighters to the presence of offensive aircraft.

Out of seventeen Skuas which took part in the raid only five returned. Damage to the ships was minimal. So a great chance was missed. You have to take risks in war and even risk your friends' lives, but these risks are only worth taking if the rewards are adequate. The Skuas could not sink these enemy ships; the Swordfish could. I would have been proud to lead the Swordfish into Trondheim following the general tactics I set out earlier, planning the attack with the two Skua squadron commanders so that they would appear to be the main raiding force and hence the target of any fighter opposition. Although we would, God willing, have been the killers, any accolades or decorations would have gone to the Skuas who would have to bear the brunt of the opposition.

During this time Debbie had moved down to Gloucester to live with her sister. I found it was a rather long way to go for weekends, and since I was very much tied to the office, sometimes never leaving it for a week at a time except for meals, I saw little of my family. I did not realise how little time was left for us to be within visiting distance.

The scene of the war now changed. Hitler had gobbled up those countries which he needed to quell before taking on his major adversaries, Britain and France. The invasion of France began, a story that is well known, and in which I had little part.

When France collapsed and the British Expeditionary Force was withdrawn a friend of mine managed to get a weeks leave so that he could go off to Dover and help with the evacuation from Dunkirk. I kicked myself for not thinking of it, although the Operations Division might have balked at the idea.

We had a Deck Landing Training Carrier, the old *Argus*, working out of Toulon. With the fall of France all but certain, all possible air power had to be sent where it could be of most use, so the *Argus* was withdrawn and her aircraft flown off to North Africa. Half of them went on to Malta, where they became that island's only air striking force. Here they made a magnificent contribution towards sinking Rommel's supply ships. The other half flew along the coast to Casablanca to be taken on another carrier. The French they encountered enroute made their passage as difficult as possible, a sad augury for future Anglo-French relations. Working with the aircraft that were detached to Malta were two cruisers, and I had a magnificent accolade to their work when I met a South African pilot after the war who had been in the RAF. He had flown reconnaissance flights from Malta to locate Italian convoys enroute to North Africa with supplies for Rommel's army. He said that when the Swordfish made contact they usually sank half the convoy, but when the cruisers got in they probably sank the lot! In the Operations Division we received reports of all these operations including the combined service successes which showed great inter-service co-operation and mutual respect. Much of this feeling of harmony was spoilt by the RAF Information/Propaganda Department which persisted in referring to the Naval Aircraft simply as British Aircraft, while giving full recognition to their own as RAF. (Our aircraft were operating under RAF control in Malta.) This was an extension of our experience in the field where both services co-operated to the full while the higher ranks always looked after their own preeminence, thereby causing discontent and interservice jealousy. The Admiralty had adopted the policy of never contradicting a Press Release issued by another Service.

With France fallen and our Expeditionary Forces

withdrawn with a disastrous loss of arms and equipment, the outlook for Britain was bleak. As far as I could see either we would be successfully invaded or it would be a very long war. I called Debbie and told her that I wanted her to follow the Government's suggestion that anyone with connections overseas should leave. If she went back to Canada I would have no worries about her when bombing started, especially if I were to be at sea somewhere and unable to know what was going on. In the event that England should fall I was under no illusions as to what would happen to officers, and I thought that I would have a much better chance of escaping overseas if I were alone. In the light of subsequent events it proved to be a good decision, for had she stayed I would have seen her for no more than an additional 14 days during the next four and a half years.

One day while I was in Harcourt's office with Ralph Edwards, Harcourt pointed to the wall map of the Atlantic and said, "Hank, there's a ship in that convoy which has ALL the available spare rifles from the USA -some 500,000 in one ship. If it is sunk I'm afraid that I shall lose my job!" It was certainly not his fault that all the eggs had been loaded into one basket, but I could understand his feelings. We anxiously watched that ship across the Atlantic and into the safety of Liverpool harbour. There waiting teams of armourers degreased them, loaded them on trucks and dispatched them to impatient Army units. At long last they could shoot again.

Another incident confirmed my belief that if you want to get something right you had best go and look for yourself. It was the height of the invasion scare, and the RAF had instituted anti-invasion patrols using Lockheed Hudsons and Avro Ansons. The former type had just arrived in quantity from the United States; the latter were somewhat slower aircraft that were often used as navigation trainers. I was assigned the task of evaluating these patrols and working out if there were any holes in our coverage that the Germans might exploit. Each day Coastal Command would report which areas had been covered and whether or not the aircraft had been equipped with radar. The importance of radar was that it could sweep a track some twenty miles wide and thus allow the patrols to cover a considerably larger area than could be done visually. At night, without radar, one could only sweep a track four to six miles wide. If our calculations were right we could safely hold our destroyers, and other escort ships that would have to deal with an invading fleet, at four hours notice for steam. This would allow a reasonable margin for minor repairs, and the crews could get ashore for brief spells of what has euphemistically come to be known as "rest and recreation".

I showed my daily analysis to Ralph Edwards and he wondered with me how efficient these patrols were, so much hung on their performance. He asked me if I could do some investigating to find out exactly how efficiently the searches were being conducted. I remembered that one of the Hudson squadrons was commanded by an old ship-mate of mine from *Glorious*, Squadron Leader Constable-Roberts. I rang him at their base at Bircham Newton and asked if I could go on a busman's holiday to see how things were done. He agreed readily and I received a warm welcome when I went down. The crew I was to fly with asked if there was anything special that I would like to see or do, and I replied that it would best suit the circumstances if they just followed their usual routine. Their eyes brightened and they confessed that they usually tried to bomb something in Holland on the way back, and indicated that they would do so this time if they got the chance. I did not object, I just wanted to see what was usual.

The plan called for this radar equipped aircraft to do two runs, each 100 miles out to sea in the general direction of Denmark, with a track spacing of 20 miles. It was after dark when we went aboard the aircraft and I asked the operator about the performance of the radar. He told me that it was not much use, and that in any case this particular set was unserviceable. To my surprise nobody seemed much concerned about this. We set off at a low altitude which was obviously best if you are looking for ships in the dark. Having completed the first run, however, we started the second run by climbing to 15,000 feet and departed from our planned track in order to fly over Holland in search of a target. Just after we had reached the coast of Holland, however, the tail gunner reported a night fighter and so we went home.

Next morning I returned to London and pulled out the RAF Anti-Invasion patrol reports. This showed that my aircraft had conducted a radar search on two runs with no sign of the enemy. In fact we had done just one run, and that without the benefit of radar. I reported to Ralph Edwards who agreed with me that we had been living in a fool's paradise, and that we had better tighten up the readiness of our anti-invasion craft in harbour. The Admiralty brought them from four hours to two hours notice of steam immediately. I felt that I had best stay well away from the wardrooms of the anti-invasion fleet as I would not be too popular there. Exactly what the Admiralty had to say to the Air Ministry on the subject I do not know -it would have been on a much higher level than I was privy to. However, I was fairly sure that I would not be welcomed so wholeheartedly were I to return to Bircham Newton.

At this time it was evident that Italy was about to enter the war and that we would have to face them in Egypt. One of our fears was that their base in Eritrea could cover the southern entrance to the Red Sea and impede our shipping through the Suez Canal. In the War Room I found the staff watching the progress of an Italian merchantman down the Red Sea. It was being shadowed by one of our cruisers and I wondered why it was being given this attention. Intelligence reports indicated that the ship was carrying a load of bombs to Eritrea where we believed there were very few on hand. The question was what to do about it. If war with Italy was declared it was simple -sink it before it reached Eritrea. Then the word went round not to worry, and sure enough it sank all by itself one day and our cruiser picked up the crew. Someone must have received a nice pay off! We later heard that Italian aircraft based in Eritrea were using 6" shells for bombs so our intelligence reports must have been true.

I attended an interesting meeting called to discuss the

experiences of a much-bombed Channel convoy which had been successfully defended by RAF fighters. At the end of the meeting one of the merchant Captains asked if we could stop the fighters from coming down to wave after their battle. "They have done a fine job for us," he said, "but we are not sure then whether they are friends or foes coming down on us and we don't know whether to open fire or not. Please ask them to stay aloft."

One day in the corridor I met my old friend and Admiral, Matthew Best who was in civilian clothes. We greeted each other and I asked what he was doing there. "Hank," he replied, "I'm a Commander now, and have come to see some of those Admirals. They have given me a bit of coast to look after." He explained that he had been chaffing in retirement with the war on, and had pestered the Admiralty for a job. Eventually they had given him one when he agreed to accept the rank of Commander. I asked what time his appointment was for and having looked at my watch said, "Sir, it's after that time now and you know you are only a Commander now!" "By God, so I am," he replied and doubled off down the corridor. I never saw him again as he died not too long after, having worked himself to death I am sure. He was a wonderful man for whom I had great affection.

As I have implied the organisation in Admiralty allowed for too many errors to occur. Unease and dissatisfaction was rife. It is little known that before the war when a change of First Sea Lord was imminent Pound was fourth on the short list of potential nominees. Having had the command of a major fleet was a prerequisite and Pound had been C-in-C Med. The first three choices fell through due either to sickness or death and Pound got the job. Would matters have been a different had one of the first three choices been available?

Then my chance to get to sea again came along. Ralph Edwards, who knew of my longing, came down to the naval Air Division's office where I was and told me of an expedition to Dakar which was about to be mounted. He said that Admiral J.D.Cunningham was in want of a Naval Air Staff Officer and that if the post attracted me I should volunteer quickly. Naturally I did so immediately.

It's Really Quite Safe

Dakar

Soon after I joined *Devonshire* at Liverpool I was on easy terms with Admiral Cunningham's immediate staff. The two major personalities were Lt.Cdr. Crease, the Operations Officer (with whom I had served as a Midshipman), and the Admiral's Secretary, Paymaster Commander Miller. I remember the latter as 'The Purple Emperor', an affectionate nickname based partly on his manner and partly on his complexion. The ship was also a vessel of character. She had come through quite a lot unscathed and the crew cherished her luck. Seamen tend to be a superstitious lot where the safety of their ship is concerned and *Devonshire's* crew cetainly weren't about to do anything that might compromise their good fortune. Hence, when the Admiralty decided that the identification letters, (which had been painted on the top of the foremost turret of all capital ships before the war), should be removed lest they aid identification by the enemy there were furious objections from the ship's company. Having a reasonable respect for superstition their Lordship's relented and directed that these letters (*Devonshire's* were DV -God Willing in Latin) might remain so long as they were dirtied to make them difficult to read. The ship also carried on its books a lucky cat. When Captain Vian had taken *Cossack* alongside the German prison ship *Altmark* in a Norwegian fjord to rescue our sailors, the cat had jumped onboard. Later when *Cossack* was sunk the cat had gone onboard *Devonshire*. Now it was watched with an eagle eye, and whenever we were alongside the gangway sentries had strict orders that it should not go ashore lest it took the luck of the ship with it. This was no laughing matter -they were deadly serious about it.

The purpose of the our Expedition was to take Dakar, an important French naval port in Senegal situated on the westernmost tip of the 'bulge' of West Africa.The operation was to be carried out by Free French forces aided by a battalion of the Foreign Legion and a Royal Marines force embarked in *S.S.Ettrick*. It was not intended, nor thought necessary, for major British forces to take part, though they were to be sufficiently strong and visible to sway the outcome. Serious fighting was not anticipated. Before embarking the Free French officers held a dinner at a hotel in London at which the toast was "Vive Dakar!". At Liverpool my first task was to go ashore in the ship's launch and pick up leaflets. There were tons of them wrapped up in brown paper bundles, many of which had been torn open to reveal slogans such as "Vive Dakar - Vive de Gaulle - Vive les Françaises Libre". Secrecy and surprise seem not to have been important factors in this enterprise.

With a screen of destroyers, the convoy sailed for Freetown from where we were to launch our attack. The two largest ships were the Dutch vessels *Pennland* and *Westernland* which carried de Gaulle and his staff. They were old coal-burning ships which made clouds of smoke and they had difficulty keeping station in the convoy. The smoke made our being sighted by submarines more likely, and their poor station keeping made the task of our anti-submarine escort much more complex. They became known as the rogue elephants. Fortunately no enemy appeared and we sailed peacfully on. Enroute we heard that a force of Vichy cruisers had escaped from the Mediterranean and sailed south along the African coast, presumably bound for Casablanca or Dakar. We sent out a reconnaisance aircraft to check on it and confirmed that they were at Dakar with the partly-finished battleship

A selection of the leaflets that were dropped on Dakar.

Richelieu. There was at least one Gloire class and two Fantasque-class light cruisers. This did not bode well for our expedition.

At Freetown our force was strengthened by the addition of the aircraft carrier *Ark Royal* and the battleships *Barham* and *Resolution. Barham* became the flagship for the assault and Admiral Cunningham and his staff transferred to her.

The plan of action, which had three main stages, was now disclosed to the participants. At dawn of the chosen day Stage One would commence with aircraft dropping leaflets on the town and its airfield, where some Free French officers would land in a light aircraft in an attempt to persuade the local populace to join us. A boat bearing a white flag would go into the port with Commander d'Argentlieu who would engage in talks with the Vichy representatives. The Commander was an interesting man who had retired before the war to become a Carmelite monk. He had been selected for this task because he was quite well known to, and well respected by senior French Navy officers, as Père d'Argentilieu.

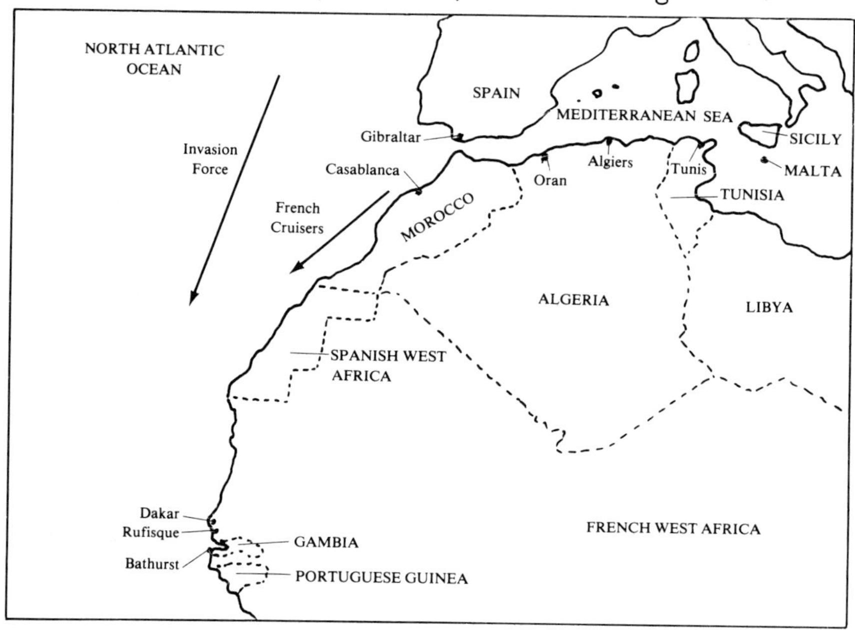

In Stage Two the battleships and transports would show themselves on the horizon, while aircraft from the *Ark Royal* would fly over the town.

If the situation demanded a Third Stage, Free French forces would be landed at Rufisque to the east of Dakar from where they would march on the town. It was presumed that this landing would not be opposed, but should resistance be encountered the Royal Marines would be in reserve to give a helping hand.

It struck me as being a rather feeble plan, and when I checked the defence intelligence it looked even worse. The Vichy French were known to have Curtiss fighters at Dakar, and I didn't see how we could expect to carry out a flypast over the town without heavy losses. I took my doubts to Admiral Cunningham and pointed out that at dawn the hangars on the airfield would be full of aircraft but empty of men. This, I suggested, would be an opportune time to bomb them which would at once ensure our own air superiority and emphasise our determination to fight. Looking at me with a rather sad, quizzical expression Cunningham said, "I know, Rotherham. I know. But I am not allowed to."

Many years later I was able to obtain more details of the initial planning of this operation from Captain Godfrey French who had been a member of the Inter-Service Planning Staff at the time it was conceived. He wrote me the following letter:

"A Directive was received direct from Mr.Churchill, which opened with the words, 'Pray let a Plan be prepared and let all preparations proceed for the capture of Dakar'. Then followed a ready made outline plan stating the forces to be employed and the dates. It was required to be presented to the Chiefs of Staff by 1100 the following day, and to the Prime Minister the same afternoon. Thus the planners were given only about 24 hours to produce their opinion. As it had to be done in conditions of utmost secrecy, time was not available for wide consultation, and they were immediately informed by the Naval Intelligence Division that by agreement with the French over the past ten years no intelligence reports would be produced about each other, and so only the scantiest of information was available. It was indicated, however, that the French in Dakar would welcome the British once they had landed, and any resistance would collapse.

"The planners worked through the night and presented their Plan to the Chiefs of staff by 1100 the next day, and concluded that provided:

1) It was an all British Expedition; and

2) Complete tactical surprise was achieved, it had a reasonable chance of success.

"The Chiefs of Staff accepted the Plan which was conveyed to Churchill by General Ismay, and Churchill aching for offensive action after our defeat in Norway gladly approved.

"The Force Commanders were then appointed. They were Rear Admiral J.D.Cunningham and Major General Irwin DSO, as Joint Commanders, the latter as he was judged to be a daring man with initiative.

"However, when the Force Commanders examined the Plan they discounted the chances and Mr.Churchill decided to change and enlarge the scope of the operation by inviting the Free French under General de Gaulle to take part. Thus both conditions prescribed by the I.S.P.S. were at once discounted..."

I have already outlined the plan in its final form. It appeared to me as though members of the Free French planning staff likened de Gaulle to Joshua whose trumpets needed only to sound to bring down the walls of Jericho.

We were close to Dakar when the day of the attack dawned. The weather was most unusual -there was a glassy calm with no swell, and there was only a few miles visibilty through a thick haze. A landing on the Atlantic Coast had earlier been ruled out because of the possibility of a heavy swell, but here was one of those days when a landing would have been simple. Anyhow, we started with leaflets, and the landing of the light aircraft. Their crews were arrested immediately and thrown into jail. Meanwhile Père d'Argentlieu, with a white flag flying alongside the French Flag, entered the harbour in his motor boat. Without hesitation he was fired on from the shore and he was badly wounded. His boat retired. This shocked the Free French beyond measure. They realised that the Vichy

French could not know who was in the boat, but they were incredulous that the French flag and a white flag would be fired on. It certainly quashed any doubt that Vichy was in full control ashore.

We went on with stage two of the plan, parading past the town in a show of force. Its batteries duly opened fire on us. We tried again, this time returning their fire, although historically it has been proven that ships cannot compete with shore batteries. The fall of shot from the French guns was pretty to watch, for to help each gun identify its shots and correct accordingly their shells contained dyes which created blue and pink splashes. They were fairly accurate, although we were only hit once on our side armour and the shell did not penetrate. One shell, however, burst just short and a splinter, a nasty jagged thing hit the mast right above my head and finished its travel by bouncing off my stomach. I felt more than ever that our 'softly-softly' plan had been ill-conceived.

Later in the day reconnaissance aircraft reported that the French *Fantasque* cruisers had left harbour, presumably to interfere with any possible landing operations in the bay. Then we heard that de Gaulle had taken his transport close inshore without telling us, and that he could not be more than two or three miles from the cruisers. Panic set in, and destroyers were sent at full speed to cover him while he was told in urgent terms to get out of the bay. Fortunately the poor visibility saved him, otherwise the Free French leader and his troops might all have been lost.

It was decided to try again the next day, using the same tactics. This time a French submarine was lying in wait and torpedoed *Resolution.* She was hard hit and had to retire. The submarine was sunk, and our force withdrew. *Resolution* had a hard time getting back to Freetown. Men had to toil in terrific heat in the propellor shaft passages to try to stop leaks, and the Engineer Commander collapsed under the extreme conditions. *Cumberland*, a 10,000 ton cruiser commanded by Captain R.R.Stuart was also in trouble. She was hit, holed and set on fire by the shore batteries. The fire was brought under control and she headed for Bathurst on the Gambia River about 80 miles south of Dakar. She had a heavy list which was agravated by a fractured fire main which continued to pour water into the ship. She finally reached Bathurst where temporary repairs were completed.

After suffering these losses it was clear that the operation was a failure, but before breaking off the attempt General de Gaulle came on board to confer with Admiral Cunningham. This meeting took place in the chart room on the bridge and both Crease and I were present. There were no recriminations, and I admired de Gaulle's attitude in a situation which he must have found most humiliating. It must have added to his burden to know later that the Free French officers who landed at the airfield were condemned as traitors. They had landed unarmed to parley with their own countrymen, the local French, to persuade them to continue to fight with them against the country which had invaded their home land. You do not normally condemn such ambassadors as traitors, nor do you fire on the white flag. However, I believe that they were eventually reprieved after a great deal of diplomatic pressure had been applied. Certainly the Free French officers I came into contact with were principled men of high calibre who did not deserve such cavalier treatment.

Could Dakar have been taken in the manner planned? Evidently not, and I do not believe that the scruples of the planners regarding bombing the hangars bear examination. It seemed absolutely ludicrous to refrain from bombing the hangars to avoid service casualties, and yet to pump shells into the shore batteries on the outskirts of the town where civilian casualties were inevitable. It is possible that the plan might have succeeded had not the French naval forces arrived on the scene -it seems likely that the presence of these ships stiffened the backbone of the Vichy adherents in Dakar who might otherwise have given in gracefully. Had there been landings at Rufisque and on the Atlantic beaches at dawn there might also have been a different outcome. As it was Admiral Cunningham had little freedom of action. The plan was not his, he did not like it, and the decision to go ahead after the arrival of Vichy warships was taken elsewhere. The intelligence reports indicating that there was strong Free French support in the town was incorrect, and indeed they were contradicted by the British Navy and Army liaison officers most recently returned from Dakar who had been sent with the expedition. Their opinion was that Dakar would fight.

It was a strange period of the war when you did not always know who were your friends and who were your enemies. Generally speaking the Colonial Governors, being Civil Servants and depending on the goodwill of the existing government in France for their pay and pensions almost always sided with Vichy. It took the efforts of someone else to change matters. There were men in French Equatorial Africa and in the French Cameroons to do this. The question is whether there was a man, or men, in Dakar with sufficient following to sway the people over to the Free French side.

Finally I wonder whether de Gaulle was the right man to lead this kind of venture. My impression was that he had great talents, but that he was not strong on tactics, nor could he be called "a leader of men". Perhaps he was already developing that remote style of leadership that made him in the years to come the very model of an enigmatic national leader. The failure at Dakar was soon to be followed by a success in French Equatorial Africa where I was to meet a French officer, Colonel Leclerc, whose grasp of tactics and powers of leadership were wholly undeniable. Leclerc's real name was Philippe Francois Marie, Comte de Hautecloque, but when France fell and he joined the Free French he assumed the name of Jacques Leclerc hoping to protect his family, which was still in France, from reprisals.

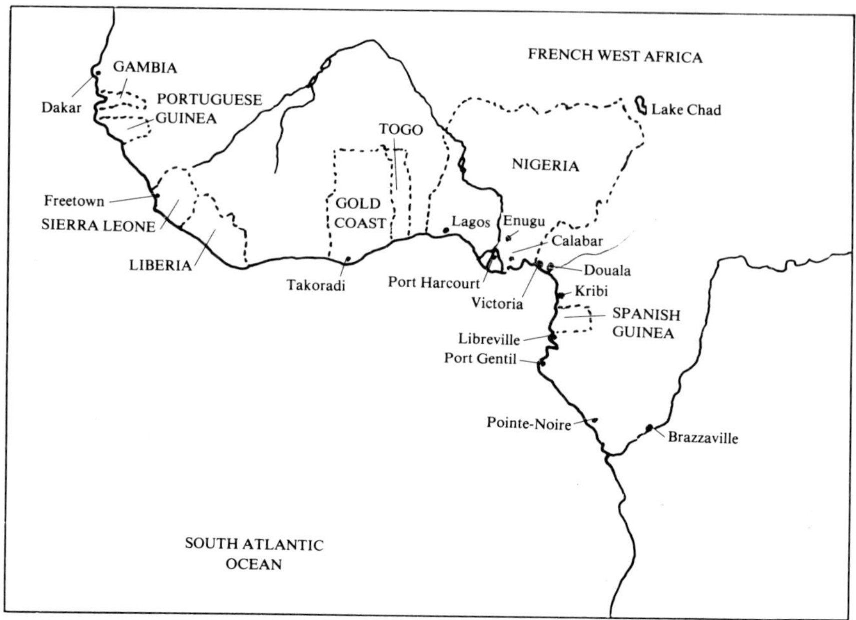

FRENCH WEST AFRICA
GAMBIA
Dakar
PORTUGUESE
GUINEA
Lake Chad
TOGO
NIGERIA
Freetown
GOLD
COAST
SIERRA LEONE
Lagos
Enugu
Calabar
LIBERIA
Douala
Takoradi
Port Harcourt
Kribi
Victoria
SPANISH
GUINEA
Libreville
Port Gentil
Pointe-Noire
Brazzaville
SOUTH ATLANTIC
OCEAN

Douala and Libreville

After we returned to Freetown from the abortive move on Dakar our attention turned to Douala, a town situated on the Vouri River bordering Nigeria. It was the capital of the French Cameroons which had just declared for General de Gaulle. Douala was likely to prove useful as an advanced base because French Equatorial Africa had split loyalties. The capital of Brazzaville had gone Free French, but Libreville, on the River Gabon, was still obstinately for Vichy. It was decided that the Free French forces with us should go to Douala to consolidate the change of allegiance there, while it was also a good staging post from which de Gaulle could fly on to Brazzaville. If necessary some of the Free French troops could be taken by sea to Pointe Noire, a port connected by rail to the capital. In the meantime the Vichy forces at Dakar flew reconnaissance flights to keep an eye on what we were doing in Freetown, and we put up aircraft to make sure that Vichy ships did not slip down the Gulf of Guinea and redress the balance of power.

We received a report that a fast Gloire-class cruiser was coming our way and *Devonshire* went out from Freetown to intercept. We picked her up during the afternoon, and she at once turned away. We gave chase, but initially there seemed little prospect of our overtaking her. Suddenly though we began to overhaul the French cruiser hand over fist. Something must have gone wrong in her engine room, for she lay stopped in mid-ocean rolling gently in the troughs of the sea. We went to action stations with all guns loaded. The turrets were kept fore and aft but were free to move. The trainers' hands were on their wheels and the range was set. We watched our adversary for any sign of gun movement. If one had moved our turrets were ready to train round at full speed and to fire as soon as their sights came on. The first ship to get off a broadside would have destroyed the other. Nothing moved as *Devonshire* closed to within 150 yards, the searchlights coming on as the daylight faded. We sent a boat over with an ultimatum -return to Dakar or take the consequences. The French Captain gave his word, and once repairs were completed he went on his way. We returned to Freetown quite elated with this small success.

It may seem strange that we did not destroy this ship when we could so easily have done so while she lay dead in the water. We were in that strange period of the War when there was hope that these men would realise how vital it was to fight on against Germany and remove their presence with all its Nazi brutality from their own country. After all, only a few months before they had been our allies and comrades.

A few days later the troop convoy, escorted by Devonshire and some destroyers, sailed for Victoria, a port almost on the border between Nigeria and the Cameroons. Its bay had water deep enough to accomodate the big transports which were to disembark their troops into smaller ships which could navigate the river up to Douala. We anchored in the bay with the transports while the smaller supply ships carried on up the river and our destroyers conducted anti-submarine patrols outside the bay. The river steamers came alongside to take the soldiery from the transports, but the disembarkation process seemed to be proceeding very slowly. Since we were worried about the rumours of Vichy French submarines in the area, the Captain of Devonshire and I were sent over to hasten things along. We first went over to Pennland, but here things were going not too badly.

They had the Foreign Legion on board and they were efficient. On board *Westernland*, however, it was quite different. Here we found the Free French, a mixture of gallant men, soldiers, playboys etc., together with quite a number of camp followers, staff car drivers, nurses etc. The bar, which was still open, was far too attractive to allow officers to get on with the job. We had it closed, which helped, and did whatever else we could to get things moving. The Captain of the ship asked us up to the bridge, complimented us for the job we had done and, presenting us each with a table-napkin memento of the ship, said, "Here is a little present for not losing your tempers." He must have suffered enroute.

At last it was all done. The river steamers had taken all the troops to Douala, and the transports sailed west with their destroyer escort. *Devonshire* went up river as far as possible and then the Admiral went the rest of the way to Douala by boat where he discussed the situation with de Gaulle. It seemed as though there was going to be no excitement, and so we set off for Lagos leaving Colonel Leclerc in command at Douala and de Gaulle established in Brazzaville. We had just arrived in Lagos when there came an urgent signal from Leclerc seeking our co-operation in taking Libreville. Admiral Cunningham sent me to talk to him and form an estimate of his abilities and the chances for a successful outcome.

The local airline provided a small four engined passenger plane for the trip, a de Havilland 'Express' I believe. Since no one knew just what we might find at Douala we flew first to Enugu to refuel so as to have enough fuel to make it back from Douala without refuelling again. It was a quiet little airfield, populated by antelopes and bare-breasted native women carrying children. In Douala I met with Col. Leclerc and our local naval Port Officer, Lt. Hooley RNVR, who acted as interpreter. The Colonel told more of his plan and explained how he intended to carry it out. For me, however, the most important part of the plan was Leclerc himself. He impressed me enormously and I had no hesitation in backing him. He had master-minded the take over in the Cameroons, and was manifestly well respected in French Africa. I wrote my report on the flight back to Lagos where I discussed it with the 'Purple Emperor' as the Admiral was ashore. My host, with splendid timing, saw the importance of the occasion and produced a haggis from his personal store. Eating such a dish in the steamy miasma of Lagos was a memorable experience.

The Free French take-over of Douala and the Cameroons was rather melodramatic. Leclerc had been just across the river at Victoria, which is in Nigeria, presumably sent there by de Gaulle. In Douala there had been plot upon counter plot and intrigue was serious. There had been one Free French plot to ensure the death of one of the strongest Vichy supporters by derailing his rail car as it passed over a bridge. The intended victim must have smelled a rat because he took one of the strongest Free French supporters along with him on the trip and so the plot had to be abandoned. English ladies going across the river to shop and meet friends took secret messages to Leclerc hidden on their persons in the best spy thriller style. Eventually the right time came and Leclerc crossed the river and seized control. With his strong and likable personality he had little difficulty in consolidating his position. Hooley, who was well respected in Douala, had been of great assistance to him.

Admiral Cunningham made up his mind to back Leclerc, and sent me back to Douala to provide liaison with the British ships which were to be involved in the operation. The British liaison officers which we had withdrawn from the Free French ships after the Dakar affair were also to return so we chartered another aircraft for the flight. This was a different type, a metal skinned monoplane, and we had a great deal of gear with us which we just managed to cram into the aeroplane. This time Enugu did not have the correct fuel for us, but we were able to reach Douala direct. On our approach to Douala we ran into the fringes of a tropical storm, something you just don't fly into if you value your life. We were just about to backtrack to Enugu, where we would have had to wait for gasoline to be flown in from Lagos, when the pilot spotted a small airstrip through a hole in the clouds at Kumba, and we made a hasty landing. Once the storm had passed we flew on to Douala where one of the most amusing and unbelievable experiences of my life was waiting to unfold.

The liaison officers returned to their ships. The four ships were the *Savorgnan de Brazza* , the *Commandant Dominé, Commandant Duboc* and the *President Houduce* . The first of these was a 'Colonial Aviso' -similar to a large frigate of 2,000 tons - armed with three 5.5 inch guns, and four 40mm and eleven 20mm anti-aircraft guns, and capable of 18 knots. The two *Commandants* were 20 knot light 'Avisos' which could be described as 700 ton gun boats, each carrying two 3.9 inch and one 40 mm and six 20 mm anti-aircraft guns. The *President* was an armed trawler with two 4 inch guns and a top speed of 8 knots.

I was quartered in the Compagnie de Bananes' building. At the time bananas were not being exported -the British government was paying plantation owners to throw their crops into the ocean just to keep the economy alive. Royal Navy ships which visited the port from time to time became known as the 'Banana Boats' because they were the only ones taking any bananas from Douala. The building had been taken over by the British to house the Naval Staff because it included a sitting room, dining room, kitchen and several bedrooms. There were four of us, and the accomodation which was extra to our requirements was at the disposal of the Free French.

We lived quite well, eating dishes such as palm oil chop. We were served by Nigerian house boys. It was acknowledged that the best house boys came from Nigeria. They spoke 'coast' or 'pidgeon' English, and so the French had to learn a little English to be able to speak to them. With the large influx of hungry soldiers supplies were pretty short, and it was some time before someone gave permission for the supply ship full of goodies for Dakar to be unloaded. Perhaps Douala had not been thought worthy of such luxuries, but until then we had to make do with such things as mashed up ripe bananas for butter.

Père d'Argentlieu was recovering quickly in the hospital, and was maintaining command of the ships from his bed. The French Air Force personnel whom we had brought with us were hard at work assembling a few

A Lysander aircraft similar to that used by the author for the recconnaissance of Libreville.

Blenheim and Lysander aircraft. Also in Douala there was a "political" general, General Spears, who was the "bear leader" for de Gaulle. He had a small staff of officers, most of whom were bilingual. Apart from advising de Gaulle his main preoccupation seemed to be with his own interests. I saw one lengthy signal to his commercial firm in England telling them of the potential trading possibilities. I was to cross swords with him later.

The first of the Lysanders was ready for flight after a few days, and a reconnaissance of Libreville was planned. It was fitted with an an extra fuel tank, the drain cock of which stuck out into the passenger seat where it might have struck a lethal blow in the event of a rough landing. As an experienced naval observer I was asked to go on this reconnaissance to report what ships or submarines were in the harbour. We planned to refuel at the small airstrip of Kribi, some 60 miles to the south of Douala, on both legs of the flight, and to cross directly over Spanish Guinea enroute. No one bothered us there although we flew over several small airfields. The weather for the trip was excellent and we had no trouble finding Libreville. We bombed the airfield for good measure and checked out the harbour. There was the sloop *Bougainville*, (similar to the *Savorgnan de Brazza*), and quite a number of barges, but nothing else. Our fuel supply did not permit us to linger so we soon turned for home. On our arrival at the hangar at Douala we were quizzed as to what we had seen, and to my horror I heard the pilot tell not just of *Bougainville*, but of 'plusieurs sous-marins'. Fortunately I was there to correct him and let it be known that these were just barges. The presence of a force of submarines would have made landing operations treacherous since we did not have any good anti-submarine ships. It appears that few military pilots have any knowledge of ships.

I made several more flights to Libreville, but all of them were in Blenheims. We dropped bombs on bridges, and usually on *Bougainville*. There were no trained bomb-aimers among the crews, however, so we had very little success. *Bougainville* generally fired back at us, but they were never very accurate. On one occasion the bomb-aimer released all of the bombs prematurely by mistake. This incensed the pilot who began a voluble argument with much waving of hands. Meanwhile the aircraft flew on by itself. *Bougainville* opened fire on us and still the argument went on. Fortunately the gunners were as inaccurate as ever, but it was not till I called the potential danger to the crew's attention that they decided to postpone their argument.

As our ships might have to enter the harbour without the benefit of navigational buoys if the Vichy French thought to lift them I thought that it would be a good idea to get some low level photography of the approaches to the harbour. To get a clear view I would stand up in the fuselage hatch with a large hand-held camera, bobbing down out of the slipstream to wind the film on to the next frame. This proved to be exhausting work, and after a few of these runs I was begining to regret that I had ever thought of the idea.

On one flight we checked out Libreville, and then went on to Port Gentil, a very small harbour some 60 miles further south. Here we did find a small submarine which even had the audacity to fire on us. Its gun was not an anti-aircraft gun though, so it was of little danger to us. We then flew up the River Gabon above Libreville just to check, but it was impossible to see much through the thick jungle canopy over the river. We ran into a series of line squalls, each of which we had to go around, and I began to worry about running out of fuel. Once we reached the coast we would be in little danger as there were airfields in Spanish territory for refuge, but nevertheless I had no desire to be interned in Spanish Guinea for the rest of the war. It turned out that we had enough gasoline to be able to overfly Kribi and proceed directly to Douala.

Devonshire had just come into the river and they sent a boat as the Admiral wanted my report urgently. I tore the pertinent pages from my notebook, stuffed them in an envelope and sent them off. On this particular day I had scribbled down a running commentary full of hopes, doubts and fears and it must have made interesting reading. Being fired on by a submarine, pushed off course by weather and threatened with the possibility of internment seemed like a meaty scenario for a day's work.

Among the Free French aircrews there was an enormous variety in experience and ability. This was understandable since most had escaped individually from France, and since then had had very little training or supervision. Their pilots and observers were officers. There was one absolutely first class pair with whom I flew, but with another crew I realised that I had never seen a pilot more relieved to get back on the ground all in one piece. I shared his pleasure at our safe return, having been aware from the time of take off that he had little experience. After years of flying one can sense a crews inexperience immediately. The next time he went flying this pilot did not return and to my great regret he took with him their best observer.

For the operation against Libreville the Admiral detached *Delhi*, a 4,000 ton cruiser with a relatively shallow draft which carried 6 inch guns. She was commanded by a good friend of mine, Captain Alf Russell, my former Commander in *Apollo*. He came ashore to discuss matters with Leclerc and our political General was there to act as interpreter. Late in the discussion Capt.

Russell was asked what he would do in a given circumstance and he gave a simple direct reply. The interpretation provided to Leclerc was incorrect so I broke in and said, "That is not what Captain Russell said, Sir." I got a very dirty look, and the answer was retranslated, this time correctly. Asked if he would enter Libreville if matters went awry with Leclerc, Russell immediately responded, "Yes, of course." His bearing during the conference gave confidence to Leclerc -he was definitely the right man for this job.

Alf later told me that British policy was that the Royal Navy should take no part so as not to further annoy Vichy, but as he said, "What can I do if Leclerc is in trouble?" In light of this official policy the actual outcome of events is of interest. *Delhi* did not have to take an active part, but nevertheless the French newspaper headlines screamed that a British cruiser had entered Libreville to assist Leclerc. Had *Delhi* assisted and entered Libreville with the *Savorgnan de Brazza* the sinking of *Bougainville* would have been a foregone conclusion, and under those circumstances she might well have surrendered peacefully without losing face. By hanging back we might have lost *Savorgnan de Brazza* and *Delhi* would have been forced to take action. So we risked our friend's lives and placed the whole operation in jeopardy, and for what? The world thought that *Delhi* had taken part anyway, because that's what the papers in Paris announced.

While we were planning the operation I was sent for by Père d'Argentlieu. From his hospital bed he announced, with a gleam of religious fervour in his eyes, his new plan for the ships and the capture or destruction of *Bougainville*. "We will enter Libreville by night!" (Although this was not impossible it was fraught with navigational dangers, a strong current and unlighted buoys being the main difficulties.) "At dawn we attack -the *Commandant Dominé* will go alongside and board, -the *Savorgnan de Brazza* will shoot, -and the *Président Houduce* will RAM!" He emphasised the last word of each phrase triumphantly. He seemed to have been trying to create a scene to outdo Captain Hornblower -imagine two ships locked together with hand to hand fighting going on while a third is shooting at them and then the *Président Houduce* ramming with all of her magnificent 8 knots! I wasn't impressed. I managed to persuade him that the poor old *Président Houduce* would be a good deal more useful just shooting her guns, and dented his enthusiasm for the boarding party which I was pleased to hear he later dropped from his plans. He was rather melodramatic and impractical. A staff course in a Carmelite cell is evidently not the best training for higher command. But he was a thoroughly charming man!

From time to time I had meetings with Leclerc and developed quite a bond with this great man, and I use that adjective advisedly. On one occasion I wanted to talk to him alone, without even our British Port Officer present. Leclerc spoke no English and my French was definitely schoolboy variety, but with him in occasional fits of laughter as I fell into the usual traps of an unfamiliar language we discussed my problem and departed with complete understanding. Next came a meeting of all three services to discuss and finalise the plan of attack. Transports were to land troops under the command of Leclerc on the coast outside the river mouth from where they would march on the town. The Air Force were to bomb any enemy troop movements. The Navy were to enter the harbour and the *Savorgnan de Brazza* would engage *Bougainville* while the Avisos were to harrass troops moving to resist Leclerc along the road by the river. The Air Force representative said that there would be no need to bother about *Bougainville*, as they would sink her before the attack. Leclerc immediately turned towards me and raised a questioning eyebrow. I responded with a coin-tossing gesture to indicate that I was extremely doubtful. Without a single word having been spoken Leclerc understood and discounted the possibility, which was just as well for the Air Force did not sink her. *Delhi* was to hold the ring outside the harbour and to defend against any interference from Vichy ships. At the meeting's conclusion Leclerc impressed upon all that no word of the plan was to be mentioned outside of the conference room. Within four hours, however, Hooley, who was not at the meeting, was able to tell me all the details. Remembering "Vive Dakar" at the dinner in London I can not say that I was particularly surprised.

The time for the attack came and everything went according to plan. The troops landed successfully and advanced under the cover of the Avisos' fire, and *Savorgnan de Brazza* fought a very nice single ship action, sinking *Bougainville* which rested on the bottom with her upperworks awash. There was fighting ashore, but the Vichy French quickly lost heart and surrendered. Delhi did not have to provide assistance.

Leclerc then sent word that he would move on to capture Port Gentil. I wanted to get down to see him to find out what RN assistance he might need. I asked for an interpreter and was assigned a young British Army Officer who I knew quite well. Unfortunately, however, the Air Force had no aircraft available so I could not go. That afternoon General Spears left for Brazzaville, and the next day my interpreter came back to see me. "Sir," he said, "You really would like to go to Libreville, wouldn't you?" I assured him that I would and he told me to come along with him. In answer to my questions he explained that the previous day he had been given orders that I was not to go, and had had to do some fast talking in colloquial French that I could not understand in order to sabotage my request for a flight. We went back to the Air Force and arranged a flight for the next day, but it turned out not to be neccesary. Port Gentil surrendered and there was to be no more fighting. I could never really fathom why it was that our General did not want me to go to Libreville, unless he thought that perhaps I might divert some of his thunder. I was disappointed as I would have liked to see Libreville from the ground after flying over it so often.

I was really quite shocked at my experiences with interpreters since I had thought that we were all on the same side. In retrospect I am glad that I chose not to use an interpreter in my confidential discussions with Leclerc. It taught me the lesson that if you must use an interpreter he should be one of your own men, someone fluent with the expressions you use and knowing their full meaning, and definitely a man you can trust who has no other loyalties.

The man of the hour was Philippe Leclerc. A Major in 1940, he was to become a divisional commander a mere four years later. He was daring, modest, simple and honest. I know nothing of his personal relationship with General de Gaulle, but the latter's behaviour following the capture of Libreville was, to say the least, rather odd. Before Leclerc returned to Douala de Gaulle sent a signal transferring him to the Chad district in Central Africa. He did not come to Douala to congratulate him or kiss him on both cheeks in the usual French fashion, nor did he send any congratulations that were made public. He simply ordered him away to what appeared a secondary place, (though of course it was to be of great importance later.) General de Gaulle's thoughtlessness almost turned Douala's French inhabitants away from the Free French cause. The people were furious about this shoddy treatment of their hero, and Hooley had to work hard with his friends to counter this danger, which eventually blew over when Leclerc made his triumphant return from Libreville.

General Leclerc (right). This photo was taken on the occasion of the official Japanese surrender in September 1945. With Leclerc is Col. Cosgrave of the Canadian Delegation.

The victory celebrations included a march-past with the Free French, the Foreign Legion and a detachment of British-led Hausas from Nigeria. The latter were, to my delight, the smartest men on parade. When all this was over Leclerc departed for the Chad, and the troops began to be dispersed. I was not to see Leclerc again, and his early death in a flying accident shortly after the war was a great loss to France. I am sure that many others besides myself mourned him.

As I mentioned earlier, there were quite a number of camp followers who were ostensibly nurses and drivers. No doubt some of them were professionals, but it was evident that there were quite a few whose duties were more in the field of entertainment. The comings and goings of some of these girls was a source of much amusement. One most attractive young woman got engaged to a senior official or Chief of Staff. She would go out with him in his car in the evening, but after returning and running up to her bedroom in our building, she would then run down again as soon as he had driven away and go off with someone else. She was a constant source of interest -in one instance I was walking past the captain's Upper Deck cabin on one of the French warships when I caught sight of her hurriedly dressing. She once said to me, "You know, we are both trying to do the same thing," and I have always wondered if by chance she was attached to our intelligence service. I saw her again years later in a London night-club, as attractive and vivacious as ever. In general I could not help feeling rather sorry for these women -they had joined an expedition to Dakar, a large city with most of the modern conveniences, but they found themselves camping out in Douala and Brazzaville, rather primitive towns deep in the tropics. I hope that they soon found their way to better places.

One day I was asked to a lunch party at a flat with a number of young French wives, and I came to the conclusion that it would have been quite easy to arrange for private French lessons. I decided, however, that any involvement in a place like Douala where everyone seemed to be fighting for his own interests would have been most unwise. The war really was more important. I was also offered a trip to the Chad district in a civilaian supply convoy by a man called Drinkwater, with the prospect of shooting big game on the way. I had a few thoughts about trying to persuade the Admiral that I would be doing vital war work by investigating the political climate in the area, but commonsense won and again the war came first. There was no question that as far as fun and games were concerned the war was a damn nuisance.

One day Colonel Montclar*, the senior Colonel of the Foreign Legion, came to see me. He was a fine man who bore many scars of wounds from the campaigns in which he had fought. He had led his battalion in the Narvik campaign in Norway, and brought it back to England when they were evacuated. With the fall of France he had taken his battalion over to the Free French cause. He told me directly, "Commander, I want a ship to take my men away." I explained to him that we knew that a ship would soon be coming, although we did not know exactly when, and asked him what his hurry was. He replied, "Half my men have to sign on again at the end of the year. It is now nearly December, and I do not know when we can get away. My men sign on for one of only three reasons: fighting, wine or women. Here there is no wine, no women and now no fighting. I must have a ship." It was true, we had drunk Douala almost dry. This was clearly a crisis; we could not afford to lose any of the Legion. I therefore sent a signal to the Admiralty putting the matter bluntly. Their Lordships did not let me down, their reply came with a date for their removal. This fine battalion which later made a magnificent stand at "Knightsbridge" in the Western Desert under Colonel Koenig, then second in command, was saved from partial disbandment.

I had the pleasure to be asked for drinks one evening by the Legion's doctor. Since, as I have said, there was little drink to be found anywhere I went happily. He opened a refrigerator (surely meant for the hospital), and pulled out bottle after bottle of Guinness stout. "Where on Earth did you get that?" I asked. "When we left England they gave us Guinness for the sick Legionnaires", he replied, "but you cannot give Guinness to a sick
* I believe this was his name.

Legionnaire." I couldn't but agree so we feasted ourselves.

I was then ordered home, and I was very pleased at how well my travel arrangements worked out. I went by coaster to Lagos, where I found *Devonshire* about to sail for Freetown. From there I took the *Monarch of Bermuda* to England. She was no longer a luxury liner, but I did not complain as I had a large cabin with 15 extra beds and a bathroom all to myself.

I heard rather a nice story during my stop in Freetown. There was a small Naval Air Station there which held spare aircraft for the Fleet and had a small liasion flight for Fleet duties. The airfield's wind sock, which was made of coloured cloth, was always being stolen and used to clothe some native's wife. Guards were set, but nevertheless the wind socks continued to disappear. Eventually they found the solution to their problem: they hired a local witch doctor to make ju ju around the mast. No one dared break the curse and the affair was settled. The Naval staff gladly paid the doctor ten shillings out of their own pocket, but on second thoughts they wondered why the Navy shouldn't pay the bill. Since there was nothing in regulations pertaining to such a payment they sent off a request to Admiralty asking for payment of ten shillings for Witch Doctor's fees. Approved, came the reply. Even in the stress of war it is comforting to know that a sense of humour and a sense of right prevails in high places.

The *Monarch* had on board a madman who was under a sentry's charge. One day he eluded his sentry and jumped overboard, and to my horror the ship was stopped dead in the water while a boat was sent to pick him up. I swear that if my own mother had fallen overboard I would not have risked this invaluable ship and the lives of the 500 men on board to rescue her, and we stopped for a madman! We were in submarine waters, and as long as we were stopped we were a sitting duck for a torpedo. Fortunately there was no submarine at hand and we sailed peacefully home.

I arrived in London just after the city had been fire bombed. I walked down to see the destruction, and for the first time I felt real anger. From then on the war changed for me. It was no longer just an exercise of my professional skills, or a proving of my theories. It was cold, hard war.

I had a few days off at home in Surrey, and was then appointed to Hatston, the Royal Naval Air Station in the Orkneys which had the job of serving the Home Fleet.

Hatston

The Orkneys in the dead of winter came as quite a shock only a month or so after leaving equatorial Africa. When I was briefed on my new job as Executive Officer at Hatston (second in command), I was told that the place was rather a mess and that Captain Fancourt and I were to clean it up. Their aircraft had a fine war record, but the station had been growing rapidly and the administration had not kept up with its development. It had been created almost overnight when war was declared because the Home Fleet needed an Air Station to serve their needs and to provide them with fighter protection. They started with a field used by Scottish Airways and a strip of main road (Orkney variety) which was widened slightly to form the main runway. Hangars and accomodation had to follow.

The weather was infinitely variable. In summer it could be quite nice -the Orcadians have a tradition of playing golf at midnight on Midsummer's day when there is still a strong red glow in the Northern sky. In winter, however, it is not so pleasant. Although it never gets bitterly cold, and there is seldom any snow because the islands are washed by the Gulf Stream, they have nasty 100 mile-an-hour gales at least twice a winter. In the middle of winter it does not get light till about ten in the morning, and it is dark again soon after three.

When I arrived I had a very quick turn over from my predecessor. He told me that his main trouble was that he could not trust anyone to do a job properly and warned that I would have to do everything by myself, which was not at all to my liking. Shortly after my arrival, however, a rather elderly Sub-Lieutenant (relative to myself that is) came into my office and asked permission to perform some job. I don't recall exactly what it was he wanted to do, but I replied that I wished that he would just get on with it and tell me about it afterwards. To this I received a heartfelt, "Thank you, Sir!". The word that I would trust people to do things for themselves quickly got around and everyone felt better.

We had a great many young officers, and with the war on our dress tended to be pretty informal. The one thing I did insist on was that all officers wore bow ties at dinner. This was not for reasons of formality, but simply because it is impossible to wear a dirty shirt with a bow tie, it shows too much.

Our Paymaster-Commander was a Welshman by the name of Ivor Dummer. He was a superb scrounger and had managed to acquire pictures and furniture from liners being converted to troop ships that would otherwise have been thrown out. These were used to fit out our otherwise stark Mess and cabins. The dentist doubled as wine secretary, and he kept us well supplied even when London was tightly rationed. He did this by bartering such things as eggs and lobster which were readily available in the Orkneys but very hard to come by on the mainland. Wine merchants seemed to be most obliging in finding stock in the furthest recesses of their cellars when offered either of these commodities. By common consent a small bomb shelter was dedicated to the safety of the wine -it being thought that it was well worth running some slight personal risk in the event of an air raid rather than face the greater perils of drought.

Almost all of our officers and men were civilians before the war, and it was wonderful how they brought skills that we lacked. If you needed some sort of specialist it seemed that all you had to do was broadcast the fact and out would come bricklayers, carpenters, plumbers, or whatever you wanted. We even found an expert keeper of pigs when we set up the Orkney's second largest piggery. We had over 100 pigs, which we fed on the swill from our Messes and rations of specially approved meal. We had very few trouble makers, and I can remember the horror of our Secretary when one managed to get himself elected to the Mess Committee. However, as I had anticipated, a little authority turned the individual in question into an autocrat who would tolerate no mischief and that was the end of his trouble making days.

For the first time in my career I found myself in a senior position where there were Wrens on the station, and I soon discovered what splendid girls they were. The Chief Wren was Mrs. Rumbelow-Pierce, a wonderful woman full of warmth and understanding with whom I soon established a firm friendship and easy working relationship. I find it hard to express how much I thought of our Wrens. When you have a contingent of men far from home in a society where there are far too few women of your own kind, there is something lacking. You can excercise men's minds and bodies by work and play, but it is not enough. The Wrens made up the family, and their presence was a steadying factor. I wonder how many wives of service men realise how much they owe to the Wrens at outlying stations. The very presence of nice girls, the possibility of talking, dancing, or singing with them occasionally made life so much more bearable and prevented a lot of psychological problems. Of course from time to time they did sleep with men. They too were human, so how could it be otherwise, but after three years of service on air stations each with over 100 Wrens, I can only recall one case of a girl getting "into trouble". And this was long before the pill. Wonderful girls, and how much we lonely men owed them. I must also pay tribute to the fact that they were both efficient and concientious at their jobs.

I got on well with the local residents. One couple, Bertie and Mabel Bain, were especially good to me. They took me to visit the Orkney Distillery, where we had drinks with the Customs Officer. He poured me an ordinary sized drink and then asked me to say 'when' as he added water. I was about to tell him to stop when I heard Bertie's whispered admonition, "Fill it up, boy, fill it up." So I did, and still it just about took the top of my head off -it was straight from the vats! I learnt a little of the long history and proud traditions of the Orkney people whose ancestors had originally come from Scandinavia. When I once made the mistake of referring to Orcadians as Scots my neighbor drew himself up to his full height, and surveying me coldly intoned, "I'll have ye know that the last time the Orkneys fought Scotland, the Orkneys won!" I spent Hogmanay (New Years Eve) with Mabel and Bertie, a night when all front doors are open to all save at midnight when a guest with dark hair and a small gift, such as an orange or a piece of coal, awaits the striking of the hour to enter and bring good fortune to the house for the coming year. You could not find better hospitality anywhere. On my last night on the island Bertie was determined to make it my best ever. "Hank," he said, "I hae'na seen ye drunk yet but I'll see ye drunk tonight." I survived just the same.

We were the terminal for the Air Ferry Flights from Edinburgh for the Fleet. The crews were ex-Jersey Air Lines who were now in Naval uniform, and they would fly through almost any kind of weather. Scottish Airways also still flew in from Inverness and there was a great rivalry to get in regardless of the weather. On more than one occasion I saw a Rapide taxi out to the runway with four men holding the wingtips in fifty knot winds. With the aircraft lined up into wind the pilot would signal to let go and the aircraft would take off going virtually straight up. On one occasion we had a Swordfish take off and then fly backwards down the runway. Figure it out: the wind was around 60 knots and the Swordfish can fly safely at 55! One day we had a senior RAF officer who was on his way to the Shetlands stop in for a visit. From the control tower he looked out at the airfield with its narrow runways (50 ft. wide) and taxi tracks (30 ft. wide) and commented, "You must have a lot of accidents." "No sir," I replied, "Actually we have very few. We have not had one for several months." He thought about that for a moment and then said, "I see, they have to try." True. Perhaps wide runways were not actually required.

A month or so after I got to Hatston I heard that I had been awarded the OBE for my efforts in the Libreville campaign. At first I was a little disgusted for the OBE was not held in high esteem -we often referred to it as the award for "Other Buggers' Efforts". Then I discovered that there were several divisions of OBE, and that the military award ranked just above an MC. Since this would give me one up on my elder brother Tom , who had just been awarded the MC, I found this entirely satisfactory. Besides, it also meant a week's leave in London to pick it up which was even better.

At this point in the war Germany had not yet invaded Russia, and the latter was considered more as an enemy than an ally. We were advised by the Admiralty that we had an active communist on the station so we decided to keep track of his activities by steaming open his mail. His letters home were full of thoughts about how to delay the war effort. But when Russia was invaded and became an ally there was an immediate change. His wife wrote to the effect that they must now work for England to help Russia. Their loyalties were clearly not with England, but with international communism and hence with Russia. We got quite a blast from a Royal Marines Security Major who was sent up to investigate because we had reported the contents of the letters to Admiralty. We were told that it was improper to open mail...presumably it was ungentlemanly. Since we knew that our man was no longer a threat we were not much worried by the scolding. Later of course, all mail was censored.

The resident squadron at Hatston was the Fleet Requirement Unit which provided aircraft for fleet exercises, such as target towing for the heavy High Angle guns, and dive bombing attacks for the short range weapons. There were two Martin Maryland aircraft which had been taken over from the French Air Force (and which still had French instrumentation) which were used for high angle gun exercises. The only fighters in the Orkneys were a squadron of Skuas, famous for their raid on Bergen in the Norwegian campaign. One day one of these aircraft was out to give the fleet some practice, but just as he went into his dive a Red Air Raid Warning was sounded -meaning that an enemy air attack was imminent. There was no time to warn the Skua pilot and just about every gun available opened up on him as he descended, Pom Poms, Oerlikons, Bofors and heavy guns. He dove through a veritable cloud of shell bursts and came through unscathed. Rather shaken he came back to Hatston where he was greeted with a signal from the C-in-C which read:

"GENERAL TO THE FLEET FROM C-IN-C HOME FLEET: WHILE I MEAN NO HARM TO MY FRIENDS, I THINK THAT THE GUNNERY OF THE FLEET WAS BLOODY AWFUL."

Admiral Tovey also sent a signal of apology to Hatston.

During the second part of my year at Hatston a satellite airfield some 15 miles away was commissioned. It was named 'Twatt' after the nearest hamlet and became the brunt of a great number of jokes. For example, when its defences were under discussion a paper was distributed by the Admiralty entitled "Chastity Belt". I have to admit I was as ribald as anyone about the place until I was told to go there and get it on a proper footing. So I was the first to hold the proud title of Commanding Officer Royal Naval Air Station Twatt, or more concisely, Commanding Officer Twatt, and my job was to make the place as efficient and happy as possible. It was right out in the sticks, practically on the edge of some cliffs. There was little to do after working hours so we made a football field, and on Sundays I would lead the young officers down to the rocks to collect shellfish or go catching rabbits along the cliffs with our bare hands. We always had a good start with new squadrons who invariably arrived thinking that "there had to be something good about a station with a name like that." Even when it rained, which was often, there were the two "L's" for consolation -Lobsters and Liars Dice -though there was very little else. Anyhow, we kept happy.

Shortly after I arrived on the scene we were sent a company of Pioneers commanded by a Welsh Major. Their job was to dig the trenches designed for our defence in case of invasion -our infamous "Chastity Belt". I was a little surprised when their Major told me that he wanted to go on leave right away. I allowed as how it was a bit soon, since the digging had not even begun. He responded to the effect that he should be given more consideration since he was the "Deputy Mayor and largest ratepayer" in his district. I was amused, but not persuaded. I later heard that he told someone that the Commander was a "very determined man."

Several squadrons came for training of various sorts during my time at Twatt, the unit I remember best being a small group of six Swordfish commanded by Lt.Bowman Manifold. He had been assigned the unusual task of spotting for the fall of shot from the monitor *Erebus* at night, and it was our job to train him. To provide them with practice in assessing the bearing and distance from the target I called upon the owner of a large and conspicuous house at the head of a deep bay, and asked him if he would mind if we made a little noise and a few flashes around him one night to simulate a bombardment. He agreed readily, and I put out a dozen men around the 'target' with stop watches and Very pistols which could fire smoke puffs. The puffs made a flash followed by a cloud of smoke and looked very much like shell-bursts. They were fired at pre-determined intervals and the aircraft noted the bearing and distance from the target. They got quite good at it and eventually Bowman and his unit returned to Erebus.

They had been spotting for their ship operating against France, and from time to time they dropped bombs. When I asked him about fighters, Bowman replied with a grin, "By day, Sir, they are amusing; by night they are ludicrous." With the Swordfish's low speed and great manoeuvrability they found it easy to take avoiding action. There was one story, perhaps apocryphal, of a German fighter who intercepted a Swordfish but could not shoot it down because he could not get into firing position behind it. He put his flaps down to reduce his speed, but still to no avail. Then in desperation he put down his landing gear, but this time when he tried to follow the Stringbag his aircraft stalled and spun into the sea. The Swordfish pilot chalked up one victory and flew home. I heard that Bowman was sent with his squadron to Egypt, and that one day while over Cairo where enemy fighters were not to be expected he was jumped by a Ju88 and shot down before he even knew it was there. A sad loss of a very fine young officer.

During this happy period of my first command King George VI flew up to visit the Home Fleet. He was scheduled to land at Hatston where he would inspect the men and have a glass of sherry in the Mess before going off to the Fleet. We from Twatt were to go to Hatston for the inspection, and we were enroute by car and truck when we saw a large gaggle of fighters escorting a passenger aircraft. He was about half an hour early and pandemonium had struck at Hatston. Our little convoy went to maximum speed. We heard afterwards that the King's ADC had commented that they were early, but the King, an old Naval man who was no doubt a little prejudiced, said, "Yes, but thank God its a Naval Air Station, things are happening." He walked around the divisions and then visited the Mess. Here he learned how we lived off the fat of the land -eggs, fresh beef, lobsters, etc. When he flew south he carried a dozen eggs under his arm as a present for the Queen.

Escorted by the author, King George VI inspects the ship's company of RNAS Twatt at RNAS Hatston, 1941.

While I was at Twatt I wanted a suitable scroll to present to visiting dignitaries, so I asked two friends, one a rhymester, Lt.Cdr. Archie Fleming, and the other an artist, Major Bertie Bass R.M., what they could do for me. I was delighted with the result, which has been carefully preserved as an heirloom. Known as "The Freedom of Twatt" it is, alas, a little too explicit for general publication.

There were very few deaths associated with flying at Hatston because it was not an operational field. There was the occasional accident, however, and one of our aircraft was caught in a severe downdraft close to Hoy Island while returning from Scapa Flow. It spun into the sea and both crew members were lost. Divers were sent down, but because of the strong current diving was difficult, and after a few days they had still found nothing. The Chief Diving Officer came over and told me that they were not having any luck, but that they would go on until they had found the aircraft and brought up the bodies. I thought about the situation for a few minutes and then told him that the station had been shaken by the loss of friends, but that because the memories of young men are short, things had settled down again. I hoped most fervently that they would never find the bodies, as if they did there would again be a period of upset with the funeral, and I could not see that that would do anyone any good. He said that they would go on looking for a while, but assured me that they would take care to find nothing. Was I right? As far as the station was concerned I know I was right, but what would the relatives think now of my action. Would they have thought that for the dignity of their sons they should have found a resting place in consecrated ground?

One morning some young aircrew from the Fleet arrived and asked if they could be flown south on leave. We naturally had a soft spot for aircrew, but that day there were just not enough seats available, so I said that they would have to wait till the next day, and that in the meantime we would make them comfortable in the Mess. They went away disappointed, but came back a little later to say that there was an aircraft that was returning to Wick and asked permission to go with it. I pointed out that they would be no further ahead because they would still have to get to Inverness to catch the train, and they wouldn't be able to do that till the next day. Probably anxious to get beyond possible recall they elected to take the flight to Wick.

A little later I received a call from the Admiralty Operations Room asking me to arrange transport for two VIP passengers who would be arriving at Scapa Flow by warship, to catch the London Express from Inverness that day. I was given their probable time of arrival and decided to send a Walrus into the Flow to pick them up and fly them directly to Inverness. Since the timing was going to be tight there was still a chance that they would miss the express train, so I phoned the railway headquarters in Glasgow to see if they could hold the train until our men arrived. There was great consternation...express trains were sacred and their departure could not be delayed. There was a solution, however. The express went by a somewhat roundabout route and it was possible for a special train to cut across and catch it at another junction. I asked how much special trains cost, and finding that twenty five pounds would do the job I agreed. I had the Admiralty look after the financial arrangements, Ŀ25 was too much for me, even to help out the war. Everything was arranged, the Walrus was despatched, and I settled down to do some paper work. After a while I heard the unmistakable sound of a Walrus approaching ...something had gone awry. The VIP's had arrived late, and so the Walrus crew decided that their slow aircraft would not make it to Inverness before dark. Quickly I called for one of our fastest aircraft, a Maryland, to be made ready. It was trundled out, and was made ready with engines running before the Walrus taxied in. We pulled the officers out of one plane and pushed them into the other along with their canvass bags...with luck she would just make Inverness before dark. But then catastrophe struck -one wheel went down into a hole and it was obvious that it would take us a half hour or more to get it out. We had a quick conference with our special passengers. They had vital German ciphers from a special operation in a Norwegian fjord, a capture of immense importance. They decided to stay the night, during which time we photographed all of their material. The next day we sent them south with the original copy, and when we had received notice that they had arrived safely we despatched the duplicates. It seemed a lot better than taking a risk of losing the only copy.

When we realised that we would not be able to get them to London the first night I called the Duty Captain at Admiralty Ops and apologised for our failure. I also asked him to cancel our special train as I thought that it might be better coming from his end. A short time later he called back to ask if things really had gone wrong as it appeared that everything was going smoothly. I told him that his VIP's were sharing a drink with me in the Wardroom. It was not till a few days later when a couple of young aircrew returned from leave that I got the full story. When they had arrived in Wick they had met up with a sympathetic airman who was prepared to take them to Inverness, although he doubted that they would be in time to catch the express. They were anxious to continue their journey so off they went. To their surprise a car was waiting when they got to Inverness and they were pulled from the aircraft and rushed to the station. There they were flung into a small train that was anxiously waiting and it puffed its way through the hills at full speed to a junction where a large train was waiting with passengers leaning out of the windows wondering what the delay was all about. They were rushed across to the right platform, pushed into the express and moments later were thundering their way to London. Pretty good service for a couple of fellows going on leave!

About halfway through my time in the Orkneys there occurred what I consider to be the most important event in my career as a Naval Observer. *Bismark*, the most powerful battleship in the world, was known to be in commission and working up. Since the time when I left the Admiralty she had been the main preoccupation of their Lordships and of the C-in-C Home Fleet. Would she try to break out into the Atlantic and harrass our convoys as had *Scharnhorst* and *Gneisenau* before her? If she managed to do so it would take a great concentration of force to find and sink her, and if she were to be joined by the other two the problem would be reaching almost insurmountable proportions. Now she had been sighted in the Skagerrak -was she on her way north for this fateful project? The finding and sinking of this vessel became the most important requirement for the future of our war effort.

Find the Bismark

It was late May when we heard that *Bismark* was moving. News came that she was refuelling in a fjord just south of Bergen as an RAF long range fighter-reconnaissance aircraft had secured a photograph of her. This put her within reach of a squadron of Albacore torpedo bombers which had been training at Hatston, so Captain Fancourt decided that he would mount an attack on the night of May 22nd. He wanted a reconnaisance first to confirm that *Bismark* was still there and to provide last minute information as to exactly where she was lying so that the torpedo aircraft could make a precise attack and withdraw quickly. Unfortunately the weather over the North Sea was bad and RAF reconnaissance aircraft had not been able to get through for the past three days. This made the need for us to conduct a reconnaissance even more vital, and Captain Fancourt selected one of our fast Maryland aircraft. They really were the only suitable aircraft for a daylight reconnaissance across the North Sea to a harbour which was known to have a recently established fighter base nearby. Pilot selection was unnecessary as No. 771's squadron commander Noel Goddard said that he would go, and his usual crew members Armstrong and Milne claimed their right to be with their pilot. Only the position of Observer was vacant

A Martin Maryland similar to the one used in the author's search for Bismark.

because they were used almost exclusively for close work with the fleet at Scapa and had no experienced man available. I asked if I might fill this spot. I knew Noel well, having paid an expensive apprenticeship to him at the game of backgammon. Our minds thought along similar lines and it would be a pleasure to fly with him.

The aircraft, in which I had not flown before, carried a crew of four. The Observer sat in the nose. The cockpit was slightly above and behind him, with the two positions being separated by a bulkhead. The telegraphist sat in another isolated compartment behind the pilot, and the fourth crew member, the rear gunner, sat in a ventral position just behind the wing. There was an intercom, but as it was failure prone, Goddard had had a speaking tube installed between the cockpit and the telegraphist positions--a bit of foresight we were to be very thankful for. The aircraft had no navigational equipment apart from its compasses which Noel had kept beautifully corrected.

I called Coastal Command to get as much intelligence information about Bergen as I possibly could. They warned me that the Germans had efficient radar against a sea approach, and a fighter airfield to the north. They also warned me that the weather was awful. Anticipating the inevitable navigational errors ahead I decided to go for some easily recognisable landfall well to the south so that even if we didn't hit it right on there would be no doubt about which way to turn once we reached the coast. George Tilney, the Ops Officer, produced an excellent photo of an island off the Norwegian coast as a suggested landfall, but when I asked him if I could take it with me he laughed and said that he did not want to lose it. I questioned his parentage, but did not press the point.

The next thing to do was to have a huddle with Noel and plan the flight. For two reasons we would have to fly low, preferably not above 1,000 feet. I would have to gauge the wind by watching the waves, and this was obviously easier to do at low level. Secondly we wanted to avoid radar detection and this also dictated as low a flight as possible. If we came under fire we agreed that we would dodge into cloud cover which we expected to be at between two and three thousand feet. This fitted with the advice we got from our gunnery experts who told me that short range guns were only dangerous if you were very low, and heavy guns were not much of a threat unless you were above 3,000 ft. Lastly we decided that we would take our departure from Fair Isle which was half way between the Orkney and Shetland Islands as it would give us the shortest possible run to Bergen.

We set course from Fair Isle in lovely weather with about 220 miles to go, and at that point it was hard to see what was worrying the RAF. After a little, however, we found out. It became increasingly cloudy and we were forced lower and lower in an increasing wind. I wanted very much to keep sight of the water as there was no doubt that the wind would be changing and possibly freshening. When we had been pushed down below 50 feet Noel said (and here I paraphrase) "Sorry, this is too much of a strain, we must go up." I did not argue as I was feeling the same way. We climbed until we were just into the clear above the clouds at about 3,000 ft. We came down again a little later so that I could get another estimate of the wind, but we couldn't stay below the clouds. The next time we tried I saw the sea in the nick of time. Noel didn't see it at all, but a startled shout from me over the intercom was enough to put him up again. We had been very low indeed, but a glimpse was all I needed to check the wind and find that it was stronger and had veered. Now we were faced with another problem. We had to get below the clouds before we reached the land or we would almost certainly fly into a cliff when we tried to go down later. Luck was on our side and just as I had decided that the attempt had to be made the clouds started to clear and we descended to 1,000 feet again without difficulty. A few minutes later my landfall island appeared ahead. I had never seen a more beautiful and welcome sight and it brought a most un-Commander-like whoop of triumph down the intercom. It was one of those days when all one's errors cancel each other out and we hit it dead on.

At about this time the intercom packed up and so from that point on all I had to guide the pilot were two buttons which operated red and green lights in the cockpit. How lucky we were that the intercom had not failed before our last descent through the clouds. We ran up inside the fjords to the anchorage, but it was bare. After we had circled to look into all of the possible holes and corners and be sure that we hadn't overlooked anything I directed Noel over Bergen harbour to see if she had moved there. This was too much for the Germans and they opened up with everything that they had. We shot across the harbour and out to sea losing height as we went. We levelled off about 100 feet above land at the outside of the harbour, passing right over a gun whose crew Milne claimed to have scattered. From there it was out to sea in a shallow dive at our best speed of around 300 knots. We had agreed to climb into the clouds but without the intercom I could not suggest this to Noel. When I looked up I could see a carpet of heavy AA shells bursting just under the clouds so the German gunners must have been anticipating such a move. I immediately became very content with Noel's decision to dive and run. We had confirmed that Bergen was clear, and since we had been warned that there was a fighter airfield to the north of the city it did not seem reasonable to search the fjords to the north and jeopardise the transmission of what news we had.

With the intercom gone I had to write down my

message, which was to go out in plain language, and slip it through a little hole to the pilot. Luckily he could use his voicepipe (voicepipes never break down) to pass the message to the wireless operator. Armstrong was transmitting on the Coastal Command frequency but he could raise nobody with my signal which read simply 'Battleship and cruiser have left'. On his own initiative he tuned to our local Hatston Target Towing frequency and disturbed the tranquility of their practice work with an EMERGENCY call which clears the air of all other traffic. To a telegraphist this succession of 'O's in morse (a succession of three long dashes) is the same as someone shouting 'SHUT UP'. The message was passed by telephone to Admiral Tovey, C-in-C of the Home Fleet, and by teleprinter to Admiralty and Coastal Command.

We set course for the Shetlands as the Albacores with Captain Fancourt and George Tilney had moved there to shorten their night flight to Bergen. Flying at 1,000 feet we aimed for the middle of the islands. The RAF picked us up on radar and suggested to Tilney that our heading would take us north of the base at Sumburgh Head. He responded that he was sure I knew what I was doing, and that I would not like to be interfered with. As soon as we sighted land we veered off to the south and landed at Sumburgh. A quick survey of the aircraft revealed to our disappointment that there was only one honourable scar where a window close to Noel's head had been shot out. The end result was nevertheless satisfactory.

I was called to the phone immediately to speak to the C-in-C Home Fleet's Chief of Staff. The Fleet flagship, HMS *King George V* and the entire fleet were waiting to slip their buoys as soon as he had had his conversation with me. I confirmed our signal, and was asked whether we had searched to the north of Bergen. I said no, and explained why we had not. Commodore Brind rang off and the fleet slipped. The hunt was on.

Goddard and I saw no reason to wait at Sumburgh, especially while there was a good ENSA theatrical show at Hatston, so we hurried back. We caught most of the show, and then went to the Mess for a drink.

When the fleet returned to Scapa Flow we recieved the

following message from the C-in-C:
"HATSTON, COMMANDER ROTHERHAM, FROM
C-IN-C HOME FLEET:
CONGRATULATE YOU MOST HEARTILY ON YOUR
DARING AND SUCCESSFULL RECONNAISSANCE AND
YOU HAVE THE THANKS OF MYSELF AND THE
FLEET FOR GIVING US THE OPPORTUNITY OF
MAKING CONTACT."
We also received a generous signal from the AOC
Coastal Command:
"ADMIRALTY FROM COASTAL COMMAND.
YOUR MESSAGE MUCH APPRECIATED AND HAS
BEEN REPORTED TO ALL CONCERNED. IT WAS A
GREAT HUNT AND WE ARE ALL EAGER AND READY
FOR MORE. THE RECONNAISSANCE CARRIED OUT
BY THE MARYLAND INTO BERGEN UNDER DIFFICULT
CONDITIONS WAS MOST IMPORTANT AND PROVIDED
TIMELY AND VALUABLE INFORMATION. I ADD MY
CONGRATULATIONS TO THE CREW."
As Captain of the aircraft I was awarded an immediate
DSO, Goddard an immediate DSC, and Armstrong, who used
his initiative to change frequency on his own got a DSM.
Alas, poor Milne who scattered the gunners got nothing
beyond a vote of thanks from the rest of us.

When I later met my old Captain, Martin de Meric,
while I was on a visit to London he told me that I had
probably made the most important "Negative" message ever
sent. Ralph Edwards, who had been in the Admiralty
Operations room at the time also told me that they had
been saying, "If only we had a Naval aircraft to get
through the weather", and then my report had come
through. It was not that we were any more skillfull than
the RAF, although I probably had more overwater
navigation experience than anyone they had available, nor
was it that we were any braver; it was, I think, simply
that we appreciated the enormous importance of reporting
this ship's movements so much more. We could understand
what a menace she would be on the high seas. We knew
that it would take a considerable concentration of ships to
destroy her as she was so much more powerfull than any
of our battleships. It was situations like this which

The author at Hatston in 1941.

convinced me that ships and aircraft which operate over the sea should all be part of the same service.

After the Bismark operation we noticed that in the newspaper accounts the RAF claimed to have made the flight to Bergen. When I went south to pick up my DSO I talked with an old acquaintance, Commander Timmins. An ex-FAA pilot who was then in the Admiralty Information Division, he told me that the RAF had refused to correct their Press Release and that it was Admiralty policy not to contradict. It was not until the Naval Information Office was beefed up with the appointment of Admiral James that a rebuttal was published. I never could understand why the RAF had this strange urge to grab the credit regardless of who had done the job.

Readers wishing to know more of the final sea search and sinking of the Bismark may find "The Bismark Episode" by Captain Russell Grenfell RN of interest.

To The Eastern Fleet

After a year at Hatston I was appointed temporarily to the staff of Admiral Somerville for passage to the East. Admiral Sir James Somerville had retired just before the war with a suspected case of tuberculosis. When he was recalled and set to work he proved to be one of our three top naval leaders along with Jack Tovey and A.B. Cunningham. Somerville was wise, kind, a great decision-maker, and shared with Cunningham a good sense of humour. There is an amusing story from the days when he commanded Force 'H' at Gibraltar in 1941 while ABC was based at the eastern end of the Mediterranean at Alexandria. Sir James was already a knight when he received a second award carrying a similar distinction for hunting down the *Bismark*. Immediately there came a signal from ABC, "What -twice a (k)night at your age!" Cunningham had just been made a baronet and given the KGCB (Knight Grand Cross of the Bath) so Somerville was able to respond, "Better, perhaps, than being barren (Baron) in the bath...?"

Admiral Somerville was to take passage to Ceylon in the carrier *Formidable*, sailing from Greenock at the mouth of the Clyde. Another carrier, HMS *Eagle*, was to sail from Liverpool with him as far as the Mediterranean. I was to join *Formidable* and be on Somerville's staff until

HMS Formidable.

we met the Eastern Fleet which he was to command, at which point I was to join Admiral Boyd in *Indomitable*.

While I was on leave between appointments I heard of *Scharnhorst* and *Gneisenau* racing up the English Channel and of the gallant but abortive sortie by Lt.Cdr. Esmonde and six Swordfish in an attempt to torpedo those ships. From friends at the Admiralty I learned that it was known that the ships had been damaged at Brest and that they would have to return to Germany for repairs. I gathered that the RAF had agreed that they would look after the Channel route, while the Home Fleet at Scapa Flow was to block them if they should attempt to go north about. The first disaster was that a submarine watching Brest had to withdraw to charge batteries, the withdrawal coinciding with the German ships leaving harbour. The next was the failure of the RAF reconnaissance aircraft to intercept them, a failure which I attribute as much to the land-based aircrews' lack of understanding of the vital importance of their task as to the poor weather. Then despite the RAF's massive bomber strength the first aircraft attack was to be made by Esmonde's slow Swordfish.

After being sunk in *Ark Royal*, Esmonde's squadron was reformed with six Swordfish and was to work up prior to embarking in a new Lease-Lend Escort Carrier enroute from the USA. They were then hurriedly moved to an airfield in Kent. I had always understood that his squadron had been borrowed by the RAF who had been assigned responsibility for stopping the German ships if they should attempt to break through the Channel. Taylor, in his book "Battle in the English Channel" states, however, that Admiral "Black" Ramsay, commanding at Dover, had demanded them. In either case they would have come under operational control of the RAF. They were the only available Naval torpedo aircraft in the South of England. It was arranged that they would attack the German ships and that they would be escorted by an RAF fighter squadron. Esmonde decided to go out at 50 feet, presumably relying on the fighter escort to protect him from enemy fighters and not realising the hordes of these that he would meet. The fighter escort did not materialise however, apparently due to the very poor weather conditions. Nevertheless Esmonde gallantly went on alone.

It is hard to understand why Esmonde did not change his tactics when he realised that he was to have no fighter escort. Flying low and being heavy laden they would be easy targets for fighters, while the clouds appeared to provide an ideal substitute cover. The low approach made it impossible to do a normal diving attack which would have left the actual point of release of the torpedoes to the last minute and hence made meaningful avoiding action by the enemy most difficult. It would also have reduced their period of vulnerability to fighters and ships' guns to a minimum. The use of cloud cover, however low, could only have helped. Such tactics would have been similar to those Robin Kilroy proposed in 1939 for our projected attack on Wilhemshaven, though it must be added that we had demanded prior practice in flying in the base of cloud cover, and Esmonde's squadron was only in the early stages of working up. In the event they were destroyed by the hordes of German fighters which had been sent out to protect the ships, long before they could deliver a worthwhile attack.

It's Really Quite Safe

Esmonde was an experienced pilot from Imperial Airways but with only a couple of years FAA experience. It is easy to criticize from the comfort of an arm chair, and surely there may have been factors involved of which we have no knowledge. It seems likely that he believed that he was on a one way mission. A devout Catholic, he went to confession before leaving. There is no doubt that he knew the vital importance of his task, and he and his small squadron went willingly. His posthumous VC, the glory of which was reflected on them all, was well earned. I think that the words of Sir Humphrey Gilbert in his moral code of Elizabethan times are apt, "He is not worthy to live at all, that for fear of danger of death shunneth his Country's service and his own honour; seeing death is inevitable and the fame of virtue immortal."

I went by train to Liverpool to call on Eagle enroute to Greenock. I stayed the night at the Adelphi Hotel, and there at the bar I met my old friend and pilot, "Rev", from my days with Glorious, Group Captain Revington. We had a drink together and I asked him what he was up to. To my surprise I found that he was enroute to the Far East and that he would be sailing in our convoy. As our conversation continued I asked him where the RAF torpedo aircraft had been when the *Scharnhorst* and *Gneisenau* ran up the Channel. With much exasperation showing he replied, "I will tell you. I was Commanding Officer at St.Eval in Cornwall and I had the Beaufort torpedo aircraft there. Now Hank, being an old FAA lag I know that ships are a fleeting target and you must be ready for them, and I knew that *Scharnhorst* and *Gneisenau* were at Brest and likely to break for home, so I told my Beauforts to train to peak efficiency and wait for the day. However, I had another task, to send bombers over France to such targets as Brest, and this I did using my other aircraft. I reported what we did but then was asked why we had not used my Beauforts. I told Bomber Command why I was holding them but was told to use all aircraft for bombing. So I did, and that is why we had no torpedo aircraft when they ran up the Channel."

It seemed clear to me that neither the Navy nor the Air Force fully realised the potential of air power or

206

understood the way to apply it. In the Navy very few senior officers had taken the trouble to analyse the potential of the air, most of them having been brought up to believe in the might of the gun and its ability to destroy attacking aircraft, despite the contrary evidence of countless fleet exercises. This combined with the fact that few Flying Personnel had risen to high rank, something which I attribute to their belonging to the wrong 'Club'. I believe that over 80% of all Flag Officers had risen through their specialization in gunnery, and there were few Torpedomen, Navigators, Signalmen or Aviators who had been promoted to senior positions. The RAF, in my opinion, had failed to realise how important it was to have officers man positions other than pilot in their aircraft. I think that the development of bomb-sights, navigation equipment, defensive guns etc., and the techniques for their use would have been much enhanced if it had been put in the hands of men who could not simply use them but could understand them and, most importantly, have the authority to demand changes and improvements where neccesary. I am convinced that had the Air Force had more 'back seat' men in its officer corps then that force, with its dedicated, brave and resourceful personnel would have been the war winner that it should have been.

I think that probably the principal reason for inefficiency, in the broadest sense, was that even up to the commencement of this war the great majority of our senior officers were imbued with the ideas of the First World War: dare everything and accept huge losses as inevitable; do not accept new ideas that might prejudice chances for promotion. Just look over the men at the top of both services and see how few were progressive and receptive to new ideas, and how they were gradually replaced by men with adaptable minds.

We stopped to refuel at Freetown in West Africa, and I was able to ask Rev to dinner. We reminisced about our days in *Glorious* and *Furious* -the days of the far off thirties that seemed a thousand years ago at this stage of the war.

When we left Freetown, *Formidable* went on alone with

two destroyers for escort for we were out of submarine waters. We took the opportunity to exercise the aircraft and their crews, flying off a squadron of Albacores one night. They went through the motions of forming up, flying off to some distant point, and then returning for a simulated attack on the carrier. Reforming at night after such an attack is always the most difficult part of an exercise as only very dim lights can be shown by the lead aircraft. One aircraft did not land on, and so a speedy analysis had to be made: where was the aircraft last seen? Was it at the first form-up or at the reforming after the attack? No-one could be sure.

The destroyers did not have enough fuel to double back and still make Capetown, and since the danger from submarines was minimal in this area it was decided that the carrier would go back while the destroyers held their course. It was a lovely clear night with a full moon over a flat sea. We retraced our course at low speed, expecting to start a search in earnest at first light in the area of the first form-up. Not long after the change of course the watch on deck was surprised to hear faint cries from the sea close to the ship. A searchlight revealed the crew of the missing aircraft clinging to one of the wheels of the Albacore...all that remained of the aircraft. It transpired that the aircraft had spun into the sea during the second form-up, and that it had gone in so hard that a wheel had been torn off. The crew of three had managed to get out safely, but their life raft sank with the aircraft. Their first stroke of luck was spotting the wheel close enough by to be able to get hold of, and the second was that, by some miracle, Formidable had almost run over them while backtracking to the point where it was thought they had last been seen.

We went on to Capetown, refuelled, and continued to Ceylon where we were to join the rest of the Fleet. In Colombo I once again met Ralph Edwards whom I had known so well at the Admiralty. He had been enroute to join Admiral Tommy Phillips who was in command of *Repulse* and *Renown*, but when both ships had been sunk by the Japanese he was instructed to wait and join Somerville. The words he said to me haunted me for years,

"Hank, I swear to you that if I had got to Tommy Phillips in time it would never have happened. Tommy never believed in aircraft, and he found out too late."

When we arrived in Colombo we were met by the cheery news from intelligence sources that a force of Japanese aircraft carriers intended to attack the harbour shortly. Faced with the prospect of coming up against the Japanese Zero fighters with which we could not compete it was obvious that we would have to try to arrange for a night engagement. Our Swordfish and Albacore torpedo bombers would be in their element at night and that could give us the edge we needed. We believed that the Japanese, knowing that there were Spitfires in Ceylon, would try to make a night approach, launching a surprise attack at dawn. I was sent ashore by Somerville to make arrangements with the RAF to set up a reconnaissance patrol that would intercept the Japanese the day before their attack so that we could attack them that night. Such a patrol line was laid on, using Catalina flying boats operating from their base at Kogala at the south end of the island.

That night I lay in my bunk thinking about the situation and trying to put myself in the shoes of the Japanese Commander who was planning the attack on Colombo. I decided that I would have flown off from a position to the south-west of Ceylon to make landfall some 20 miles to the south of the city so that there would be no doubt which way to head along the coast for the attack. To my horror I realised that the patrol line we had set up would not intercept such an approach. I hastened ashore the next morning to reposition one of the Catalina flights to cover this gap, and I slept much better that evening feeling that all contingencies were covered. Formidable sailed and joined up with the rest of the fleet which consisted of the carrier *Indomitable*, the battleship *Warspite*, (capable of about 24 knots), and four of the 'R' class battleships which could do about 20 knots. The latter had originally been designed for work in the North Sea and had rather short endurance, a factor which was to prove disastrous. Other ships in the fleet were the cruisers *Dorsetshire* and *Cornwall* and a number of destroyers.

It's Really Quite Safe

I flew onboard *Indomitable* to give Admiral Boyd news of the impending Japanese attack and details of Admiral Somerville's plan to engage them by night with torpedo aircraft, and then to send in the battleships. We lay in ambush for three days, but then with the 'R' class battleships running short of fuel and water we moved south to Addu Atoll. When we arrived there we received a signal from the Catalina on the rearranged patrol line which indicated that the Japanese were moving in for the strike. We were like a boxer caught on the wrong foot. We sped north as soon as we could get refuelled, but we were too late. Colombo had been hard hit, although forunately we lost only an old destroyer and *Hector*, an AMC (Armed Merchant Cruiser.) On our way north a formation of high-flying aircraft appeared on our radar, and then vanished. The next day we picked up the survivors from their targets: *Dorsetshire* and *Cornwall* had both been dive-bombed and sunk by overwhelming swarms of aircraft.

With the benefit of hind-sight one wonders whether Somerville should not have sent the old 'R' class battleships off to refuel by themselves and held Warspite and the carriers for the anticipated night action. It was, after all, the carriers which were to have done the job. He was, of course, faced with the possibility of great criticism from his seniors who were imbued with the idea that the battleship was all powerful.

The Catalina which reported the Japanese carriers got his signal off but went in to get better information and was shot down. A shame, had he been more alive to the dangers of fleet fighters he might have been wise enough to get out quickly and come in again from another bearing, taking a quick look on each occasion. Fortunately the crew was picked up by the Japanese, so they survived, although in most unpleasant conditions. Years later when I was in Ottawa I was able to take the pilot, by then Group Captain Birchall (RCAF) to lunch and apologise for being the cause of his spending years in a Japanese prisoner of war camp. I had checked on the position of the aircraft which made the intercept: it was the one I had had moved over. The Japanese used the exact game plan I would have used if I were in their shoes. It appears that Naval minds of different nations do think alike.

After their attack on Colombo the Japanese moved east and intelligence told us that Trincomalee was their next target. The Commander-in-Chief of the East Indies Squadron, Admiral Arbuthnot, had a small carrier, Hermes, under his command there, and she was ordered to sail out to sea and to return only when the anticipated attack was over. We thought that she had been sent round to the other side of the island where she would be safely out of the way, so it was with great shock that we learned that the Japanese striking force had seen her while they were on their way to Trincomalee and after rearming had returned and sunk her. It was a terrible and unnecessary loss.

The Japanese next raided the Bay of Bengal, but they missed their main objective -our fleet with its carriers. We had suffered severe losses and deep humiliation, and Ceylon, which was under our protection, had been heavily bombed. The results might have been quite different if the Japanese had not been three days late. With our fine night fighting aircraft and our force of heavy ships, obsolescent or not, to follow up, we might have secured a resounding victory. Such is the nature of war.

Faced with a fleet with a good deal more air power than ourselves Somerville took the only option available to him -to keep the fleet in being. We withdrew to Bombay, crossed to Kilindini in Kenya, and then returned to Colombo. We exercised our aircraft continually, and like a cautious boxer we kept to our side of the ring and only occasionally jabbed at our opponent. On one foray into the Bay of Bengal we shot down a Japanese flying boat which had been picked up on radar, but then blotted our copy-book by damaging one of our own Catalinas. This shadow-boxing was at least taking some pressure off the Americans in the Pacific, but we were not accomplishing a great deal. A success was obviously needed, and this led to the decision to take Diego Suarez -a magnificent harbour in the north of Madagascar- from the Vichy French. The ostensible reason was that if we occupied Diego Suarez it would be denied to the Japanese raiders

It's Really Quite Safe

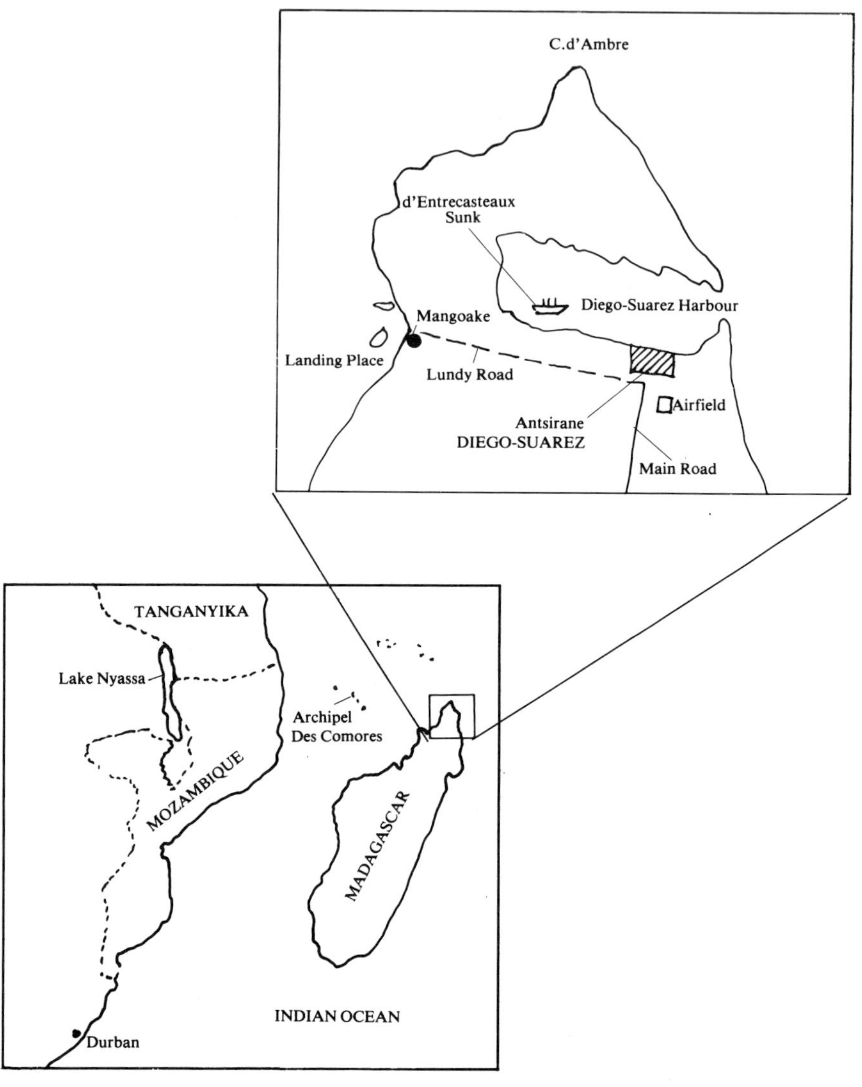

and submarines which were already operating in the Indian Ocean. This base would have been of enormous advantage to them in their attempt to cut our lines of communication between Egypt and Ceylon and around the Cape of Good Hope. It was anyone's guess what the Vichy French would do.

Unlike the Dakar expedition, this was to be an entirely British affair. We made a rendezvous with the assault fleet, and the orders were flown over to Admiral Boyd in Indomitable. When I settled down to read them I was horrified to discover that we would be repeating, in part, our tactics at Dakar. The plan called for us to drop leaflets over the airfield at dawn to warn the French before we bombed. I thought this was just too much, and so I went to Boyd and described for him the results of our earlier, similar action. I pointed out to him that all good Frenchmen would be in bed with their wives, girlfriends or mistresses at dawn, so we might just as well bomb the hangars at first light and ensure air superiority for ourselves. I was heartened by the fact that Boyd took my advice, for when we attacked we bombed the hangars immediately. No one was killed and we had complete air superiority thereafter.

Diego Suarez harbour was formed by a strip of land to the west which hooked around into Cap d'Ambre to form the north side of the harbour. The town of Antsirane was to the south of the harbour, as was the airfield. Our attack was to be made on the western shore. Here there was a small sheltered harbour with a difficult approach. It was covered by a shore battery and the approaches had been mined. The plan called for entry into this harbour to be made at night, with the mines to be swept and dimly lit marker buoys to be installed to guide the assault transports. It was a difficult job, but it was well executed. So well, indeed, that the French gunners had to be roused from their sleep by the landing party! The advance across the peninsula followed.

General Sturgess of the Royal Marines was in overall command of the landing, while the force ashore was led by Brigadier Frankie Festing who later became Chief of the General Staff. The naval forces were commanded by

Admiral Syfret. At first things went well, but the attack bogged down when the main French position was reached. Sturgess decided that he should go to the front to discuss the situation with Festing, and I am told that he went out on the back of a dispatch rider's motorcycle. It was agreed that a diversion was needed, so Sturgess returned with the following request to the Fleet.

Admiral Syfret was asked to send in a destroyer with an assault force of Marines from *Ramillies*, and this he agreed to do. The destroyer Anthony ran the gauntlet of the batteries at the harbour entrance and landed the Marines at the quay in the town of Antsirane, then escaped under heavy fire. This diversion caused considerable concern among the French, and their main defence line was soon pierced.

In the closing stages of the battle the French sloop *d'Entrecasteaux*, which was in the harbour, was reported to be firing on the flank of our assault troops, so our aircraft were sent in and sank her. *Ramillies* shelled the last of the forts into submission, and then the naval force steamed around to enter the harbour. I had just gone below decks to change when I heard a short blast on the siren and the ship healed sharply to port. A French submarine had fired a torpedo at us and we had had to take violent evasive action. Fortunately for us the torpedo missed, and the sub was quickly sunk by one of our destroyers. The battle for Diego Suarez was over.

The next day, having heard from our aircraft that the *d'Entrecasteaux* was resting on the bottom with most of her upperworks above water, I asked Admiral Boyd if I could take a party of aircrew to see if there was anything worth taking out of her with particular reference to codes and cyphers. He approved, and so we sailed off in a cutter with a large crew. On the way a lone French soldier fired a few rounds at us, but no damage resulted and we reached *d'Entrecasteaux* safely. Apart from a few rather bloated bodies scattered around the quarterdeck it was evident that the ship had been abandoned in a hurry. We found their steel cypher box where it had been dropped before it could be thrown overboard. This was a great haul, for along with the very valuable cyphers there was a

Top: *HMS Illustrious with four Swordfish ranged on the foredeck.*
Bottom: *HMS Indomitable at Gibraltar.*

signed copy of the report of the commanding French Admiral at Oran, written shortly after the fall of France when Britain was trying to persuade their fleet to join ours. Their Fleet based on Oran in North Africa, if an enemy, could cut our communications with Egypt. This threat had to be eliminated. Force "H" based on Gibraltar was sent to parley with them with the hope of persuading them to join us, or leave the Mediterranean for, say,

Martinique. (This would put them out of the reach of the German Navy who would probably have been delighted to take them over.) The almost unthinkable alternative was for them to be sunk where they were by our Fleet. Captain Troubridge, the Captain of the Indomitable, had been the Naval Attaché in Paris before the war and he felt that this report would be very useful after the war because it showed that from the very first the French had considered us as enemies, and that they had intended to fight us rather than join us or have their Fleet immobilised. They therefore played for time, negotiating with a Captain who had previously worked with them as allies until they were ready for action. How quickly allies can turn to enemies. I had always heard that the French Navy had had no love for us since Trafalgar and this story seems to bear out that theory.

The carrier *Illustrious* came to relieve *Indomitable,* and Admiral Boyd was pleased to be able to return to the ship from which he had earlier launched his attack on Taranto. It was decided, however, that the Eastern Fleet Carrier Force was to be broken up, and Admiral Boyd had to return to England by way of Canada and the United States. I would have liked to have been able to go with him in the hope of seeing Debbie on the way, but it was not to be. Instead I was sent to work with Brigadier Festing on a plan for the full scale occupation of Madagascar, and transferred to *Albatross*, a veteran seaplane carrier which had about half a dozen Walrus amphibians. It looked as though there would be a little excitement in taking this large island from the French.

Madagascar

The Japanese threat had begun to recede, but there was still fear that their submarines might use the ports of Tamatave and Majunga. Furthermore the attitude of the Vichy French in Madagascar had not mellowed at all and there seemed to be reason to believe that they might well cooperate with our enemies. There had been a curious incident at the fall of Diego Suarez that suggested that such cooperation could already be an established fact. An unidentified aircraft had overflown the harbour, and *Ramillies* and a tanker had been torpedoed and damaged by either a French or Japanese submarine. At that time it was believed that the Japanese had a submarine capable of carrying a small aircraft for reconnaissance, and we did not want to take chances on such a combination astride our supply routes. Madagascar is a very large island indeed, measuring some 1,000 miles from north to south, and 350 miles across at its widest point. Its capture needed detailed plannning, so we went to a government building overlooking the harbour in Mombasa (Kenya) to put the plan together.

The 29th Brigade under Festing was to carry out the initial landings, backed by East African troops, while a squadron of Albacores was to be ready to land as soon as an airfield could be captured. We had one worry, and this was that ships needed unloading and reloading ready for the assault as all the wrong things were on top. Since there was no large crane available anywhere near at hand to unload our heavy supplies from the cargo ships, a floating crane was sent for from Bombay. It was despatched unescorted, at its top speed of eight knots. As it had to maintain radio silence for fear of attracting the attention of enemy submarines, there was an anxious wait before its wobbly derrick poked up over the horizon.

At length the day for final briefings before our departure arrived. It was well done and the plan was very clearly laid out for everyone by General Sturgess who was to be with the Fleet. As the briefing concluded he said, "Well, gentlemen, is everything clear? No further questions? Well then, that is all. Good Hunting!" We dispersed to our ships to pass the information on to our own units and to set sail for the operation.

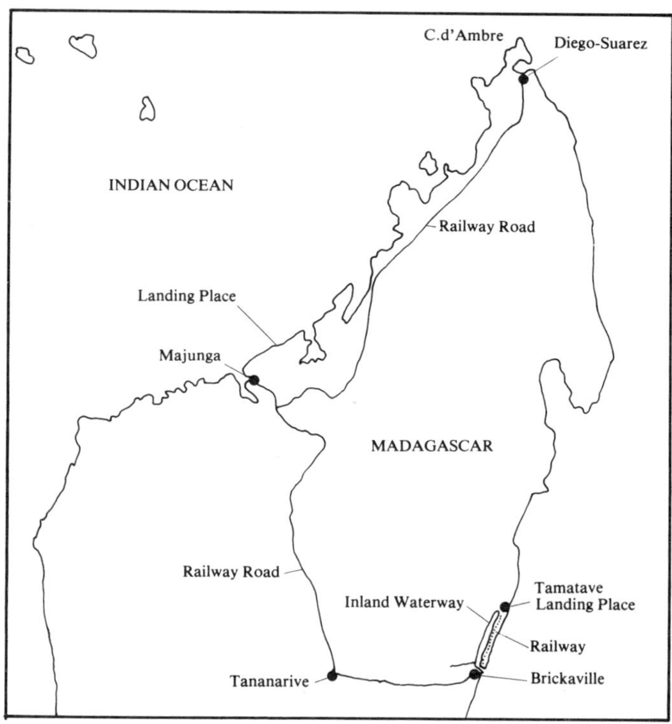

The first landing was to take place at Majunga, a river-mouth harbour on the west coast of Madagascar. We were to creep in to the coast north of Majunga and anchor close to the shore. We were led by *Albatross*, piloted by its navigator, Commander Smythe. He did a lovely job of the approach to an unlighted shore, placing the ships behind us most accurately. I give full marks to the merchant ships carrying out this manoeuvre which was quite foreign to their usual procedures. They had to let down their anchors slowly until they reached bottom, with no rattling of chains which might have warned of our approach.

Two battalions, one the Lancashires under the command of Colonel Stockwell, landed and commenced their advance. They quickly overran a small airfield on which our aircraft landed at dawn. As soon as the initial landing was complete the ships weighed anchor and again led by Albatross we moved down to Majunga where we anchored off the town. As dawn broke the lighthouse keeper on a small island off the harbour woke up and fired off a flare, perhaps as a warning signal to the town. We had been warned that there might be a gun on this island, and since we were no more than half a mile from it there were a few nervous moments while we waited to see what might happen. One of our destroyers had been assigned the task of knocking it out should it dare to fire, but no evidence of a gun appeared and all was well.

Our troops advanced against very little opposition and entered the town. The French troops withdrew to the opposite side of town to take up a defensive position between Majunga and the capital of Madagascar, Tananarive, in the centre of the island. When our troops sought quarters in Majunga Lt.Cdr Smallwood, commander of the naval aircraft ashore, and Colonel Stockwell, commander of the advancing troops, were allocated a house which belonged to a prominent Vichy supporter who had been flung into jail. Smallwood later told me that in the best traditions of submission to invading hordes the housewife had indicated unmistakably that ravishment was anticipated, eagerly, in the circumstances. For better or for worse, however, the Vichy supporter was released

before nightfall and temptation removed. A similar disappointment happened to my friend Major Bertie Bass. While leading his company in Burma they entered a village where they were met by the Headman who offered him a very attractive young virgin as the rights of the conqueror. "Alas, Hank," he said, "the advance had to go on".

With Majunga dealt with we had to turn our attention to Tamatave on the east coast. The assault troops were relieved by the East Africans and re-embarked for the voyage to the far side of the island. Our force, which consisted of one battleship, one aircraft carrier with a destroyer escort, *Albatross,* and the transports, sailed north-about round Madagascar. The 'harbour' at Tamatave was a roadstead, (ie. an offshore anchorage), sheltered by islands, and a night entry was considered to be too hazardous. A garrison was known to be in the town, and in view of the fact that the shore was studded with strong points it was felt that attempting a landing without first softening up the defences with gunfire could result in severe casualties. At daylight our destroyers were brought into the roadstead. The landing parties were in their boats lined up less than a half a mile off shore, and the transports with the reinforcements lay outside them. Further off, but still in full view of the town, was the battleship, and we had aircraft flying overhead. We tried landing an envoy under the white flag as at Dakar, but his boat was fired on and retired smartly with no casualties. We demanded surrender, threatening to bombard for half an hour before landing if there was no capitulation. The Chef de Région refused, and would not yield to any persuasion.

Opposite: *HMS Albatross being overflown by a flight of Walruses.*

Top: *The invasion force off Tamatave.*

Bottom: *Landing craft of the invasion force move past a cruiser and a destroyer off Tamatave.*

Top: HMS Albatross, which acted as the headquarters ship, and two transports lying off Tamatave.

Above: This group of four photographs shows the remains of a railway bridge that was blown up by the Vichy French in order to impede British forces during the invasion of Madagascar.

The word came to open fire and the bombardment began. The moment the first gun fired up went the White Flag. A cease fire was ordered immediately, fortunately for the inhabitants before the battleship had commenced firing. As it was there were about 30 civilian casualties. After we had landed it was discovered that the entire defence force had been removed the day before to augment the defences at Tananarive in their stand against our troops advancing from Majunga. I subsequently heard the Chef de Région boast that, "My honour is bathed in blood", but as it was not his blood, but French blood he could have saved, I thought this to be a particularly vainglorious claim.

The naval phase of the operation seemed to be over and I was itching for something useful to do. The Vichy French had taken most of the railway engines inland to the capital and then blown a bridge over a ravine so that our troops advance would be slowed. The army asked whether the navy could move two engines by boat to the other side of the breached line, and I was given the job. There was a point where the railway ran along an inland waterway close to the coast. From there we thought we could take a small locomotive to Brickaville on the other side of the blown bridge. I went down to inspect the chosen loading site where there were a few barges, and found the natives were hard at work and doing a very good job of making a rail siding down to the water. A local Frenchman commented that they would never have worked so hard for them, so perhaps our intelligence was right on this occasion that the ordinary folk of Madagascar were not deeply loyal to the French.

I had a working party of shipwrights and seamen with me and we set to work joining two barges together. They were lashed together with ropes, and then several lengths of rail were placed across them to form a platform. Each of these was tied down with more ropes which ran underneath the barges. More lengths of rail were then secured to this rudimentary platform to form a track for the locomotive. The ends of these rails protruded from the barge and were joined to the track on the siding with a loose coupling. Work on the barges and the siding was

Top: The makeshift barge being connected to the hastily prepared siding in preparation for the arrival of the engine.

Bottom: With the engine safely on board the barge and the tug ready, the naval crew pushes off.

Opposite: Some of the shipwrights and seamen from Albatross who formed the construction crew. The author is in the cab (centre).

completed at about the same time and the smaller of the two available locomotives was driven down. To show our confidence in this contraption we had an army officer ride in the engine and I stood on the barges. All went well, and our engine was duly secured.

We had two small wood-fired tugs, (which really looked more like large canoes), to tow us and for a time we did well. The tugs had earlier been sent to survey the passage ahead and had reported that there was sufficient depth of water. However, despite the fact that we drew only a couple of feet we grounded and stuck fast. I sent one of the tugs off to fetch shovels, and the next morning we dug ourselves through to deeper water. We went on, arriving at Brickaville the next afternoon. We had sent word of the height of our rails above water and a siding was ready for us to link up to. As soon as we had made the connection our little engine steamed ashore whistling proudly. To our chagrin we discovered that the army had captured another locomotive, so ours was no longer really needed, and we were reprieved from bringing the second, larger engine. I remember that night -sleeping in a cot that was two feet too short in a dirty little hut in thick jungle. I was glad to get back to Tamatave the next day.

Top: Laying tracks down to the waters' edge.
Bottom: An aerial view of the siding down to the river.

The resistance at Tananarive collapsed quickly and the French governor moved to make his last stand at Fort Dauphin. Our headquarters staff was being moved to the capital, but with the campaign almost at an end I appreciated that my days in Madagascar were numbered and very shortly I received a signal by way of *Albatross* that I was to make my way to Diego Suarez to join an RAF transport ship bound for Ceylon. It seemed that my next job would be the command of an air station there.

Brigadier Festing said that if I could get myself to Tananarive he would lay on an aircraft to take me to Diego Suarez.This was a gesture which I much appreciated. We had got on very well together and I had the highest respect for his abilities. The more he thought about the trip the more it appealed to him, and eventually he decided to come with me to the capital. He commandeered an engine and one coach to take us down the coast to the broken bridge, where we were to transfer by car and ferry to Brickaville. Enroute we stopped to bathe in the sea (nice being conquering troops), and then went on in our wood fired engine, driven by the General, with his railway expert and myself crammed into the cab along with the engine driver and stoker. We stopped for wood by the side of the tracks and then went on our way. It was like living a childhood fantasy! After a night at Brickaville we went the rest of the journey to Tananarive by rail -in a 1920s vintage roadster on railway wheels! I took leave of Festing the next morning when one of Smallwood's Albacores flew me to Diego Suarez. I was sad to leave Festing, he was a wonderful man and I thoroughly enjoyed being on his staff. I am glad to say that later, when he was passing through Ceylon, he got in touch with me and we relived old times.

I went aboard the RAF transport at Diego Suarez and found a large detachment of air force personnel and some VADs (volunteer nurses aids of the Volunteer Aid Detachment) destined for Ceylon. We had a pleasant, almost peace-time, voyage by way of Addu Atoll. Having been there before with *Indomitable* I was able to persuade my fellow passengers that it was a well-know resort with country clubs and polo grounds. I don't think they were too impressed when they saw that it was nothing more than a rocky coral lump with hardly a shrub on it!

The other engine captured by the army.

Katukurunda

s soon as I arrived in Colombo I called at the small office of Commodore (Air) Elliot, finding to my pleasure that his staff officers were Robin Kilroy, my former CO at Lee, and Dicky Dakeyne whom I knew from my days in *Apollo*. Ceylon, now re-named Sri Lanka, is about 250 miles long and 130 miles across at its widest point. It is a beautiful tropical island that lies between six and ten degrees North latitude. The east and north-west sections of the island are (or at least were) malarial, and were affected only by the north-east monsoon. The south-west section of the island, where my new station Katukurunda was located, was subject to both the north-east and south-west monsoons, the latter being the more violent. The area receives an average annual rainfall of about 120 inches, with 30 inches falling in each of the months of May and November. This amount of rain may have been too much for malarial mosquitoes, for the area was relatively healthy, although I found the heat and humidity most debilitating, sapping one's ambition to do a great deal of anything. Experience eventually made me make fourteen days of up-country (ie. inland above 3,000 ft ASL) leave mandatory every six months. Even so, it was hard to maintain initiative and efficiency. The coastal plain was covered with cocoanut plantations, the low-lying hills grew rubber and some 'low-country tea', and the inland hills were covered with tea. Most of the plantations were run by Englishmen who were generally short-staffed because most of the young planters had gone off to war. Their loss was our gain, however, because it meant that there were quite a few unoccupied bungalows which we were able to use as small leave camps.

The day after I arrived in Colombo I went down to survey my new command at Katukurunda, which was about 30 miles south of the city. There I found a small airfield with a single airstrip fashioned from Kabuk, a local clay used for roads. There were three officers and thirty men, and I was somewhat surprised to find that the Wardroom Mess was the verandah of my one-bedroom bungalow! By the time that I left two-and-a-half years later the station had grown to be our largest Royal Naval Air Station, housing 300 officers and 3,000 men including 100 Wrens, 1,000 Italian co-beligerants (ex-prisoners of war) employed on construction, and about 1,000 Singhalese. We could accomodate more than 100 aircraft and had a RN Aircraft Repair Yard. We had built two Wardroom Messes, and a theatre as well as all the housing for the personnel.

Officers from the early days at Katukurunda.

Like Hatston, Katukurunda had three main functions: we provided a small reserve pool of aircraft and crews for the fleet carriers; we took in carrier squadrons for rest and training; and our repair yard was constantly busy preparing aircraft for embarkation and repairing others which had been damaged. Unlike Hatston we had many local problems, we could not go home to see our families, and there was a constant threat of a Japanese invasion.

One of the main problems we faced was the heat and humidity. It made long term aircraft storage impossible -anything that was left enclosed quickly rotted or mildewed. We had to keep electric light bulbs burning in our clothes closets at all times, and anything hung out to dry, such as parachutes, had to be placed in a draft or they remained damp. Aircraft engines stripped down for inspection could not be left with any bare metal parts exposed overnight -they had to be oiled every evening to prevent the onset of rust.

The training squadron at Kat. Their task was to supply replacement aircrew to the fleet. The aircraft is an Avenger.

Officers of the Repair Yard with Commander Manners-Clarke (front and centre).

I found it a little trying at first to be away from active operations against the enemy, but soon buckled down to the minutiae of a support unit. With a great deal of help from others I organised team sports such as soccer, field hockey,and cricket, as well as activities such as sailing, bathing, theatricals, brains trusts and lectures. We even started a base newspaper. I saw my job as being there to encourage and advise and to develop initiative in others to get things going. Basically I felt I had to create an atmosphere in which others would do more than duty demanded. I tended to worry about 'my' people most of the time, and when someone once asked the padre how I behaved in church he replied, "The Captain is most attentive until he has read the lesson; then he thinks about the Station." I think that was a fair comment. I worked hard and played hard, and mixed closely with both the officers and the men.

Our local paper was named "Two-Six", a title lifted from the nautical order "Two-Six-Heave" commonly used when exhorting a team of men to pull together. A poem written by a young officer, which was published in our Christmas & New Year 1943/44 edition, points out how important it was to make the place as happy as possible:

MEMORIES OF ENGLAND

Oh England! How in simple line
Recall the beauty that is thine?
Sweet memories of that pleasant land
Reaching to this distant strand.

Many great and famous men
Found the urgent need to pen
Lay or simple verse in praise
Of England; seen thro' memory's haze.

The day I sailed I saw a verdant land.
I gazed from hill and meadow to the sand;
And I saw England --as indeed I know her --
A land of beauty, bloom, and simple splendour.

My thoughts again went back to boyhood's days
When in the summer's heat I'd often laze
Upon my back in some sweet meadow cool,
Dreaming of a deep translucent pool.

I walked the sweet and scented wood
Pretending that I understood
The language that the wild birds speak,
And learned the wiles of rabbits meek.

How can a writer's pen portray
A picture of a lamb at play?
Or --however hard he try,
How catch the seagull's plaintive cry?

It's Really Quite Safe

> And should I dream, or stop to pray
> Beneath the hot sun's scorching ray,
> I think of those old country bowers,
> Or of traditions that are ours.
>
> But now I'm far away from that,
> And who shall say I do not care?
> For though I've seen the waters blue
> And lovely birds of brilliant hue---
>
> Oh, how my poor heart would resound
> To hear my footsteps homeward bound
> To that green isle which I recall.
> This absence taints my heart like gall!
>
> J.Quinlan, S/Lt (A)

It was not surprising for men this far from home to feel homesick, especially not during the Christmas season, and I was pleased that the site of our airfield was one of great potential beauty. There were many days when I sat on my verandah with a cup of tea and watched the sun rise over Adam's Peak, a conical mountain in the centre of the island. Johnny Johnston, the civil engineer responsible for the actual work of construction, readily accepted my instruction that no trees were to be cut down without my approval. I felt that they were neccesary for both shade and beauty. Johnston and I saw eye to eye that our buildings had to be light and airy, and we often rejected Admiralty designs. We were constantly at work together selecting sites and designing buildings, and we must have covered a good many miles together doing site surveys to determine the optimum location of buildings with regard to ease of access, comfort of living, and military considerations. My bungalow became the place for final acceptance meetings with all concerned present. Things would be thrashed out over a gin, and once final agreement was reached there were no amendments.

Top: An aerial shot of the campsite at Katukurunda.

Bottom: Another view of the camp. In the right foreground is the first real Wardroom.

One of the things we had to contend with was the local penchant for graft. Johnny complained to me that every Kangani, or foreman, took a percentage of the wages for each of his gang, and that a gang of men passing dirt in baskets from the diggers to the truck had to be at least twelve strong, regardless of the distance. Even if the distance were a mere ten feet they would form a semi-circle to accomodate the required twelve men or women! Additionally all of the Kanganis had dead men on their books. Johnny told me confidently that he would break this system by having inspectors as they did in England, but later reported that they had beaten him at his own game, "The inspectors now have dead men on their books and we are worse off than ever!" We were obliged to accept local custom.

A Company of Royal Marines acted as our defence force. They had a permanent camp and a strong point complete with weapons pits and trenches on the edge of the runway. I found it very comforting to have a detachment of these magnificent men right on the airfield, for the rifles which we had been issued were so old and worn that the bullets rattled down the barrels once they got hot. In the event of attack we would surely have had to wait till we saw 'the whites of their eyes' as the saying goes. We were rather concerned about the possibility of an airborne landing, so to support our Marines we cooked up a means of booby trapping the runway. We made a number of tripods, on each of which was placed a wooden trough long enough to hold two 100 lb. bombs set nose to nose about two feet apart. The idea

Opposite: The Captain's bungalow with a corner of the hockey field (which also doubled as a parade ground) just beyond.

Top: The control tower at RNAS Katukurunda. The "Affirmative" flag is flying, indicating that conditions were O.K. for flying.

Bottom: A few badly damaged, yet unexploded, bombs after an explosion in a bomb dump. Sabotage was suspected, but never proven.

was that in the event of an impending enemy attack these contraptions would be placed on the runway, where any landing aircraft would knock them over thus causing the bombs to collide with one another where upon they would explode. I tested the device by using a jeep and a long rope to pull it over: it worked well.

Our Kabuk surfaced runway was fine for light aircraft such as the Swordfish and Spitfires, but when we began to receive Avengers and Corsairs in increasing numbers we found that it could not stand the weight and was starting to break up. It looked as though we might have to close the airfield while a heavier runway was built, until the Royal Marines Staff Officer in Colombo mentioned that he had seen a metal-plank runway in use in India. Enquiries turned up enough of this material to cover our surface and a supply was rushed to us. The Royal Marines, who complained of being tired of being just a defence unit, asked if they could lay it, and in just a few days of hard work they provided us with a runway which would take just about anything which might be sent our way.

Opposite: A caricature of the author drawn for the station paper shortly after his first solo flight.

Top: An Avenger making a practice deck landing with a batsman at Kat. The metal planking used to strengthen the surface so that it could take these heavier aircraft shows to advantage.

Centre: A Barracuda in dispersal among the palm trees at Katukurunda.

Bottom: A Swordfish about to land on a carrier –the batsman has just signalled "cut". While at Kat. the author learned to fly this type of aircraft.

It's Really Quite Safe

We had some troubles with our large Transport Section. All of our drivers and mechanics were local civilian Singhalese, and there were only a couple of servicemen in charge. It had become clear that we were using far too much gasoline, so I asked my Royal Marine Company to use their dispatch riders to trail our trucks and find out what was going on. They were instructed to do nothing more than observe until a full report could be prepared so as not to tip off the drivers. The report was conclusive, gasoline was being syphoned out of the trucks on a regular basis, --we were being robbed blind. Thinking that it would be wise to warn other units of this abuse I forwarded my report to the Admiral, and was astonished when, rather than being thanked for the warning, I received a sharp reprimand for allowing it to happen in the first place. I attributed this to the Admiral living in a sheltered society and not yet appreciating the nature of the Singhalese.

Another nuisance peculiar to this area was the poison pen letter --an invariably anonymous letter which accused someone in authority of some evil deed. On one occasion we received a General order warning us that information had been received that cooks throughout the island were being bribed to poison us. "Scratch, I bet that came from an anonymous letter." I said to my secretary. He agreed, so I called the Admiral to suggest that this might be the source of the information and that it should be ignored. Enquiry showed this to be the case and so we ignored the threat.

The airfield was situated on low lying flat land along the coast, separated from the sea by a road and a railway. The runway ran southeast-northwest to be in line with the southwest monsoon. This was fine except that the wind only blows from the southwest at the break of the monsoon. Therafter it veers around to the northwest and never blows from the southwest again till the next monsoon season. This made landings for aircraft with a tendency to weathercock rather difficult. I set about gathering statistics, and after six months I was eventually able to persuade the authorities that we required a second runway. It was opened shortly after I left.

Top: The Operations Room at Katukurunda.

Centre: An Avenger (JZ199) over the rice paddies of south-west Ceylon.

Bottom: The author (3rd from left) in attandance at the marriage of a young pilot and a volunteer nurse (VAD).

It's Really Quite Safe

During my stay we only had two fatal accidents, although there were several narrow squeaks. I was on the airfield at the time of one of the fatal accidents -an Albacore had been caught in a gusty cross-wind and wound up upside down on the edge of the runway. I jumped in my car and raced over, arriving just behind the ambulance and the crash tender. I can still see clearly the image of a young VAD, who without thought to her own danger from fire, was right under the aircraft, half crouching, half on her back, helping to ease the terribly injured observer out of his cockpit. He died later in hospital. The pilot, who had escaped unscathed, was in a state of shock and distress. I thought it was fortunate that he was one of the few men on the base who had a wife there to give him comfort as he had married one of our VAD's.

A close call occurred when an Albacore experienced engine failure at night while actually in the circuit. It just vanished, and as its circuit would have taken it out over the sea we thought that it had probably gone down there. I was in the control tower watching the landings, and in the hope that it might have force-landed along the coast and I immediately drove down to the beach with the crash tender following to look for them. Surely enough the crew was on the beach, waiting to greet me. "Here we are, Sir. Did you come to fetch us?" Rather an anticlimax. Their engine had cut and the pilot had put down in shallow water from where they had waded ashore. They had picked the only safe place for a dead engine landing away from the runway.

In another case a young pilot landed with his engine boiling over and in immediate danger of seizing up. We asked if he had been low flying, a suggestion which he vehemently denied. When we told him that he had better remove the palm leaves from his radiator intake he had to agree that he had indeed been a trifle low.

As I mentioned earlier, I decided that all of our residents should take fourteen days leave every six months. Although there was a Naval rest camp at Diatelawa it was being used by men from the ships, and furthermore it was not very high so it was better that we find places of our own. I had become friends with a number of local planters, and through them I managed to 'borrow' some unoccupied bungalows. We ran these ourselves, sending each party up with a Petty Officer who would stay over so that there was always someone there who knew the ropes. They would take their own food and rations of rum and beer, and found themselves in the middle of a tea plantation in lovely surroundings with lots of interest going on. Best of all it was cool, Dear God, cool. I cannot say too much for the work done by these planters on our behalf. Apart from the groups of men we sent they almost always had a couple of men on leave billited with them in their own house, and I find it hard to imagine anything more trying than sharing ones home with a constant flow of strangers with whom you have little or nothing in common. This, however, was their contribution to the war effort, and we were grateful.

We had sleeping space for 150 men in our rest camps which took care of our needs. I used to make quick visits whenever I could. I recall one short sick leave I took when I had been down with Dengue fever. I called on the planter and arrived just in time for tea with him and his wife. My host allowed that I didn't look too well and spiked my tea with a little of his closely guarded, rationed scotch 'for medicinal purposes'. I must say it helped a lot.

The author with a 3½lb. trout caught while on leave at Horton Plains. This was the record trout for the year there. Trout lived in the rivers above 3,000 ft ASL where the water was relatively cool.

Palm trees and outrigger canoes lend a 'tropical paradise'
look to the beach which was used for recreational swimming.

When the war in our zone turned to the offensive I had the opportunity to meet Lord Louis Mountbatten who had been appointed the Supreme Commander for the Far East. A short Combined Operations Course was being held at Mountbatten's headquarters in Kandy, the ancient capital of Ceylon. One of his ADC's was an old acquaintance of mine from Admiralty days, and as Mountbatten always wanted to meet Commanding Officers from important bases or ships I was asked to lunch. This was my first and only opportunity to meet him, and I found him to be a most gracious host. There were a dozen or so guests, and to my surprise we were all warned that nothing of any secrecy was to be discussed because Chiang Kai Chek's representative would be present and anything that he heard would doubtless go straight to the Japanese. Sometimes one could do without allies; this was one that was obviously very doubtful.

From time to time when we were not harbouring squadrons of aircraft we would be asked to take men from ships for a week or two. They had a rather rough time aboard ship and we did our best to make their time ashore pleasant, arranging daily swimming parties and organising games. Before the war it had been found that bathing on the coast near Colombo could be dangerous during the south-west monsoon because of the heavy seas and strong undertow. A standing order had therefore been issued by the Commander-in-Chief to the effect that no Naval person should swim in the ocean during this monsoon. I needed bathing desperately for the well being of my men. I had found a place with coconut palms on the foreshore, a lovely gently sloping sandy beach, and calm water at a temperature of about 80°F that was sheltered from heavy seas and sharks by an offshore reef. It was a perfect place for men to forget about the war for a few hours. After arranging for life-savers I requested special dispensation from the standing order on swimming for Katukurunda. I was refused. I was furious that the authorities, who were quite prepared to risk the lives of men by sending them into battle, would not take this minimal risk while making them happy and healthy. I debated what to do, then decided to cross my fingers and carry on swimming. There was only one swimmer who got into difficulties, and my life-savers rescued him. No doubt I would have been hung from the nearest yardarm if anything had gone wrong, but I was lucky. I'm sure that Admiral von Scheer would have approved..."rules and regulations are made for those who need them."

With a war on you never know what is going to happen next. Fortunately one of our biggest challenges occurred after we were fully organized. One day I went up to Colombo to visit the Head Office, arriving in the late afternoon, and expecting to go to a party with some of the staff that evening. When I arrived I was greeted with the news that at 9.00 am the next morning we were to get some 50 to 60 aircraft from a carrier, and that all their ground crew were to be brought to us later in the day when the ship had entered harbour. Up to then they had not thought it advisable to use the telephone line, but agreed that it would now be safe for me to do so. I called Katukurunda and gave the full particulars to my Commander, Charlie Long. That being done I asked where the party was. "Aren't you going back to the Station?" I was asked. "Not necessary," was my reply, "All arrangements will be made by my Heads of Departments who are entirely competent." Let me tell you of the men in in whom I had so much confidence.

Good officers for Air Stations were hard to come by and I had to be somewhat ruthless until I got the right men for the job, many of whom had to be found locally. Eventually I had Charlie Long, a planter from Kenya who had retired as a Midshipman, as Commander; a South African Sub-Lieutenant as First Lieutenant in general charge of the Living Quarters; a Warrant Officer Gunner (T) as Wardroom Mess Secretary; a Chief Engineer, Cdr. Manners-Clarke in charge of the Repair Yard; an old time civilian Flying Instructor "Hilda" Hilditch as Cdr (A) in charge of all aircraft on the ground and in the circuit; Lt.Cdr.(O) Patterson, our only regular, in charge of the Operations Room and all aircraft outside the circuit; a bank manager as Paymaster Commander in charge of all pay and messing; and a garage man from Inverness who ran our large Transport Section quietly and efficiently. With a

Left: The author and Charlie Long on their way to a wedding.

Below: The author (left), Exec. Officer Cdr. Long (saluting), and Repair Yard Officer Crd. Manners-Clarke seeing off Admiral Sir James Somerville (shaking hands with Operations Officer Lt.Cdr. Patterson.

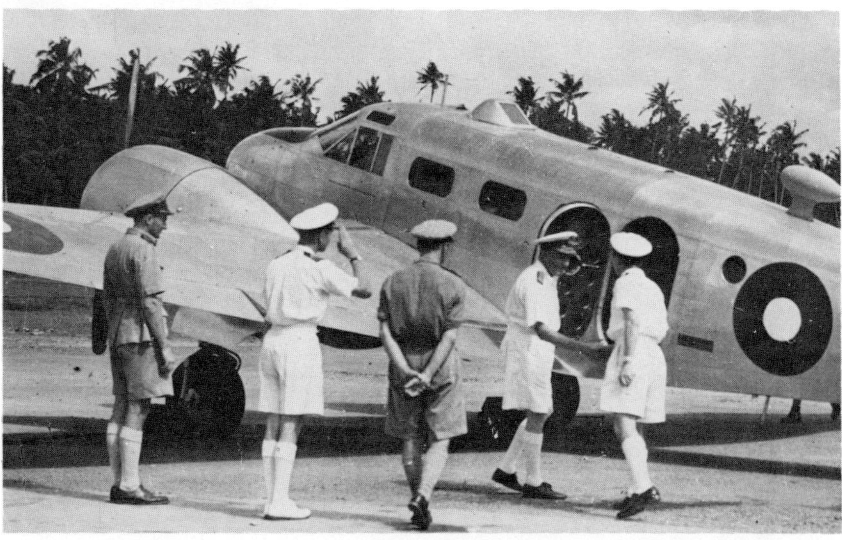

team like this my presence was unnecessary, indeed it would probably have interfered with the rush job they had in hand if I had started to ask questions. We had our party in Colombo, and I got back late that night and was down to the airfield at 9.00 am to see the aircraft land. Everything had been arranged.

It's Really Quite Safe

Manners-Clarke was a practical engineer who, it was rumoured, had in younger years competed in the "Wall of Death" -riding a motorcycle around the vertical sides of a small enclosed circuit, a popular event at county fairs. He did a great job; everything they turned out flew well. I treasured all of these men and guarded them jealously, particularly the South African. He was far too far from home to get promoted, but I refused any officer senior to him who might have tried to take over his job.

The Station Doctor was Reg Bennett. He was a sailing expert and designed and supervised the building of boats in our shops. We sailed on the local river, the Kala Ganga, and Reg organised a sailing team and led us to victory over the team from the Colombo Yacht Club who were seldom beaten. Our Torpedo Gunner, Mr. Williams, was the confidant and adviser for young aircrew, and in his capacity as Mess Secretary was largely responsible for setting the tone of the Mess. From the Lower Deck there were the Master at Arms, the Senior Rating responsible for discipline, and the Presidents of the Chief and Petty Officers' Messes with whom I talked whenever our paths crossed on the Station. Lastly, there was the Captain of Marines, in command of the fortified camp on the runway, who was responsible for our safety. My own constant companion was Tina, half bulldog, half bull terrier. She was tough, naughty, and faithful.

Above: The author in his spacious office, with faithful dog Tina asleep at his feet.
Opposite: One of the sailing boats designed by the Station Doctor, Reg Bennett.

In looking back over my experiences during the war years one of the things which struck me was how useless were many of the formerly retired officers and men that came back into the service, particularly those who had retired on their pensions and done little more than visit their local pubs to tell stories of their past accomplishments. Those who had taken up civilian trades had learned new skills, kept their minds alive, and were generally of great value. How much better off we would have been at shore stations such as this if the Admiralty had encouraged the very competent young men who had joined for the war to rise quickly to jobs of importance where technical fighting knowledge was not essential. Instead we were faced with the unpleasant, but essential task of asking to have inefficient officers replaced until we eventually got what we wanted.

It's Really Quite Safe

The author (right) with
C-in-C Eastern Fleet,
Admiral Sir James Somerville.

Admiral Somerville, who was still commanding the Eastern Fleet, used to visit us from time to time. He would tour the station as work went on as usual, and then we would gather as many men as we reasonably could and he would give them a pep talk, at which he was a master. I found his visits to be great morale boosters.

In 1943 we were sent two Wren officers, the first of our Wren contingent, and they were given a small two room bungalow for quarters. One night Singhalese thieves broke in and removed most of their belongings while they slept. It was rather scary for them, and so from then on they called at my bungalow and collected Tina each night. With her they were quite safe. Another robber broke into one of the Royal Marine Officer's rooms and was jumped by the awakened officer. The intruder promptly stabbed him, narrowly missing his jugular vein. The Royals were aroused by the noise, and seeing their wounded officer they dealt soundly with his assailant. At the subsequent trial the robber pleaded self-defence, claiming that it was he that had been attacked. To my everlasting disgust he got off with a year or so in prison.

When we were advised that 100 Wrens were to be posted in to the station we had to set about building a

Top: The "wrennery" seen from across the main road.
Bottom: Wrens marching past during Sunday Divisions.

Wrennery. Unfortunately there was no space left within the camp itself, so we had to set it up on a small hill just outside the station. If I had had my choice I would have put it right in the middle of the camp to make sure that no slippery natives could break in. Instead we had to put up a high barbed-wire fence around their building and have two armed guards inside the fence. There was an attempt made to break in, but it was foiled by the guards. It seemed a shame to have to put our girls behind barbed-wire, but they understood the need for it. Shortly after they arrived some aircraft came in from a carrier, and they were absolutely delighted when they called the station for landing clearance and heard a female voice in reply. The presence of English girls at Kat made us very popular, and had another indirect benefit. There were a lot of native women working on the station, and as time passed they became more and more attractive both to me and to others. With the Wrens among us this attraction faded which, I am sure, avoided many complications. Our girls took full part in the station, they were smart on parade and deadly on the hockey field...no one's shins were sacred.

There was one interesting incident involving a Wren which I remember. One of the girls had apparantly fallen in love with an RAF pilot who had been onboard the same ship on the way out, but he had had to go to India. One day an RAF aircraft arrived unheralded and landed without permission. It taxied around, a small female figure ran out from behind a palm tree, climbed in through an open door, and then the aircraft took off and disappeared to the north. Young Lochinvar had captured his bride. Strangely enough there was nothing we could do about this desertion because Wrens did not come under the naval Discipline Act. As far as I could see we depended strictly on their goodwill for their good behaviour. Thank God they had lots of goodwill.

I fear that I may have overstressed the social values of our Wrens and overlooked the jobs they did. There was no doubt that they worked efficiently and concientiously, but they also did a priceless job of raising the morale of us men in outlying stations. The Navy owes them a great debt.

For our entertainment we built a large theatre where we could show movies or have touring entertainment companies perform. Shortly after it had been opened I met the President of the Petty Officer's Mess and stopped to ask him how he liked it. "Very nice, Sir, very nice, " he replied, "But you know we have lost something. Every night we used to have something on in the Mess --a whist drive, a darts competition, a sing song, or something. Now,

The large theatre at Katukurunda where movies and touring performers entertained the troops.

Sir, we just go to the movies." It was true, we used to make our own fun, and I think that we were the happier and more of a team for it. It was nevertheless necessary for our many visitors from the Fleet seeking relaxation. Whenever live shows came to entertain us I would get up to thank them at the end of their show. I enjoyed this because it gave me an opportunity to talk informally to my men, and I would usually ask them for cheers for anything that I could think of. One evening we had the Colombo Amateur Theatrical Society on stage, all of whom I knew quite well. One very attractive member of the chorus line always put a foot wrong at least once per show, and sure enough she did the same this time. I leant across to whisper some comment about it to Charlie when she looked down and shouted at me, "Shut up!" The whole theatre burst into loud applause.

Visiting ENSA Theatrical Parties usually stayed two nights so that we could have two performances. We accomodated them on the base, the men in the Officers Cabins, and the women in the Wrennery. One troupe included a married couple who were quite persistent about sleeping together. With our accomodation arrangement this would have been very difficult, but Charlie Long settled the matter diplomatically. "You know," he said, "The Captain has not seen his wife for nearly four years," at which they backed down.

However, back to the war. The oil refinery at Palembang on Sumatra became a primary target for the High Command, and they decided to attack it with a squadron of long range bombers. For this purpose they borrowed a squadron of US aircraft, Liberators or Flying Fortresses I believe, which had the necessary range. They were to fly from RNAS China Bay, at Trincomalee on the east coast of Ceylon, and for this purpose the runways had to be lengthened and bulk fuel tanks installed. The aircraft arrived, refuelled and departed on their 1500 mile trip to the target. Destroyers were sent out to patrol along their track just in case they ran into any trouble. Reports had it that only one aircraft located the target, and very little damage was done. They returned to Ceylon before going once more about their business.

A month or two later two R.N. carriers met up with an American carrier and launched an attack supported by fighters. Palembang was, I believe, put out of action for some time. This incident demonstrated to me that when you can use carrier borne aircraft you should do so, they are so much more deadly than long range heavy bombers. Bombers have to risk unpredictable weather, and from my experience, including this affair, their navigation over the sea is uncertain. Carrier aircraft, on the other hand, can be brought much closer to the target and sea navigation is their forte. Using a mass of aircraft in low level attacks certainly proved more devastating than sending in a handful of bombers to attack from high altitude.

When our carriers returned from this operation I was given a couple of days warning that they would disembark at Kat, and it was requested that I arrange for them ALL to have four or five days leave. This meant making accomodation arrangements for some 100 officers, a similar number of lower deck flying crew and petty Officers, and God knows how many others. The scramble was on. I called my two best friends among the planters, Reg Notley and Tiny Whitelaw, and asked them if they could each find some houses up country to take 50 officers. We cleared our rest bungalows for the flying crew and Petty Officers, and the Army lent us space in a camp for the remainder. Reg and Tiny both asked me why I wanted this help, and for security reasons I could tell them only that it was worthwhile. This was enough and the planters all did their best to accomodate as many men as possible. Even the Grand Hotel in the Hill Station Nuwara Eliya provided us with four free rooms. Once again I was made aware of how much I owed to the friendly nature of these plantation owners. Their houses were always open to me, and in this place where local habits and customs had to be carefully respected I found their advice invaluable.

There was a small civilian aircraft on the field, a BA Swallow. It had dual controls and Hilditch suggested that he might teach me to fly. This was a suggestion which I accepted eagerly, and after $4\frac{1}{2}$ hours of dual instruction I went solo. I always wondered how many there were watching from behind palm trees when I did my first solo landing. Headquarters in Colombo advised me that what I was doing was illegal despite Hilditch's qualifications as a flight instructor. The rules and regulations specified that only RAF instructors could teach naval officers to fly, and I was warned that I would be in trouble if I were to crash the aircraft. I told them to keep their eyes closed as I did not intend to stop. As far as I was concerned it was a very good thing for the young officers to see that the Old Man could also defy gravity entirely alone.

One day I accompanied a large striking force from Kat which was carrying out a mock attack on one of our carriers which was coming into Colombo. I was travelling a good deal slower than the striking force and suddenly found myself in the midst of a melée of dog-fighting Corsairs. It was rather alarming because there was nothing I could do to avoid these fast aircraft except keep a steady course so that they could avoid me without complications. Fortunately someone said something to the effect of, "My God, look what's among us!" and they moved off. I then flew past the carrier at deck level which resulted in a betting match as to what sort of aircraft it was I was flying. It seems that despite my helmet and goggles I did not escape recognition. The Admiral was the winner of the betting. I met him at a party at the Colombo Club that evening and he rushed over and said, "A BA Swallow, right Hank?!" He was right and claimed his round of drinks.

My fun with the Swallow came to an end the next time I went on leave. When I got back Manners-Clarke informed me that he was very sorry, but that they had had to condemn the aircraft due to its condition. I told him that that was nonsense, that I only flew it gently, and that I wanted it again. "I thought you might say that, Sir," he said, "so I had it cut in half". He had too. I guess it really was dangerous.

A bit later we found a Swordfish with dual controls and we managed to get it to Kat so that I could continue my flying. By the time I left I had logged some 40 hours solo, which I reflected was almost enough to qualify me as a navigtor for a Wellington squadron.

Towards the end of my time at Kat we heard to our grief that a well known and admired Admiral had been killed in a crash while being flown to France by the Naval Communications Squadron. Although the initial Press Release did not include the name of the pilot, whom we understood had also been killed, Hillditch said, "Sir, I bet it was ----", mentioning a wartime pilot I had known. I asked him why and he replied, "I had the job of converting him to heavier aircraft, but I thought he would never make a safe pilot and proposed to fail him. He was well connected though, and I was told to pass him. I'll bet it was him." And surely enough, when the name was released Hillditch was proved right.

One of the weekly functions I established was a curry lunch in my bungalow for the senior officers each Sunday. My Head Boy, James, was one of the best curry cooks in Ceylon. He was a bit of a reprobate, but a charming one. I would invite about 15 guests each week from the circle of planters and their wives, Station, Squadron or Wren officers, civilian construction supervisors or members of visiting ENSA groups. They were always mixed affairs and proved to be lively and popular. It was customary for a curry lunch to be served in the Wardroom on Sundays as well, and afterwards we would drive down to the beach to swim and sun-bathe.

In December 1944, Admiral Sir Geoffrey Layton, C-in-C Ceylon, decided to inspect the sation. He was reputed to be a man who put great store in appearance, and I was rather apprehensive about how I would be able to ensure his approval. Fortunately we had been drilling a little smartness into our young men, so we formed as large a Guard of Honour as we could and had them fall-in at the main gate in their best uniforms for the C-in-C's arrival. He expressed pleasure when he inspected them. As soon as the Honour Guard inspection was finished we led the Admiral indoors and quickly dispersed the men around the Station. I next drove him on an inspection tour of the base, and wherever we came across a member of the guard they would present arms smartly. As a result we got a very fine write up from Sir Geoffrey. I think that if I had tried the same trick with James Somerville I would have been out on my ear in a jiffy, and rightly so.

One of the less pleasant tasks of a Commanding Officer is dealing with dicipline. We had very few problems, including a couple of Courts Martial which resulted in officers and men being discharged from the service. There were a few trouble makers which had been sent out from the U.K. before their sentences for previous misdemeanours had expired. These men I interviewed immediately, pointing out that we liked to keep this a happy Station and that they would be very welcome if they cared to join in, but stressing that if they did not I wouldn't hesitate to throw the book at them. They all settled in.

There were a couple of problems I found noteworthy. One of these was a young man who had been very foolish and certainly merited punishment. However, he was very young, and something told me that although he should be taught a lesson, clemency was needed. When the time came to pass judgement I said gruffly, "Remanded for punishment", a phrase that usually meant a Warrant and a severe punishment. After the lad had been marched off I went into a huddle with my Master at Arms who was a great psychologist. Next day when the young man was

Admiral "Clem" Moody inspecting an honour guard,
followed by the Officer of the Guard and the author.
This was the same guard used to "entrance" Admiral
Sir Geoffrey Layton.

brought back for sentencing I gave him a reprimand. "That was just right, Sir", commented my M.A.A., "He was crying his eyes out all last night." The other problem I found a good deal tougher.

A Special Repair Party had arrived on the station. These were men who, because they were not the brightest, had been trained how to service just one type of engine. Unfortunately we had none of their particular brand of engine on the Station, so they were being employed on general work. Two of them were very keen to fight the war, but since there was no war here they decided to go where there was. They had heard that the Russians were fighting and so they decided to go and join them. They took a days leave and promptly disappeared. In due time they were posted as deserters. They crossed by ferry to India, and thence, by stringing a good line, they secured the assistance of the Military Railway Officers and obtained passage by way of Madras to the Khyber Pass in northern India. This proved too cold for them, so they travelled across to Persia, which they found to be too hot. Discouraged they came back across the straights to Ceylon and gave themselves up. While they were away I had received a letter fom the father of one of them. His son had written to explain what they proposed to do, and he in turn wrote imploring me to recover them, give them their just desserts and set them back on the straight and narrow again. I was in a quandary -legally they were deserters and we could have locked them up and thrown away the key. But they were not criminals. I rather admired their spirit, but their actions could certainly not be condoned. After I had heard the case I went to my Admiral, and after quite a battle managed to persuade him to let me handle it the way I proposed. The next day, therefore, I had the Ship's Company fallen in, all very formal. Then the appropriate Articles of War were solemnly read and a sentence of 90 days detention was proclaimed. They were marched away, but after they had gone just a few yards I called them back and announced that the Admiral had granted a suspension of sentence subject to good behaviour. The general reaction was positive, I felt better, and discipline had been maintained without these two simple yet resourceful lads going to jail.

One last story of my time at Kat concerns Christmas day 1944. Being a holiday it was, of course, likely to be rowdy, so Charlie and I decided to lay on an Old English style football match -one half the station versus the other half, with the field being the whole station. We figured that having a wild time playing round and through the huts would take some of the devil out of them. Once the match was under way I went off to the airfield to pass Christmas greetings to those who had drawn sentry duty, and to the Royal Marine Camp. When I returned all seemed quiet. My car was stopped by a small group of young men who, very politely, asked if they could throw me into the water tank. The decision was entirely up to me, but I said, "Approved." They took my watch and hat and then threw me in, had a good cheer and then pulled me out again. Having had a hunch this sort of thing might happen I had James set out some clean clothes, so I dried off, changed, and went about my rounds. Altogether I went into the water tank three times that day, always after permission had been granted. After all, everyone else was jumping in or being thrown in. These water tanks were scattered around the Station for fire protection. Fortunately James kept a clean dry uniform ready so I remained respectable. Many years later I told this story to a Canadian Army Colonel, and I'm afraid that he did not approve. For me it exemplified the Navy's way of living: we were a team, and this was a day when we could let our hair down and have fun with one another.

After I had been at Kat for about a year I felt that I had done my time ashore, so I asked for a relief. When none came I went to Colombo and pointed out that Katukurunda was far too big to be commanded by a Commander and suggested that they find themselves a Captain. They spiked my guns on this approach by making me an Acting-Captain.* It was some consolation, but not exactly what I had been aiming for. From time to time thereafter I would ask for relief, and eventually I was told that the Captain of a 'baby' carrier was to take over and I would get to take the carrier home. "Relief at last!", I thought, but it was not to be. This particular Captain did not have a great reputation and the C-in-C refused to accept someone who might destroy the morale of such a large air station. So I had to stay. To be thought so indispensable was comforting, but I was starting to feel caged. No one was sent from England, but eventually the Admiral took pity on me and found a Captain, a good one, to take over. After the war I met a Captain in South Africa who shed a little light on the subject for me. He said that he had been offered command of Kat, but when he made enquiries to Admiralty about the place all they could tell him was that the Captain had a hockey field outside his bungalow, so he asked for another appointment. Such was the knowledge that England had of their largest Naval Air Station.

When eventually I was relieved, after two and a half years, Admiral Moody sent for me and said that he had decided that he would send me on leave to Canada so that I might see Debbie again. He was such an honest man that I had great difficulty in getting him to change my orders to read that I was travelling on duty, so that I could get a little priority. Eventually he agreed, however, and after just four days of travel by DC-3 and the like (spent mostly sleeping on top of mail bags) I arrived in Canada.

Some thirty years later I returned to Katakurunda, this time with Debbie. The airfield was no more, and the

* *For a space of six months the author was the youngest Acting-Captain in the Royal Navy.*

The author with the "Captain's Car", a Packard. Several of these luxury cars, which had originally been intended for some Sheiks, found their way to Kat. after their ship had gone aground.

hangars and the repair yard had also disappeared. The camp was still there though, now being used as Ceylon's Police Training Camp. I introduced myself to the Sergeant on duty at the gate, who shook my hand warmly and provided a young constable to show us around. The camp had been improved; buildings that were once temporary had been made permanent, and two new playing fields had been created. The only major change that I noticed was that the Petty Officer's Mess, which had had a very fine site, had been replaced by a large statue of Buddha and had become their temple. We had tea with the Camp Superintendant and his wife in my old bungalow. He had been a young constable in the nearby town of Kalutara while I had been there and reminded me of a time when he had come to me for assistance in closing down a local brothel. My memory was dim, so I said I hoped that I had been co-operative, and he assured me I had. My hockey field / parade ground was now used as a parade ground only, but the place was in beautiful shape and my heart was very full when we left. Part of me would always be there; when you build and shape a community from almost nothing, how could it be otherwise?

*Sport was a significant part of life at Katukurunda.
The above photos show the soccer team and the Royal
Marines Tug-of-War team. Both teams were Ceylon Champions.*

When the author returned to Ceylon in 1975 he found that RNAS Katukurunda had been converted to a Police Training Camp. He was graciously welcomed by the Police Commandant seen here.

Debbie and son Tony, aged 3.

Reunion, and a New Ship

After more than four years apart Debbie and I met again on the platform of a railway station in New York, and there seemed to be something symbolic in the detachment of such a meeting place. We knew less about one another then than we had when we were married. She had been able to tell me little of her day-to-day life in her letters because she had been working in a munitions office, and I had been in a similar position. Social events, old times and innocuous happenings made up the bulk of our correspondence, and it was fortuitous that we were able to catch up on part of the lost years and get to know one another again before we returned to Montreal to see my son. Tony was at the top of a short flight of stairs when I came through the front door and he launched himself into my arms. It was odd to be presented with a well-grown and active boy when the last memory I had was of a baby who could neither walk nor talk. I had trouble at first in responding to 'Daddy'. The first few times I did not realise that it was I who was being addressed and looked around for some venerable father-figure. Then reality dawned. I was Daddy.

The last part of my leave was spent at the family skiing cottage in the Laurentians, and there one frosty morning there came a letter from the Admiralty saying they had a ship for me. I went to Ottawa where I found Seymour Stead, a former shipmate in *Furious*. He was able to arrange a last-minute flight for me so that my leave could be stretched to the utmost. I made arrangements for Debbie and Tony to follow by sea, sailing from New York to Liverpool aboard *Rangitata*. I was able to meet them on their arrival and whisk them off to Belfast where I had found an apartment in a country house. My new command was an escort (or 'baby') carrier undergoing conversion in the Belfast shipyards, and we would have some time together before she was completed and ready for sea again.

HMS *Trouncer* was being fitted out as the Assault Carrier Flagship for the invasion of Malaya. A single screw vessel of some 15,000 tons (after conversion) she had only 8,000 horse power to drive her along. I found she handled much like a picket boat, except when the wind blew, in which case she was more like a sailing vessel in which the sails were always set and could not be trimmed. A bit of a handful. The conversion included putting in a large operations room, cabins for staff officers, new radio equipment, and Bofors guns on new gun sponsons. The latter were to replace the small calibre Oerlikons and give us better protection against Kamikase bombers.

She was lying at Harland and Wolfe's yard, and my first job was to make an inspection and see what we had to deal with. The living quarters were definitely spartan. The men had bunks and a cafeteria, and a bathroom which consisted of a row of washbasins with a row of toilets behind them -cleverly designed so that while you were shaving or brushing your teeth someone else could be right behind you at their 'devotions'. Nowhere was there any room for either officers or men to gather for the kind of social life which I found to be so much a part of naval seagoing experience. I had a word with the shipbuilders, and they agreed to improve things by creating meeting and reading rooms from the existing living space.

The use of bunks was partly to blame for the shortage of recreational space. The hammock was looked upon as old fashioned but it does have its advantages. Many were the times while I was in destroyers that I would have gladly traded my bunk for a seaman's hammock. When a ship is moving heavily in a rough sea a hammock swings comfortably to maintain its position relative to the vertical, while a bunk moves rigidly with the ship and you have to hang on to the rails for dear life to avoid being pitched onto the deck. Hammocks can be quickly stowed so that sleeping space can double as eating or playing space, an important consideration where space is at such a premium. Hammocks have been known to be used to stop leaks too -the loss of a bed being a small price to pay to save the ship from loss or the crew from a swim.

The staffing of a ship is even more of a headache than the staffing of a shore station, but I was told that I could ask for any particular officers that I wanted. I recruited my Commander (Flying), Tony Ford, during an enforced wait for weather in the Isle of Man, and I found a first class chaplain at the naval air station at Eastleigh. It was VE-night and I was impressed with the way in which the padre kept youthful excess within proper limits during their celebrations. At about two in the morning I put it to Reverend R.A.Lowry that there was a vacancy for him if he cared to go to sea. He was overjoyed at the offer, and we clinched the arrangement over breakfast, squaring it with the Chaplain of the Fleet and filling in the necessary documents later in the day. He proved to be, literally, the best man aboard, capable of solving any problem from drink to homesickness. Naval padres wear no badges of rank, by tradition they bear the rank of the man to whom they are speaking. Lowry was able to get on close terms with young ordinary seamen and redfaced oldsters in a remarkably short time. He was sincere, discreet and a great source of fun.

In May I attended a most interesting Air Co-operation Course held at Old Sarum near Salisbury. It was conducted by a mixed-service staff and was attended by Commanders and Captains, or their equivalents, from all three services. The atmosphere was excellent as we were told how each service could help the other in the field. The only sour note came when Wing Commander Varcoe proceeded to tell us, in no uncertain terms, how Bomber Command was winning the war. The students, all experienced men, were silent. After he had departed our senior instructor, a Group Captain, told us that in future they would not invite Bomber Command to appear but would instead use their own staff to explain how bombers could help. The other speakers were all from overseas commands such as Africa, Egypt and Burma, and their theme was the excellent co-operation which all three services had shown in their theatre of war. They were refreshing to listen to. Remembering past experiences this confirmed my opinion that while rank and file and their commanders would always work together, once you got into the higher brackets instincts of power took over to the detriment of inter-service co-operation and goodwill.

I was fortunate with the Heads of Departments who were sent to join the ship. Jim Hayes, the Commander, and Partridge, the Chief Engineer, were splendid and reliable people, and we were blessed with a well qualified dentist. At one stage there was a prospect that our Admiral-to-be was going to bring two extra staff officers with him, and that our dentist would have to be put back on the quay-side to make room. I came aboard to find 'toothie' almost in tears at losing his chance to go in the ship. He even volunteered to sling a hammock in some corner or other, but I told him not to worry -come Hell or high water he was coming with us. I then got on to Admiralty and made a strong plea to keep him, saying that we would find accommodation. I knew from my pre-war days that a toothache in mid-ocean can be a serious matter, and I was relieved when the Admiralty gave in gracefully.

While we were still fitting-out in Belfast I had the chance to meet Debbie's two brothers again. The eldest, Lieutenant Commander John Stairs, was the Captain of a frigate, and when I knew that he was coming to lunch one day I warned the quarterdeck that my brother-in-law was coming onboard and arranged that he be properly piped aboard. When he arrived he received the salute which, as Captain of his own ship, was his due. When his younger brother, Sub-Lieutenant Bobbie Stairs of M.T.B.'s, made his visit a few days later I gave no special instructions. The Officer of the Watch, however, was taking no chances. As far as he was concerned all brothers-in-law

The author with Commander Jim Hayes on board Trouncer.

must be Captains, and so Bobbie was ceremoniously piped over the side. He was embarassed, but carried off the situation with proper aplomb, returning the courtesies with enormous gravity.

When VJ-day came there was a sense of sadness as well as joy. Everyone had been keyed up to go out and finish the war. They had become a team, and now there was a sudden vacuum. Our VJ celebration party was an affair of mixed emotions, however release was to come. The Admiralty decided that as the ship was designed as a tropical Headquarters vessel with special awnings and extra accomodation it should go east just the same. There was the usual 'working-up' period, which included a trip to Glasgow to load a cargo of aircraft engines. Since it was going to be a long voyage I decided to allow night leave to each watch. I was warned that my trust might be misplaced and that under the circumstances we might lose men to desertion. In the event no-one deserted. Three were late returning, but the sum total of their lateness

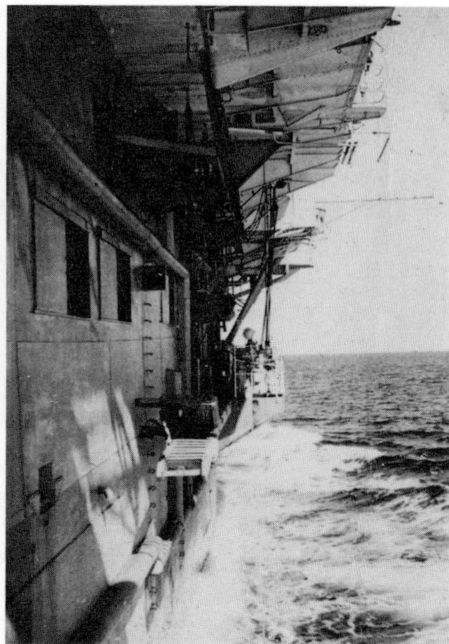

Two shots of Trouncer's bow as she set off on her maiden voyage.

was only an hour and a half. As I leant over the rail as *Trouncer* pushed aside the waters of the Clyde I had the same thought that had come to me in *Iron Duke's* picket boat: you can trust men who trust you. In twenty-one years I had advanced from picket-boat to escort carrier, but the principle of leading men by trust still held true.

H.M.S. Trouncer
at Sea

Trouncer made a brief stop at Gibraltar, which gave us a chance to load some sherry for the Mess. We were there just two nights, during which time the Admiral, Sir Victor Crutchley VC, kindly asked me to join him and his wife for dinner. After we had had dinner the three of us sat before the the fire talking. The Admiral was making a lot of statements with which I strongly disagreed, but just for once, I held my peace. His wife, who was sitting across from me, said, "You don't agree with my husband do you?" I had to admit that she was right, and we all had a laugh about it. It was a pleasant evening.

Our next stop was Malta, and here I had my first ship-handling crisis. We were to berth at the far end of the Grand Harbour and there was a following wind. Tugs had been ordered, but when they arrived it was obvious that someone had taken the term 'baby' carrier too literally. These tugs were so small that they could have been used regularly for little more than hauling the garbage barges out to sea. *Trouncer*, with all her 'sails' set got between the buoys, and I had just worked her into position where we could secure when a gust of wind caught us and we began to drift towards the beach which was a mere 100 yards off. One of our tugs had just succeeded in getting a wire to us, but did not have the

Top: HMS Trouncer berthed in Malta's Grand Harbour in 1945.

Bottom: A view of part of the ancient fortifications of Grand Harbour —something which brought back memories of his first days as a cadet aboard Iron Duke to the author.

Opposite: Divisions on Trouncer's flight deck.

power to hold us. With our single screw and tremendous windage we were in real danger of grounding, and all that came to mind was the well-known parody of the Rules of the Road --"when in danger, when in doubt, wave your arms and run about." Then out of the corner of my eye I caught sight of the ocean-going tug *Roysterer* steaming purposefully out of French Creek. "Yeoman!", "Sir", "See that tug; signal HELP!" The response was immediate. The big tug got her line aboard, gave a tweak and we were up to our buoys. A close run thing.

While we were in Malta I decided that I should arrange for a talk to the Ship's Company like the one given by Charles Savory aboard *Durban*, to warn our young men about the perils of VD. I did not think that our ship's doctor could put it across, so I gave the talk myself by means of a loud speaker on the Flight Deck. I thought that it was unnecessary to include the little white lie about knowing of the horrors first hand, and our subsequent record indicated that I was probably right. At any rate when we left Malta we received a very favourable write up from the Colonel in charge of the Royal Marines Police which said that we were the best behaved ship they had had there for a long time.

It's Really Quite Safe

Our next stop was to be Port Said in Egypt at the entrance to the Suez Canal. I was in my cabin changing uniforms just before we were to enter harbour when suddenly the ship heeled over with full rudder and I was called to the bridge. I rushed up to find that we had reversed course and were headed out to sea at full speed. An emergency signal had been received directing us to go to the aid of a liner that was on fire, and very properly my navigator had turned the ship around immediately, before it got into narrow waters.

Even at full speed it took us a couple of hours before we came in sight of the *Empire Patrol*, which was burning furiously. During our dash to the liner's last reported position we had received further signals which told us that she had 450 Greek evacuees from the Deodecanese Islands on board who were being shipped home. Our boats were swung out, and our aircraft were brought up on deck from the hangar in order to make room for the rescued. Blankets, camp cots, mattresses, clothing and food were made ready for distribution.

The following narrative of the subsequent events of the rescue were written by Reg Notley, my old plantation friend whom I was giving passage back to Ceylon. He wrote:

"On Saturday afternoon, September 29th, at about 1:15pm, HMS *Trouncer* was a few miles off Port Said when instructions were received to proceed as quickly as possible to help the *Empire Patrol*, a ship on fire nearly fifty miles away. The *Trouncer* swung around and was soon doing her best speed. On the way preparations were made to deal with the emergency as information had come through that there were nearly five hundred Greek refugees on board. Boats were got ready, the aircraft in the hangar were brought up on the flight deck, blankets, camp beds, mattresses, clothing, hot drinks and food were all got ready in the hangar to receive any people who might be rescued.

"By about four o'clock the *Trouncer* was at the scene. The *Empire Patrol* was burning furiously and people were seen on the forecastle and the stern. The *Trouncer*'s boats were lowered and were soon picking up many of the

274

Empire Patrol burning fiercly as Trouncer comes to the resue.

passengers who had jumped into the water during the first panic. Strong swimmers from the *Trouncer* had received permission to go into the water to help and there were a very large number taking Carley floats out and collecting people and bringing them to the boats and floats. With so many keen helpers this did not take long and soon the boats were going alongside the *Empire Patrol* and taking people off the stern and stem of the ship, she was like a furnace midships and the fire was spreading rapidly. It was quite apparent that the passengers had to be coaxed to go over the side, and many were let down by ropes as they would not trust themselves to ladders and scrambling nets. The *Trouncer's* boats had a very difficult task as there was a high swell running, a certain amount of broken water and the sides of the ship were very hot. Paint was peeling off in large flakes and in many cases burning as it fell into the sea. One of *Trouncer's* boats with two Carley floats and several swimmers had a most difficult time of taking survivors out of the water where they were being sent overboard by the Chief Officer who was isolated on the forecastle with about fifty passengers. This Chief Officer of the *Empire Patrol* did splendid work with the

Above: Trouncer's bow
was too high and the
sea too rough to permit
the safe transfer of
passengers directly
from ship to ship.
Left: Survivors are
brought on board from
life rafts.
Below: Survivors on
a Carley float.

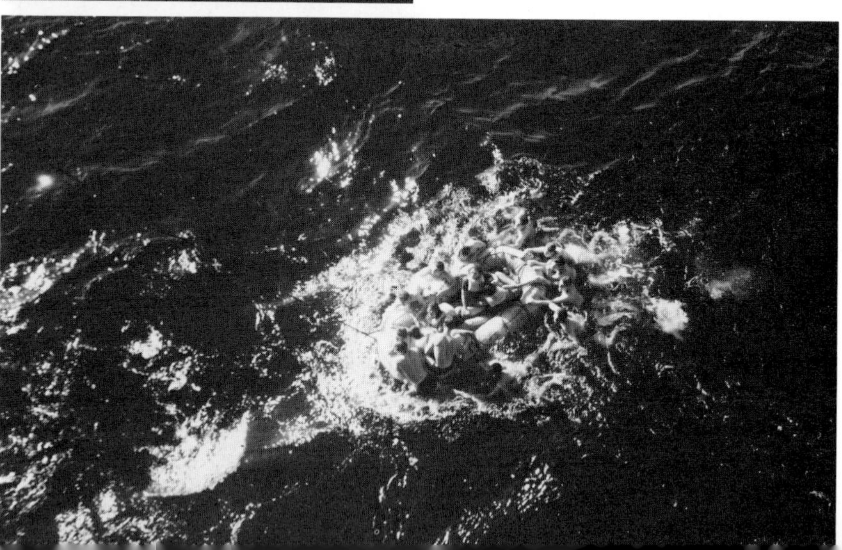

fire gaining on him the whole time. He had to force most of the people overboard and they were picked up quickly by the waiting boat and swimmers. The water was very hot and it was difficult for the boat to get near the sides of the ship.

"On the stern there was more room and the Captain and officers got the passengers over without too much difficulty. First came the babies and children, tied up in cloths and lowered to the boats. I saw several children of about ten years who came down ropes "hand over hand". Many of the women and children came aboard *Trouncer* absolutely dry and this alone indicates an excellent handling of the boats in a heavy swell and a breaking sea. An attempt was made to accelerate the taking off of passengers so that more searching could be done in daylight. The *Trouncer's* bow was laid alongside the stern of the *Empire Patrol* but the heavy swell and the height of *Trouncer's* forecastle made it apparent that the method of removing passengers by boat could not be improved upon.

"The Captain was the last to leave the *Empire Patrol* and before he left the portholes in the stern were showing the fire raging beneath the deck. The fire broke through the deck a few minutes after the Captain left. It was now dark and the *Trouncer* used searchlights to locate survivors who were in the sea. An aircraft had been giving positions of boats and rafts which were then picked up. The search went on during the night and the next morning. One woman was picked up after she had, with a lifebelt, been in the water for at least twenty-four hours.

"I am a civilian travelling in the *Trouncer* and it appeared to me that my observations might be of interest as they are from an entirely different angle from the official reports. Many points may be inaccurate but the following are things which struck me most forcibly:

"An aircraft carrier seems to be the most unsuitable type of craft that could be deployed on the work of taking passengers and crew from a blazing ship. Throughout the whole operation the handling of the *Trouncer* can only be described as magnificent, it seemed that not only the personnel but the ship herself entered into the spirit of the job. I consider Captain Rotherham's handling of the ship and personal direction of such a difficult task is beyond praise.

"From the Commander to the most junior rating there was a wonderful example of teamwork and complete understanding. To one who has worked very large labour forces for the last twenty-five years this was most outstanding, especially as I understand that the *Trouncer* is on her first voyage since being commissioned.

"The swimmers who spent hours in the water, the crews handling boats and their officers could not have done better if they had been practicing for many months.

"When the survivors arrived they were taken charge of by sailors who were off duty at the time and it was a moving sight to see how they looked after the aged women and comforted them. There seemed to be keen competition to look after the babies and children. The injured were dealt with most promptly by the medical officers and their staff.

"The arrangements made for receiving the unknown number of survivors and providing them with beds, clothing and food worked so smoothly that one would think that it was almost a usual occurence to have 420 passengers put on board with only three hours warning.

"The *Trouncer* saved 420 people from horrible deaths --this could not have been done without the utmost efficiency and skill on everyone's part. I consider that I have been privileged to have been able to see the British Navy doing such a magnificent piece of work.

(signed) R.C.L Notley, October 2nd,1945.

All this went on without my exhortation or direction after my agreement with Heads of Departments as to what had to be done, made before we reached *Empire Patrol*, bar occasional discussions. During this time I never left the Bridge save to go to the fore end of the Flight Deck from where I conned the ship while laying her bows alongside *Empire Patrol*.

Towards the end of the operation we were joined by a 10,000 ton cruiser commanded by Gerald Langley. He was far senior to me, so I considered his asking me what I

Top: A passenger in the water about to be picked up by Trouncer.

Bottom: Rescued passengers are made comfortable on Trouncer's hangar deck.

wanted to do upon his arrival, and later signalling that I should complete the report (a privilege reserved for the senior officer present) as it was my show, to be a kindness not all would have shown. After the rescue work was complete we closed his ship to take onboard a few that he had picked up, lying across his stern while a boat made the transfer. A small (1,000 ton) sloop was lying alongside the cruiser, and it shoved off and started to go astern without looking. When her Captain looked around and saw us in the way for the first time he grabbed his loud hailer and called "Get out of my way!" Quite a request for them to make of a ship of 15,000 tons with just 8,000 horsepower! I was tired and told my Yeoman to make rather a rude signal, then changed my mind and said,"Don't make that." "No, Sir," came the reply, "I didn't think you would." So we made a more polite one. "What do you think I have? Four wheel brakes and a supercharger?" He went away chastened, I hope.

Of the 450 souls on board *Empire Patrol* we lost only 30. When I had first seen her I did not expect that we would do nearly that well so I was very happy. I was also extremely proud of my crew, many of whom were on their very first voyage. They had responded magnificently to a real emergency and I could not have been more pleased.

We returned to Port Said with the survivors, and there I had to complete a report and have dinner with the senior officer ashore to fill him in on the events. By the time I crawled into my bunk I had been on the go for 42 hours. It had been a long day.

The next day we continued our journey, passing through the Suez Canal. We stopped in Cochin in southern India to disembark some unwanted aircraft and engines, and then

went on to Colombo. We stayed there for a week, during which time I went down to Kat for curry lunch and to have a look around the place again.

Then unexpectedly we were ordered to return home by way of Durban and Capetown. For the trip to Durban we were given a few passengers. There was also a Wren officer who wanted a trip home, but she was told she could not travel alone with all those lecherous sailors. I commented that I could keep any eye on one, but not on thirty. Little did I know that I would have thirty Wrens on board when we left Capetown!

One of our passengers was a tough young South African. He had been captured by the Japanese and had worked on the Burma Railway. I asked him briefly if he wanted to comment on his experience as a prisoner of the Japanese and all he said was, "If you had a sense of humour you lived, if you hadn't you died."

When we were a short distance from Durban, steaming

Opposite: The Suez Canal.

Below: Equator crossing ceremonies on board Trouncer -King Neptune and his court arrive on the aircraft lift.

Equator crossing ceremonies on Navy ships were often elaborate productions; Trouncer's were no exception.

into a head sea, *Trouncer* dropped heavily into a breaking rogue wave. The forward end of the flight deck was bent and the catapult was rendered inoperable. My thoughts were black. Was it my fault? Should I not have slowed the ship down and made Durban the following day? Captains have these agonies of self-doubt when things go wrong, perhaps that is why so many go down with their ships. I will always be grateful for the intervention of Tony Ford at this juncture. He came up to the bridge, and for the next fifteen minutes quite deliberately engaged me in a fairly banal conversation. I knew that his purpose was to convey sympathy by presence, and I thanked him for coming up. Of course I never found out whether this was just a spontaneous gesture by an old shipmate, or whether he had drawn the short straw in the Wardroom for the role of Captain's comforter!

Because of the damage we had to stay longer than planned at Durban to effect repairs. I was amazed at the overwhelming hospitality we received. The war was over, but the town still hung out the welcome mat for servicemen. Their leave committee came on board as soon as they heard that our stay would be prolonged and asked whether we would grant leave, and if so, to how many. They also wanted to know how many men would like to go to the country and how many to the city. We gave them the numbers (400 each watch), and by the next morning it was all arranged. When we left we saw that the "Lady in White" who sang to departing ships from the breakwater with a megaphone was still in business. I sent her a personal message of thanks in case we might be one of the last RN ships to call there.

At Capetown we took on a very mixed bag of personnel and cargo. There were 300 men, 30 Wrens, some boxed aircraft, several hundred tons of raisins and Christmas puddings, and three million pounds (sterling) worth of gold. Stowing the cargo took a little planning. It was arranged that the men would be housed in the hangar, the Wrens would be put in a cabin flat, and the raisins and puddings would go in the lower hold. The boxed aircraft we put on the flight deck to edge the hockey field, and the gold was stowed in an upper deck magazine. Jim Hayes and I brought out our slide-rules and from our combined calculations we determined *Trouncer* to be seaworthy. As one of the Port Authorities jokingly remarked, however, it was lucky that warships did not carry Plimsol marks!

The arrival of the gold was occasion for some small drama. We had been asked to arrange for an armed guard on the jetty when the gold arrived, with the qualification that it be 'unobtrusive.' I racked my brains for a scheme whereby armed men could be unobtrusively hanging around a jetty in broad daylight, eventually coming up with the idea of having the sailors smarten up their rifle drill. Then the gold convoy arrived -trucks surrounded by armoured cars and motor cycles. The sailors, with bayonets fixed, formed a ring of steel around the precious cargo while it was hoisted onboard. Once it was in the magazine I ordered the door welded shut, and for good measure put a 24 hour guard on it.

On our way home we were instructed to call at St.Helena. Apparently they had not had a supply ship for three months and the islanders were getting short of food, particularly meat. We gladly landed what could be spared and were requested to give passage home to some men whose leave was long overdue. Despite the fact that we were very crowded I had made up my mind to take them until the news filtered through that there had been an outbreak of polio just before our arrival. I asked the doctor whether there was any risk of bringing the disease on board, and he admitted that it was a possibility. In view of our crowded conditions I decided, reluctantly, that we could not accept the risk and so we sailed on without those men who had no doubt been looking forward to spending Christmas at home. St.Helena was a forbidding place. Its high cliffs and swooping seabirds gave it an air of desolation, and I even felt a twinge of sympathy for Napoleon who had spent the last six years of his life in exile there.

After leaving St.Helena we set course for Freetown. We were scheduled to make landfall at dawn on a coast that had no adequate shore lights nor even lighted buoys. We consulted the "Pilot", that wonderful book which tells you all about a coast, its dangers, the currents etc. It said that very occasionally there was a set towards the east at a high rate. Since there were dangers to the east I decided to allow for the maximum known current. It was just as well, for we experienced just this set and arrived accurately off the harbour. Provide for the worst and you will keep out of serious trouble.

When we had docked at Glasgow the unloading of the gold turned out to be a real anticlimax. A man in a black coat and striped trousers came aboard and produced a letter of introduction from the Bank of England. He arranged to come back in the evening when the sealed door had been breached, and said that he would have two trucks waiting at quayside. He asked if I would provide a Petty Officer as escort if he could not get a policeman to go with the gold to the station. I felt that my responsibilities were at an end, and that I shouldn't have to put this burden on one of my Petty Officers, so I refused. Fortunately he got his policeman and off they went. What a contrast to Capetown!

While we were at Glasgow I had planned to take a day or two's leave to go to Somerset to see Debbie. She was expecting our second child in February. *Trouncer* was to be moved to a different berth, but it was to be accomplished with the use of tugs and without raising steam, so I saw no great need of my presence. Admiral Jaggers Troup had other ideas. He called me in and asked whether it was my intention to go on leave while my ship was being moved. I pointed out that we would not be raising steam so there would be nothing that I could do whether I was there or not. He was not moved and told me bluntly that if the ship were damaged in any way during this move he would personally see to it that I was Court Martialled. Naturally enough I stayed on board. Later on we moved the ship down to "The Tail of the Bank" at Greenock, and while we were there we had to make yet another move up to Faslane for oil, so again there seemed to be no chance for leave. This time, however, I was sent for by another Admiral, Rear Admiral H.E.Horan DSC. He asked me why I had not put in for a few days leave, as he knew that I had not had any. I told him about our move to Faslane, actually a little tricky, and his response was to ask if I could not trust my Commander. Of course I could trust him, after all he had commanded a destroyer. So the Admiral told me to go on leave and give my Commander a chance. Something tells me that he had heard about my little run in with Troup.

Troup's sort of attitude was quite prevalent. There were a lot of senior officers who thought that the Captain had to be there at all times just in case something happened. In *Formidable* our Captain slept in an armchair on the bridge each night that we were at sea. Would he have been in a fit state of mind to take immediate action in the event of danger? Could he not trust his Officer of the Watch? Is it not better to give one's Second in Command a chance to find out about handling the ship when the situation is relaxed instead of waiting until the Captain goes sick when he may be catapulted into a difficult situation without adequate training? In retrospect I do not think that I gave my Commander enough chance to learn how to handle *Trouncer*, a temperamental vessel. I once heard of a Captain of a carrier who was visited at sea by his Admiral who flew in with the Captain's relief.

It's Really Quite Safe

The Admiral said that he had come to the conclusion that the endurance of the carrier was the endurance of the Captain. He would not delegate authority, so he had to be removed. The Admiral flew ashore taking the old Captain with him.

The military machine that had been set up to combat Germany and Japan was now being dismantled with some speed, and *Trouncer* was employed in the ignominious business of dumping surplus aircraft at sea. These were brand new American aircraft, but the United States didn't want them back, there were just too many of them. It seemed like a dreadful waste, but worse was to come. *Trouncer* was also of American origin, and as she lay at the Tail of the Bank off Greenock discussions were held as to what should, or should not, be taken out of her before she was returned to her builders. When I heard how little was to be removed, when so much was British I protested. The reply was that there was no more room in the Store Houses. We had cabins full of furniture, including the Admiral's. I was asked whether I would like it. Would I indeed? So Naval Stores very kindly sent it south for me by rail. We broadcast round the ship for anyone who would like a radio or anything else we had to dispose of, and anything which might be dutiable such as our Wardroom's wine stock was allowed through Customs at minimum duty. I was curious as to why they were being so co-operative and they explained that we were doing a job for our country and they just wanted to help.

One of the Customs men told me that they hated to charge people who had crossed the Atlantic on duty and had returned with small dutiable items, but that they had to be extremely careful or some twit might enquire of the authourities whether it was all right that they had not been charged and then the poor customs officer would be in for the high jump. "Once Lady 'Alifax comes back with 'er 'usband," he elaborated, "and she brings back a pair of shoes for the Queen. Now, I can't charge the Queen for a pair of shoes, but I was worried that she might own up in London, and then I would get into trouble". Whatever you may think of them when you try to smuggle, Customs men are just as human as the rest of us.

Next we were sent to Trinidad to load aircraft for return to the U.S.Navy at Norfolk. Here I met up with my old friend Inspector Ogier who years before had led me round some of the local dives. Now he was Chief of Police, and I invited him aboard for a drink. He insisted that I come to his office instead. There he explained that there had been an upsurge in violence in Trinidad, almost amounting to revolution, but that the Police were a jump ahead of the trouble makers. He told me that he and a colleague had met one of the ringleaders at a party and had managed to get him drunk, (something Ogier was quite capable of). The man became so drunk that he boasted of their plans, after which they continued to ply him with drink until he had forgotten what he had said. It was a change to hear of such a humane way of interrogating a suspect. Anyone who knew this friendly Channel Islander would have expected nothing different.

Enroute to Norfolk we stopped at Bermuda to pick up some more aircraft. We were the largest ship ever to berth in this awkward little harbour, and we did so without the aid of tugs. Luckily there was little wind and what there was we could use to our advantage. Nevertheless I told the port Captain that I would not leave until he could give me another day with just such a favourable wind.

Shortly after we arrived at Norfolk to give *Trouncer* back to the U.S. Navy and pay off, I received a cable telling me of the birth of our second son, Gib (Gilbert) and that all was well. The day before we dispersed a Supply Rating came to me and told me that he had come to collect my binoculars which, he said, were on loan from the U.S. I thought that Uncle Sam could afford to lose one pair, so I told him that they could not be found. I heard no more about it. I have them to this day; they are very good ones, wonderful for bird watching. Then I left my one and only sea command to return to England (via Montreal) to my family. *Trouncer* was cranky, under-powered, and sluggish, and sometimes almost un-manageable, but she was all mine, and had been since conversion to a carrier Flagship a year before.

HMS Trouncer's first voyage.

Canada

When I returned to London, Seymour Stead, who was now on the staff of Canada House, told me of a job coming up in Ottawa as the Deputy Director of Naval Aviation. The Canadian Fleet Air Arm was a new force and they had no senior naval aviators. I was told that as soon as I got settled in I would take over as Director, and therefore should retain my rank as Acting Captain. As Debbie was a Canadian I found this move most attractive, so I told Stead that I was available. In due course they asked for me and I was appointed. At first sight this appointment appeared to be a plum and a sure road to advancement. I had not reckoned on the fact that recommendations from a Royal Navy Admiral or Captain would far outweigh those from the heads of a foreign or sister service, big or small, regardless of its contribution to the Battle of the Atlantic. As far as the R.N. was concerned I was in a backwater. It was fortunate for me that I knew many Canadian Naval Officers and liked their way of life. I was particularly fortunate when Admiral Grant, a man I knew and admired as a leader, became the Chief of Naval Staff. Any difficulties or differences I had were of a professional, not personal, nature, and this was confirmed by our decision to stay in Canada and start a new career later.

It's Really Quite Safe

I arrived in Ottawa in June, 1946 and was horrified to discover that Canada had fallen into the same trap as England had after the First World War. The RCAF were providing all of the shore accomodation and storekeeping facilities for Naval Aircraft at Halifax, under RCAF command. I protested this arrangement at a Staff meeting, pointing out that we had tried this in the U.K. and found it most impractical, to say the least. I was told that they knew about that, but that even if we weren't able to make it work in England they could in Canada. This I doubted, so I set myself the task of getting the Air Station at Halifax transferred to the Navy. It was not long before a number of incidents showed that I was right: when money is short it invariably goes to the controlling service. I began keeping a scrap book in which I recorded everything that went wrong because of split resonsibility. It included pictures of wings lying on a cement floor instead of being in a proper rack, and many other affairs. Eventually the RCN came to the same conclusion and wanted to take over, so I took my scrap book to Admiral Grant. He took the matter up with the Minister of National Defence, the RCAF gave in, and the station was turned over to the Navy.

The effect of the war on the Canadian Navy was traumatic. Before the war it had been a tiny service and it had expanded rapidly to become a major force without which the Battle of the Atlantic could not have been won. One of the results of this rapid expansion was that almost all of the pre-war permanent force officers, regardless of their efficiency, had gone to the top. Some, I believe, went far too high for their capabilities, and they blocked the promotion of many of the wartime officers, most of whom were not asked to stay on in peacetime. In the Fleet Air Arm there were no pre-war officers, and I could see that we were going to be left with no experienced pilots and observers if they all returned to civilian life at the end of their short service commissions. I was worried, and went to the Chief of Personnel to explain my concern. I thought that we should be going after the men that we wanted as Permanent Force Officers. His reply was most abrupt -to the effect that if these officers didn't ask to stay on then they weren't wanted. I was sure that without some encouragement to stay the more ambitious men would go off to greener fields, leaving the Navy with just run of the mill aircrew. I thought this to be rather short sighted, so when I visited a base in England where squadrons were training before joining our carrier I talked to the squadron commanders and told them that if they had what it takes and were interested in long service there could be a good career ahead of them in Canada. One or two did apply, so we at least had them to carry on the good work. War experience is so vital, and so easily lost if there is not someone in reasonably high quarters to carry the torch.

Recruiting was difficult in the years immediately following the war, and as far as I was concerned the unattractive uniform was a large part of the problem. The Canadian Government did not want money to be wasted on dress uniforms which would not be needed in battle, a foolish economy which did much to undermine morale. I was talking to a couple of younger officers who had been in the army before the war. They had just been to a wedding togther and had worn their outdated Regimental uniforms. Several other young men at the wedding had been attracted by the uniforms and expressed interest in joining the regiment. The attraction was the uniform -there can be few more potent builders of morale than being able to push your chest out and feel proud of your unit in a smart uniform.

Another foolish economy was the cancellation of long range cruises by RCN ships. *Uganda* had been sent on a cruise round South America and eulogistic reports extolling the wonderful effects of these visits on trade had come in from Consuls, Trade Representatives, etc. I saw some of these reports and they reminded me of the farewell speech we had been given on our visit to Rosario. There was also a report of our sailors having a good time, and the immediate reaction, (straight from Mackenzie King I believe), was that there were to be no more such cruises. Canada had better things to do with its money than to send its sailors off to exotic spots to have a good time. At the same time the custom of allowing Commanding officers an allowance for the entertainment of visiting dignitaries, senior officers and the like was stopped. All entertainment costs had to be fully justified and documented. This created a possible small cash saving, a huge amount of paperwork, and a loss of morale.

One summer the cruiser Sheffield came into Canadian waters, and following the custom of years past they were asked if they would take some personnel for training. They of course agreed and some University Cadets were sent. Then despite all of the similar pre-war experience someone started to worry about how these cadets would react to the "strict" discipline of an RN cruiser, and they were all required to submit reports on their experiences. I was delighted by one of these -the cadet wrote that he had enjoyed himself and learnt a lot, but that what had really impressed him was that hardly any orders were given, only requests. I chuckled, this is normal for RN ships. Orders are reserved for emergencies because it makes for a friendlier atmosphere. Of course God help the little bastard that does not comply with such a 'request'!

To my distress I discovered that while I was in Ottawa the Royal Navy decided that the Fighter Direction Branch and the Navigation Branch should be joined together. I was dismayed because I could see no similarity in the work of these two branches. The Navigator has to be a calculating and cautious man concerned with the safety of the ship whatever the wind or unforseen currents may do. The Fighter Direction Officer works in an ops room where his fighters and the enemy aircraft they must intercept are displayed on a fluorescent screen. His charges move at hundreds of miles an hour, and decisions have to be made in split seconds. I could not understand why anyone would want to marry these two seemingly incompatible specializations, unless someone was empire building. It seemed to me that the Observer Branch, which was itself in immediate danger would have been a more suitable bedmate for the Fighter Direction Branch. I brought this up at the weekly staff meeting, but since the head of the Staff Meeting turned out to be a Navigator my suggestion fell on stony ground indeed. I had a little more success in my efforts to keep the Observers Branch alive after the R.N. decided to follow the RAF idea that the pilot could do everything. I fought this move tooth and nail, arguing that a brain was needed in the back seat in order to develop the use of the highly technical electronic equipment being installed. I won, and we set up our own Observers' School, and the RN reinstated the Observer Branch a year later. Unfortunately this experience did not prevent the RCN from abolishing the Observers after I and my successor had gone.

During these battles I visited the Naval Air Station at Shearwater and watched an air display. That evening the wife of one of my friends asked if I had heard a remark made by someone standing behind us, "That fellow Rotherham would crucify himself for a cause." Perhaps I did. It was so easy if you were competent, or sometimes even if you were not, to gain advancement by "kissing the ass" of your Seniors. That way, however, the cause of efficiency, particularly in war, was prejudiced to the extent that lives and battles could be lost. It could not be my way. Fighting for the development, or even for the existence, of a new and modern technique of war against the prejudices of the proponents of entrenched methods is never easy, no matter how obvious it may appear that it is the weapon of the future. I was encouraged to find that the RCN were not nearly as hidebound as some of the more senior specialists of the RN, particularly those of the Gunnery Branch. Being a smaller service, however, they were understandably prone to adopt the advice of their larger contemporaries.

It had been arranged for the RCN to acquire some Hawker Sea Furys, the latest word in propellor driven shipboard fighters, as a lead up to jet fighters. They cost a good deal of money, and when there came one of those apparently inevitable delays in production the U.S.Navy offered us some surplus Hellcats. This was a good aircraft, but not a patch on the Sea Fury. It was an attractive offer, but I thought it would be a retrograde step for our small but efficient Air Arm. I hurredly wrote to Admiral Matthew Slattery, in charge of the supply of R.N. aircraft telling him of the danger of the contract being lost. Luckily he was an old friend and he lost no time in arranging for enough aircraft and spares to be diverted from delivery to the RN to form a squadron for us. The Sea Fury then developed some troubles with its Bristol Centaurus engines and I had to go over to the U.K. to sort things out. The engine manufacturers convinced me that they had cured the problem and I was able to return to Canada satisfied that my initial faith in the aircraft was sound. During my investigations one of the Test Pilots told me that he had proof of the rugged strength of this aircraft, for when he had had to force land one in Windsor Great Park he had knocked down several oak trees with it. With a twinkle in his eye he added that they were not the usual 500 year old trees, but some recently planted replacements.

When New York's Idlewild Airport (now J.F.K. International) was to be opened it was arranged for an aerobatic team of R.N. aircraft to participate in the official ceremonies. 400 Squadron was shipped across to Shearwater with two Sea Hornets, two Sea Furys and a Vampire, and here they reassembled their aircraft and practiced for the display. The Sea Hornet's pet trick, flown by Lt.Cdr. Fisher, was to do a loop, starting from low level and shutting off one engine and then the other as he climbed through the loop and restarting them on the way down. His announcer at Idlewild gave a blow by blow description of this, saying, "Now he is shutting off one engine...and now the other...you see, it saves petrol". I obtained permission for the team to come to Ottawa and they put on a terrific performance over the Ottawa River off the Rockliffe Heights. I felt that the Navy had scored one up over the RCAF even if we had had to use the RN to do it. At that time the RCAF had no aircraft that could even come close. The pilots came to our house for a party that evening and were a delightful team. It came as a great shock when, a few days later while they were waiting for embarkation at Halifax, Fisher came out of the clouds in his Hornet and went straight into the sea. We never found out why, he had not been doing anything 'clever' at the time. He had served with me in *Trouncer*, and I had found him to be a brilliant pilot, a good officer, and a very nice man.

One incident which occurred while I was in Ottawa

could have had a similarly tragic ending, but fortunately ended happily with amusing overtones. Soon after we arrived we made friends with Captain Jack Raby, the US Naval Attaché, and subsequently with his relief, Captain Ben Custer. One day Ben decided to fly to Churchill (in northern Manitoba on the shore of Hudson's Bay), and he asked his good friend Captain Sir Robert Stirling-Hamilton, the RN Representative on the British High Commissioner's staff, if he would care to join him. On the return flight something went wrong and they had to make a forced landing hundreds of miles from anywhere. For a week they were lost, and the Diplomatic Corps was in a tizzy. To start with they had broken all the rules in the book: they did not have proper survival equipment; and then, despite the fact that they were an impossible distance from any settlement and knowing full well that every possible aircraft would be out looking for them, they left the aircraft (the only thing likely to be spotted from the air) and started to walk. God only knows where they thought they might get to. Miraculously they found a deserted trapper's cabin and soon after they were seen by a search aircraft and recovered. Perhaps it was the US Army Air Force Sergeant who was with them that had most to do with their rescue. He was deeply religious and prayed continually for their rescue. When you break ALL the rules you need some help from "Above".

Two Sea Furys and two Sea Hornets over Niagara Falls.
This Royal Navy aerobatic team came to North America
to participate in the opeining of New York's Idlewild
airport and put on displays at several locations in Canada.

It's Really Quite Safe

After all had ended well we found to our joy and delight that Ben had written articles for the US Naval Air Publication over the signature of Gran' Paw Pettibone. These were about the misadventures of errant young naval pilots, criticizing their actions and giving advice on what they should have done. I often wonder whether this last escapade of his was ever published and commented upon by some later Gran' Paw Pettibone. As he was no longer a young pilot he probably escaped criticism.

In 1948 the new Minister of Defence, Brooke Claxton, took over his office in the 'temporary wartime buildings' which housed National Defence Headquarters. (These temporary buildings were finally torn down in 1982.) He did not find his office sufficiently elegant, so he sent for Harold Beament, the well known war artist, and asked for his advice on a colour scheme. Harold, an old friend of mine from Durban days, told me over a gin at the Mess that he was absolutely furious about this "insult". He was an artist he insisted, not some damn house painter! I was able to laugh him out of his anger, and as I also knew Brooke Claxton I was glad to be able to act as a buffer between the two. However, I don't think Brooke Claxton ever got any advice on his decor.

I found what I thought to be sound thinking among the RCAF; they were certainly not nearly as dogmatic and domineering about their ideas as the RAF. I was pleased to find that Air Commodore Claire Annis, with whom I frequently shared a drink, thought that there was a clear case for Officer Observers in aircraft, and that they should also take their place within the command structure. Altogether I found that there were many people with whom I was able to discuss methods and tactical needs, and I hope that my contribution was as valuable to them as I found their ideas were to me.

In December 1947 my last chance for promotion to Captain came up and I was duly passed over, and so my hopes of any future rewarding service with the navy came to an end. I had thought that with five years of apparently successful service as an Acting Captain, and having been loaned to the Canadian Navy as a Captain in an extremely responsible position that I stood an excellent chance of being promoted, if for no other reason than for the Admiralty to demonstrate to the RCN that they had sent them one of their best. I was not alone, every single officer loaned to the RCN in the capacity of expert advisor was later passed over, something which I found very strange. War is a great leveller but as far as I was concerned it ended a year too early.

My relief, Captain Lentaigne, also FAA of course, knew of my great interest in High Bombing and so told me of the job he had just come from. He had been in charge of testing our bombs against a captured German cruiser. Equipped with tail fuses, these bombs were timed to explode some 40 feet after passing through an armoured deck so that they would detonate right in the vitals of the ship. He told me that the tests had revealed two defects. The first was that often the effect of the bomb being 'squeezed' as it passed through the deck armour would literally squeeze out the fuse. It would be left on deck and the bomb would not explode. The second defect caused the bomb to explode on impact in spite of the supposed time delay. The reason for this was attributed to insufficient delay having been built in as a direct result of the inaccuracies of the methods used to establish the actual delay needed in the first place. Before the war bombs and their fuses had been tested by firing them from a gun at an armoured plate at very close range. Subsequent investigation revealed that during acceleration in the gun the striker mechanism in the fuse would be driven to its rearward extreme and therefore would take longer (here we are measuring in thousandths of a second of course), to come forward and exlode the bomb on impact. This gave an entirely false impression of the time delay, for in a bomb falling from an aircraft the striker would naturally rest in its full forward position. What a pity that no one thought to test our bombs in realistic conditions **before** the war. How many brave lives were lost dropping these bombs to no avail, and how many German ships lived to fight another day and inflict even greater casualties.

Now my concern was to get out of the Navy when my term in Canada was complete, and to find an occupation outside the service which would fulfil my needs both mentally and financially. As it seemed that there were far more opportunities for a retired officer in Canada than in overpopulated England Debbie and I decided that we would seek our fortune here. This decision was helped by the fact that I had actually been longer in Canada than any other country including England since 1924 when I went to sea, and that my previous longest stay was in Ceylon. I also had many friends in Canada by this time, whereas in England I had very few outside the service. As my tour in Canada came towards its end I was warned that there was a shortage of Observers in the navy and that I might have a great deal of trouble getting out, so I pulled out all the stops. I got Brooke Claxton, who had been my late father-in-law's partner, to write to his counterpart, the First Lord of the Admiralty, while I appealed personally to Admiral Harcourt, (Director of the Operations Division in 1940), who was at this time in charge of all officer appointments. I told him that I did not think that I could bear reverting to Commander after five years of service as a Captain. Eventually all was well and I was retired with the War Service Rank of Captain.

After retirement I emigrated officially, joining the retired list of the RCN, and the Naval Officers Association. When I went to the Naval Reserve Division in Toronto to be inducted I was asked to swear allegiance to the Queen, something which I had never been asked to do before. Unlike the British Army and Royal Air Force, the Royal Navy is the King or Queen's Navy and they are not sworn men. I was surprised, but quite content, to find that the RCN do swear allegiance.

I was honoured when the Association sent me as a representative to the Defence Conference in Ottawa where experienced men with war service records discussed the interests of their services. At one of these meetings which was on Naval Affairs only we pressed for a second aircraft carrier. The Minister of National Defence said at the end of the meeting that soon we would be lucky to have even one. There was a hush, and the Minister was about to leave when one of our back benchers spoke up. "Sir, you can't do that, you will be breaking up the team." The back-bencher had of course spent the war years protecting convoys and hunting submarines. Brooke Claxton sat down again and stayed a half an hour longer while we told him how ships and aircraft worked together against submarines and surface ships, how they must know each other, serve together, have the same interests at heart and be able to discuss their work over a drink more often than in the solemnity of a Conference Room. There you usually have to pull your punches lest you offend some senior officer with preconceived ideas. The Navy kept their carrier.

There was one very amusing moment during a tri-service meeting which was a wind up affair at the end of general discussions. The RCAF opened with the following resolution:

> 'As the RCAF is the most important of the
> three Services it is proposed that priority in
> Defence Funds should go to that Service.'

We were all rather taken aback and a deep silence ensued. Then Billy Bishop, the First World War Fighter Ace and a VC winner, bless him, saved the day. He said quietly, "Don't you think that is a bit too much to ask these fellows to swallow?", and we went on to other things.

It is probably fortunate that I was not at NDHQ when Paul Hellyer was planning to unify the services as I would undoubtedly have qualified myself for immediate dismissal from the service (if not crucifixion) as happened to some of my friends. The Navy's reaction at the time is well known. Several senior officers were obliged to retire because of their outspoken opposition, but surely it was their duty to represent their misgivings. The thought seemed to have been that by combining the services there would be a saving of manpower, but there was little consideration given to pride of service or tradition. As to savings of manpower there are very few who are capable of being expert in one job, so how they could be expected to be efficient at two or more is hard to see. And putting them all in green uniforms made them strangers to their colleagues in other countries. It might seem that doctors could be interchangeable, but the problems found aboard ship are quite different than those found when flying.

It's Really Quite Safe

It was not just the senior officers who were opposed -the feeling went right through the Navy to the extent that years afterwards when I went to dinner at the Naval Reserve Division of Montreal, HMCS *Donnacona*, I found every one of the young Reserve Officers to be wearing navy blue Mess kits, having purchased their own. It is from such men, and retired naval personnel and their friends that funds have been raised to purchase uniforms, instruments and regalia to outfit the naval 'Bands in Blue' which are now forming across the country. It is heart warming to get copies of Reserve Officers' quarterly publications keeping us up to date with naval thought, and this continued interest runs right across this vast country from sea to sea. Naval traditions are alive and well in Canada.

After retirement and probably as some recompense for my services in Ottawa and afterwards for the Naval Officers Association I was grateful to receive the Coronation Medal, awarded by Ottawa.

Epilogue

After retiring I tried working for large aircraft companies, but found that coming into the civilian world late in life and being set in my ways, I was unsuited for such employment, as indeed I think would be most retiring officers. In 1955 we settled in Knowlton, a residential holiday resort some 60 miles south east of Montreal. Here I worked for myself, buying a hardware store, and later getting into real estate. I found that as long as you had some grey matter and initiative you could do well in small business, and as the training of a Naval Officer led one to mix with the locals and work with them towards the betterment of the community, such involvement made the earning of a good living easier and more pleasant. Now at what should be a firm retiring age of seventy-eight I find myself still fully employed, not for financial gain, as I have made enough to support us, but for Community projects.

I have been asked if I have any regrets. Yes, but only small ones. I would have liked to have played hockey for England; I would liked to have been at the Battle of the River Plate in *Apollo*, she was so battle efficient as to have been in her element in a situation such as that though she had been paid off long before; and of course I was bitterly disappointed at not being promoted to

Captain. Perhaps my greatest regret, however, was that I was unable to take a more offensive part in the war, within the FAA, and make use of the skills which I had developed in peace time. However, surely the Admiralty was in a box -the FAA only became a real part of the Navy in 1939. It was small -senior expert officers were desperately needed to guide the vast expansion for war - and also expertise was needed to lead and direct offensive operations. I fell between the conflicting needs -it was lovely to be promoted to Commander so young, and again to Acting Captain for five years - but then I could not use my skills personally -and how I would have liked to lead the Swordfish into Trondheim that dreadful day when the concept of the attack was so misguided. Perhaps I was of more value to my country as a director of affairs, but as to my own satisfaction I have doubts. However, my being passed over for promotion made me get out of the navy and prove that I could do it again in private life. So I really find that I would have changed very little. Naval life between the wars was grand, you had little money but you had a wonderful life among fine people. You worked hard and you played hard. Seeing how well I did in the short time that I was on my own in the Real Estate business I think that I could probably have made a great deal of money in civilian life if I had started earlier, although I would not have traded my life in the Navy for this reason. Canada has been kind to me and it has been a good place to bring up our four children.

Acknowledgments

I would be the first to acknowledge the debt I owe to that eminent Naval Historian, the late Captain Stephen Roskill R.N., who insisted on a copy of my early manuscript being sent to Churchill College, Cambridge, for their Archives, and who encouraged me to get my memoirs published, writing a foreword for me, as he said that I had told of so many things that no one else knew; and coupled with him, Mr. Corelli Barnett of Churchill College who wrote to me, "We shall indeed be very grateful to have your memoirs in the Archives Centre where they will constitute an important addition to our coverage of Naval History." I should add that a copy of the manuscript was also demanded by the Public Archives in Ottawa.

Two others who helped me greatly were Captain Godfrey French R.N. who wrote for me the story of the planning for the Dakar Expedition, and Reg Notley, one of my best planter friends of Ceylon who with others helped me so much there, and who wrote the account of the *Empire Patrol* rescue work. I had given him passage back to Ceylon after leave in England.

I also acknowledge the encouragement and advice of Admiral Sir Conolly Abel-Smith, Air Marshal Tony

Dudgeon, Duncan Hamilton, and the Fleet Air Arm Museum where captain Dennis White and his secretary, Gaynor, did everything to help. Others who have helped with encouragement and information have been Commander Seymour Stead R.C.N.(R), and Godfrey Smith, both of Malmesbury, Major Dick Partridge R.M. whose book "Operation Skua" brought back many memories and supplied some insight into our knowledge of that sad day at Trondheim; and Mrs. N.B.J.Stapleton who allowed me to use a photograph of the *Royal Sovereign's* Picket Boat from her husband's book "Steam Picket Boats", and the Maritime Museum at Greenwich for giving permission to publish the photograph of *Iron Duke*, my first ship, and Rick Johnson of **The Hangar Bookshelf** who helped to adjust several accounts of operations where passage of time had dulled my memory.

But finally, my wife Deborah, who has read and reread every word and every amendment to help make it readable; and my friends at Knowlton who have continued to encourage me.